Dictionary of Legal Terms

Spanish - English

English - Spanish

AF713742

Diccionario de Términos Jurídicos

Español - Inglés

Inglés - Español

By

Julio Romañach, Jr.
Attorney at Law
B.A., J.D., Louisiana State University
Member of the Louisiana State Bar Association

Part I. Spanish - English
Part II. English - Spanish

Jura Division
LAWRENCE PUBLISHING COMPANY
P.O. BOX 25073
BATON ROUGE, LA 70894
(504) 344-2897 FAX (504) 769-7515

©1989, 1992
COPYRIGHT 1989, 1992
Julio Romañach, Jr., All rights reserved.
Published by Lawrence Publishing Company

es propiedad

No part of this publication may be reproduced in whole or in part, or stored in a retrieval system, or transmitted in any form or by any means, electronic, mechanical, photocopying, recording, or otherwise, without written permission of the publisher. For information regarding permission, write to Lawrence Publishing Company, P.O. Box 25073, Baton Rouge, LA 70894

ISBN 0-9633610-0-7

Printed in the U.S.A.

To:
Paula, my wife, without whose unending patience, encouragement, and editorial assistance this work would never have been completed.

Cristina and Marta, my daughters, who make all my undertakings meaningful.

Author's Preface

When I began to practice law, I encountered a serious deficiency in the technical materials available to the lawyer engaged in international, transnational, admiralty, or immigration practice: the lack of a trustworthy bilingual dictionary of legal terms, Spanish - English and English - Spanish. The general Spanish - English dictionaries are simply inadequate to serve the needs of the practitioner who must translate the precise technical meaning of a legal term from one language into another. The problem is compounded by the difference in legal systems between the United States, on the one hand, and Spain and countries of Latin America, on the other. Thus while all American jurisdictions, with the exception of Louisiana, have a system based on the common law, Spain and the Latin American countries are civil law jurisdictions. The difference in systems accounts for differences in legal terminology that transcend the language barrier.

In preparing this dictionary, I have studied with great care the civil, commercial, penal, labor, and administrative codes of Spain and the Latin American republics. I have also perused innumerable treatises, articles, cases, and legal documents of every sort. My experience as a research attorney at the Center of Civil Law Studies of the Louisiana State University School of Law and at the Louisiana State Law Institute has been invaluable in the preparation of this work, since I have had the opportunity of comparing legal drafting techniques in both Spanish and English, on a continuous basis, for several years.

I have worked on the preparation of this dictionary for over a decade. I sincerely hope that it will be of assistance to the members of the bar, translators, interpreters, and anyone who needs to translate Spanish language legal terms into English or English language legal terms into Spanish.

Part I Spanish - English

Parte I Español - Inglés

A

Abalienar. Alienate;assign.
Abanación. Sentencing an individual to exile.
Abanderamiento. Registration of a foreign owned ship. By this process, the ship acquires the nationality of the state of registry.
Abandonar. Abandonment; desertion; abandon; desert.
Abandonar la instancia. Abandonment of an action.
Abandono. Abandonment; desertion; waiver of rights.
Abandono de bienes. Abandonment of assets by the owner.
Abandono de buque. Abandonment of ship; limitation of liability by abandonment of the vessel.
Abandono de la acción. Abandonment of the action
Abandono del hogar conyugal. Desertion or abandonment of the family home.
Abandono de servicio. Desertion or abandonment of his position by a public official.
Abdicación. Abdication.
Abdicar. To abdicate.
Abigeato. Theft of livestock.
Abigeo. One who steals livestock or beasts.
Ab intestato. Intestate; without a will.
Abjuración. Renunciation under oath.
Abjurar. To renounce under oath.
Abogacía. The practice of law.
Abogadear. To practice law with little or no dignity.
Abogadesco. Pertaining to the lawyer (usually derogatory).
Abogadil. *See* Abogadesco.
Abogado. Lawyer; attorney; solicitor; barrister.
Abogado del Estado. Attorney that represents the interests of the state.
Abogado fiscal. State attorney; district attorney.
Abogar. To represent or defend in a law suit.
Abolición. Abolition.
Abolicionismo. Abolitionism.
Abolicionista. Abolitionist.
Abolir. To abolish.
Abonar. Guarantee; to satisfy; to pay.
Abonaré. Promissory note.
Abono. Partial payment; guaranty; security.
Abono de tiempo de prisión. Credit for time served pending trial.
Abordaje. Collision of vessels.
Aborto. Abortion.
Abrevadero. Servitude of passage for watering animals.
Abrogar. Abrogate.
Absolución de la demanda. Judgment for the defendant; dismissal of the action.
Absolución de posiciones. Answers to interrogatories.

Abstención. Abstention; recusation.

Abuso. Excess; abuse.

Abuso de autoridad. Abuse of authority by a public official.

Abuso de confianza. Breach of faith; abuse of confidence.

Abuso del derecho. Abuse of rights.

Accesión. Accession.

Accesorio. Accessory.

Accidental. Nonessential; casual; accidental.

Accidente de trabajo. On the job injury suffered by a worker.

Accidente "in itinere". Accident suffered by a worker on the way to or from the employment site.

Acción. Action; share of stock.

Acción cambiaria. Right to use executory process derived from a bill of exchange.

Acción criminal. Criminal proceeding; criminal action; prosecution.

Acción cuanti minoris. *See* Acción estimatoria.

Acción de goce. Share of stock giving the holder certain rights to participate in the profits of the corporation. The corporate charter may give voting rights to the holders of such shares.

Acción de simulación. Action to declare the nullity of a simulated act.

Acciones alternativas. Claims pleaded in the alternative; alternative actions.

Acciones comunes. Common stock.

Acciones con valor nominal. Par value stock.

Acciones nominativas. Shares of stock issued in the name of a given person.

Acciones pagadoras. Shares of stock the value of which has not been completely paid for by the shareholder.

Acciones preferenciales. *See* acciones preferentes.

Acciones preferentes. Preferred stock.

Acciones sin valor nominal. No par value stock.

Acción estimatoria. Action for a reduction of the purchase price for hidden defects in the thing purchased.

Acción hipotecaria. Hypothecary action.

Accionista. Shareholder.

Acción mixta. Mixed action; action based on a right that is both personal and real.

Acción negatoria. Action by the owner of real estate, who believes his property to be free of encumbrances, against another who claims to have a servitude therein.

Acción pauliana. Action by the creditor to nullify the debtor's fraudulent conveyances.

Acción penal. Criminal action; criminal proceeding.

Acción personal. Personal action; action based on a credit right.

Acción petitoria. Petitory action.

Acción pignoraticia. Action derived from the real right of pledge.

Acción popular. People's action. This action may be exercised by any citizen in cases involving issues of general interest.

Acción posesoria. Possessory action.

Acción prescriptible. Action susceptible of prescription.

Acción real. Real action.

Acción redhibitoria. Redhibitory action; action to dissolve sale for breach of warranty of hidden defects.

Acción reivindicatoria. Reivindicatory action.

Acción rescisoria. Action to rescind or dissolve an act, agreement, contract, etc.

Acción resolutoria. Action to dissolve an act, agreement, or contract, etc.

Acción revocatoria. Revocatory action.

Acción subrogatoria. Action by the creditors in subrogation of the rights of their debtors against third parties.

Aceptación. Acceptance.

Aceptación de árbitros. Acceptance by a person to serve as arbitrator.

Aceptación de herencia. Acceptance of the inheritance.

Aceptación de peritos. Acceptance by a person to serve as expert.

Aceptante. Accepting party; one who accepts a bill of exchange; offeree.

Aceptar. To accept.

Aclaración de sentencia. Explanation of a judgment by the court that rendered it; reasons for judgment.

Acordada. Order or administrative resolution, of a general character, issued by a higher court in the exercise of its supervisory jurisdiction over lower tribunals.

Acrecer. *See* Acrecimiento.

Acrecimiento. Accretion; Increase in the share of one or more coheirs by virtue of the incorporation of the part of others who, for any reason,do not receive their share.

Acreditado. Diplomatic agent who after presenting his credentials, has received the *exequatur* ; one who has received credit; one who gives a credit right to another and receives a sum of money in return therefor.

Acreditante. One who extends credit; one who acquires a credit right by paying the holder a sum of money therefor.

Acreedor. Creditor.

Acreedor común. Ordinary creditor; common creditor.

Acreedores de la masa. Creditors with rights to the assets of a bankrupt estate.

Acreedor hereditario. Creditor whose credit burdens succession assets.

Acreedor hipotecario. Creditor whose right is secured by a mortgage.

Acreedor ordinario. Ordinary creditor.

Acreedor pignoraticio. Creditor whose right is secured by pledge.

Acreedor privilegiado. Lien or priviledged creditor.

Acta. Act; entry; record.

Acta notarial. Notarial act; annotation made by a notary outside his protocol to preserve a record of statements or facts.

Activo. Totality of a person's assets.

Acto administrativo. Administrative act.

Acto de administración. Act of administration; an act that tends to preserve the economic soundness of an enterprise or an estate.

Acto de comercio. Commercial act.

Acto de conservación. Conservatory act.

Acto de disposición. Act of disposition; transaction involving alienation, encumbrance, or waiver of rights.

Acto de emulación. An act performed with the sole intent of prejudicing another.

Acto de gestión. *Negotiorum gestio;* voluntary management of the affairs of another.

Acto de gobierno. Discretionary action of the executive destined to solve a political problem.

Acto de mera tolerancia. Sufferance by the owner of a thing of the use of his property by a third person, tolerated because of friendship or mere courtesy.

Acto de reconocimiento. Acknowledgment.

Acto de última voluntad. Testament; will.

Acto discrecional. Discretionary action by an administrative agency.

Acto entre vivos. *Inter vivos* act.

Acto ilícito. Unlawful act; act contrary to law; crime ; tort.

Acto inexistente. Juridical act lacking an element that is essential to its validity.

Acto inter vivos. An act which does not depend on the death of the parties performing it for its effectiveness.

Acto jurídico. Juridical act; human act that creates, modifies, or extinguishes rights.

Acto procesal. Procedural act; an act capable of creating, modifying, or extinguishing procedural rights.

Acto propio. An act made voluntarily; the implications and effects of such an act may not be denied to the prejudice of third parties by the person that executes it.

Actor. Plaintiff.

Acto reglamentario. Act performed in accordance with a set of rules or regulations.

Actos del estado civil. Acts that create or affect the civil status of a person.

Actuación. Procedural act; proceedings of record.

Actuario. Officer in charge of service of process.

Acueducto. Servitude consisting of the right of having water flow through the property of another en route to one's own property.

Acuerdo. Resolution; decision; agreement.

Acumulación de acciones. Joinder of actions.

Acumulación de autos. Consolidation of actions; joinder of actions.

Acusación. Accusation; indictment; filing of charges or information against.

Acusación particular. Accusation by a private individual.

Acusador particular. One who is a party to a criminal trial on the side of the prosecution.

Acusador público. District attorney.

Acusar la rebeldía. Taking a default; notification to the court that a party is in default.

Adhesión. Adhesion.

Adhesión a la apelación. Action to intervene in an appeal to obtain reversal of a lower court judgment insofar as prejudicial to the interests of the intervening party.

Adición a die. Resolutory conditions in a contract of sale whereby the seller reserves the right to rescind the contract if a buyer is found who will pay a higher price.

Adjudicación Judgment; adjudication; award.

Adjudicación en pago. Giving in payment.

Adjudicador. One who adjudicates.

Adjudicatario. Person who is awarded a thing in an adjudication.

Administración. Administration, especially of the executive branch of the government.

Administración de justicia. Administration of justice.

Administración de la sociedad de gananciales. Management or administration of the community of gains.

Administrado. Person whose assets are administered by another.

Administrador. Administrator.

Administrador judicial. Judicial administrator; a person put in charge by the court of administering property subject to litigation.

Administrar justicia. Administration of justice by the courts.

Admisión. Admission.

Adopción. Adoption.
Adoptado. Adopted person.
Adoptante. One who adopts.
Adoptar. To adopt.
Adoptivo. Person related to another by adoption.
Adquirente. One who acquires.
Adquirir. To acquire.
Adquisición. Acquisition.
Aduana. Customs; customs office.
Adúltero. One who commits adultery.
Adulterino. Child born of an adulterous relationship.
Adulterio. Adultery.
Adulto. Adult.
Adventicio. Patrimony acquired through the collateral line or by legacy.
Afectar. Burden; affect.
Afianzamiento. To guarantee; to post bond.
Afianzar. To post bond; to guarantee; to stand as surety for.
Afidavit. Affidavit; declaration made under oath.
Afinidad. Affinity; relation by marriage.
Afirmación. Statement; affirmation; assertion.
Aforado. One who is governed by special laws.
Aforo. Appraisal, usually for tax purposes; inspection of a commodity by customs agents.
Agente. Agent; mandatary.
Agente consular. Consular agent.
Agente de la autoridad. Government agent; public servant.
Agente diplomático. Diplomat.
Agio. Illicit benefit derived from unlawful commercial or securities activities.
Agiotaje. Illicit speculation; illicit commercial or securities activity.
Agiotista. One who habitually participates in unlawful commercial or securities activities.
Agir. To file a complaint in a court of justice.
Agotamiento de crédito. Exhaustion of credit.
Agravante. Aggravating circumstances.
Agraviado. One who has been harmed or prejudiced.
Agraviar. To cause lesion, harm, or prejudice.
Agravio. Grievance; harm; prejudice; wrong.
Agregación de expedientes. Incorporation of part of the record of a judicial proceeding in a different case.
Agresión. Assault; aggression.
Agrimensor. Land surveyor.
Aguas territoriales. Territorial waters.
Aguinaldo. Gratuity given to employees on certain holidays; bonus.
Aislacionismo. Isolationism.

Ajuar. Furnishings and other movables normally found in a house.
Ajustar. Settle; compromise; adjust.
Ajuste. Settlement; compromise; adjustment.
Ajusticiado. One who has been executed through legal process.
Albacea. Executor of a will.
Albacea dativo. Court appointed administrator of a succession.
Albacea testamentario. Testamentary executor.
Alcaide. Warden; person having custody of prisoners at a jail or penitentiary.
Alcalde. Mayor.
Alcaldía. Mayoralty.
Alcance. Deficit; reach.
Alcanzado. Person heavily indebted.
Al despacho. Notation of the time when a pleading or document in a judicial proceeding is submitted to the court or a judge for decision.
Aleatorio. Aleatory.
Alegación. Allegation; argument; pleading.
Alegar. To allege; to argue.
Alegato. Argument; pleading.
Alegato de bien probado. Writing wherein the parties to a judicial proceeding make their final argument on the resolution of the issues before the court.
Alevosía. Specific intent; malice aforethought; aggravating circumstances.
Alevoso. One who commits a crime under aggravating circumstances.
Alguacil. Marshal; sheriff; bailiff; court officer.
Alianza. Alliance.
Alienable. Alienable.
Alimentante. One who owes an obligation of support to another.
Alimentista. One who is owed an obligation of support.
Alimentos. Alimony; child support; action for alimony or child support.
Alimentos definitivos. Permanent alimony or child support.
Alimentos provisionales. Provisional support; alimony *pendente lite.*
Alindamiento. *See* alindar.
Alindar. To set the boundaries of an immovable.
Almacenes generales de depósito. General warehouses authorized to issue warehouse receipts.
Almoneda. Auction.
Alodial. Allodial.
Al por mayor. Wholesale.
Alquilar. To lease.
Alquiler. Rent; price of a lease.
Alta traición. High treason.
Alteridad. Characteristic of the law which assumes a relationship of at least two parties.
Aluvión. Alluvion.
Alzada. Appeal.

Alzado. A debtor that fraudulently conceals his assets from his creditors.

Alzamiento. Concealment of assets by the debtor.

Allanamiento a la demanda. Admission by the defendant of the allegations made in the petition by the plaintiff.

Allanamiento de morada. Entry of a dwelling by an investigating officer usually for the purpose of conducting a search therein.

Amancebamiento. Concubinage.

Amancebarse. To enter into concubinage.

Ambito territorial de la ley. Territorial scope of the law.

Amenaza. Threat.

Amigable componedor. Mediator; conciliator; arbitrator.

Amigable composición. Mediation; conciliation; resolution of a dispute brought about through mediation.

Amillaramiento. List of property owners for tax assessment purposes.

Amillarar. Formation of a list of property owners for tax assessment purposes.

Amnistía. Amnesty.

Amojonamiento. Setting of landmarks.

Amonestación. Warning.

Amortización. Amortization; recuperation of or compensation for the capital invested in a business or enterprise.

Amortizar. *See* amortización.

Amovible. Public official that is subject to removal from his position.

Amovilidad. Removable character of a public employee.

Amparo. Protection of a right; action seeking enforcement of an individual right protected by the constitution, alleging infringement of such right by the government; possessory action against a trespasser.

Ampliación de la hipoteca. Making the mortgage extend to other assets of the debtor.

Ampliación de sentencia. Amendment of a judgment by addition of items omitted by oversight.

Analogía. Analogy.

Anarquía. Anarchy.

Anatocismo. Capitalization of interest; interest over interest.

Anclaje. Duties paid by vessels to anchor in port.

Anexión. Annexation.

Angaria. Mandatory delay imposed by the state on foreign vessels anchored in its ports so that they may perform a public service; right of a belligerent state to confiscate property belonging to the enemy or enemy nationals within its territory.

Animo de lucro. Intent to obtain an economic benefit.

Anotación. Annotation.

Anotación de crédito. Notation of credit.
Anotación preventiva. Precautionary recordation; preventive recordation; preventive inscription.
Antecedentes penales. Criminal record; prior arrests and/or convictions.
Antedata. False date placed on a document which is prior to that on which the document was executed.
Antedatar. To antedate.
Antefirma. Indication of the employment, office, or position before the signature.
Antejuicio. Preliminary proceeding.
Ante mí. Before me.
Anteproyecto de ley. Early version of a bill prior to that in which it is introduced as projected legislation.
Anticresis. Antichresis.
Antijuricidad. Illegal action; unlawfulness.
Antinomia. Contradiction or opposition between two laws.
Antiparlamentario. Contrary to parliamentary rules or practices.
Anualidad. Sum of money that must be paid on an annual basis pursuant to a contract or by operation of law.
Anulabilidad. *See* anulable.
Anulable. Subject to annulment.
Anulación. Annulment; nullification.
Anular. To annul.
Anuncio. Legal notice.
Aparcería. Sharecropping.
Aparcería rural. Sharecropping.
Apartamiento. Abandonment of an action or claim.
Apátrida. Stateless person.
Apear. *See* deslindar.
Apelable. Appealable.
Apelación. Appeal.
Apelación en ambos efectos. Denotes the suspensive and devolutive effects of an appeal.
Apelado. Appellee.
Apelante. Appellant.
Apellido. Surname.
Apeo. Setting of boundaries.
Apercibimiento. Admonition; warning.
Apersonarse. To make an appearance before the court.
Apertura a prueba. Period in judicial proceedings during which the parties may offer and introduce evidence.
Apertura de crédito. Opening a line of credit for; opening of credit.
Apertura de la sucesión. Opening of probate proceedings; opening of the succession.
Apertura del testamento. Opening of the will.
Apoca. Letter of payment or receipt.
Apoderado. One who holds a power of attorney from another; agent; mandatary.
Apoderado judicial. Attorney.

Apoderamiento. Empowering.
Apoderar. Empower; grant of power of attorney.
Apología del delito. Justification for the commission of an act classified as criminal under applicable law.
Aprehender To arrest; seize.
Aprehensión. Arrest; seizure.
Apremio. Mandatory injunction; order.
Apresamiento. Seizure, specially of a vessel.
Aprisionar. To imprison.
Aprobación. Approval.
Aprobar. To approve.
Apropiación. Appropriation.
Apropiar. To appropriate.
Aprovechamiento forestal (de una finca). Timber estate; utilization of the timber of a particular parcel.
Apuesta. Betting.
Arancel de honorarios. Tariff upon which the fees of certain professionals is calculated.
Arbitrador. Arbitrator; mediator.
Arbitraje. Arbitration.
Arbitraje forzoso. Forced arbitration.
Arbitraje voluntario. Voluntary arbitration; conventional arbitration.
Arbitrariedad. Arbitrary; arbitraryness.
Arbitrario. One who acts arbitrarily; arbitrary.
Arbitrio judicial. Judicial discretion; authority of the court to decide matters within its jurisdiction.
Arbitro. Arbitrator.
Archivar. File.
Armador. One who operates a vessel for profit (shipowner; charterer).
Armas prohibidas. Illegal weapons.
Armisticio. Armistice.
Arquear. To measure the carrying capacity of a vessel.*See* also arqueo.
Arqueo. Carrying capacity of a vessel; audit; inspection.
Arraigo. Landed property; bond that must be posted by a foreign defendant who owns no property within the jurisdiction.
Arras. Earnest money.
Arrendador. Lessor; landlord.
Arrendamiento. Lease.
Arrendamiento de servicios. Lease of labor; contract of hire.
Arrendamiento por aparecería. Sharecropping.
Arrendamiento rústico. Lease of rural property.
Arrendamiento urbano. Lease of urban property.
Arrendatario. Lessee; tenant.
Arrendaticio. Pertaining to the contract of lease.
Arresto. Arrest.
Arribada. Entrance of a vessel to the port of destination or to a different one.
Arribada forzosa. Entrance of a vessel to a port other than the one of destination due to accident.

Arribada voluntaria. Entrance of a vessel to the port of destination.
Arriendo. Lease.
Artículo. Article.
Artículos de previo pronunciamiento. Incidental matters that must be disposed of prior to a decision on the merits.
Ascendientes. Ascendants.
Asegurado. Insured.
Asegurador. Insurer.
Asegurar. To insure; to enter into an insurance contract.
Asentamiento. Judicial possession of the assets of a defaulting defendant given to the plaintiff; an entry or inscription made in an official registry.
Asentar. To affirm; to found; *see* also asentamiento.
Asertorio. Oath affirming the truth of a fact.
Asesinato. Murder; assassination.
Asesino. Murderer; assassin.
Asiento. Entry; inscription; recorded entry; seat.
Asilo. Assylum.
Asilo diplomático. Diplomatic assylum.
Asistencia letrada. Assistance of legal counsel.
Asistencia marítima. *Sui Generis* contract arising from the assistance given to a vessel in distress by another vessel.
Asociación. Association; corporation.
Asociación en participación. Type of partnership *In commendam.*
Asociado. Member of an association.
Asunción de la deuda. Assumption of the debt.
Asunto. Case; judicial proceeding.
Atentado. Abuse of process; criminal contempt; assault; attack.
Atentado contra la autoridad. Attack or intimidation against government officers.
Atentado contra la libertad. Act against the right of freedom.
Atentado contra las buenas costumbres. An act contrary to good morals.
Atentado contra la seguridad de la nación. An act against the security of the state.
Atestación. Testimony; attestation.
Atestado. Police report; investigation report.
Atestiguación. Testimony; attestation.
Atestiguar. To testify.
Audiencia. Hearing.
Ausencia. Absence; Absenteeism.
Ausente. Absentee.
Autenticación. Authentication.
Autenticar. Legalize; attest to the authenticity of .
Auténtico. Authentic.
Auto(s). Hearing; trial; judicial proceeding.
Auto cabeza del proceso penal. Initial judicial action in a criminal proceeding.

Autocontrato. Contract made by an agent acting on his own behalf and on behalf of the person he represents, or one made by a representative of two different individuals.

Auto definitivo Definitive hearing; final judgment.

Autodeterminación. Self determination.

Autonomía. Autonomy.

Autonomía de la voluntad. Autonomy of the will.

Autopsia. Autopsy.

Autor. Author; ancestor in title.

Autoridad. Authority.

Autoridad de la cosa juzgada. *Res judicata;* authority of the thing adjudged.

Autorización. Authority.

Autorizar. To authorize; notarial attestation.

Auxiliar. Assistant.

Auxiliatoria de pobreza. Judicial resolution authorizing a person to litigate without paying costs due to poverty or lack of means.

Auxilio marítimo. *See* asistencia marítima.

Aval. Payment guarantee made in a negotiable instrument, usually as an accomodation party.

Avalado. Maker or drawer of a negotiable instrument that has been guaranteed by another.

Avalista. Guarantor of a negotiable instrument.

Avalúo. Appraisal; evaluation; fair market price.

Avenencia. Compromise; settlement; conciliation.

Avenidor. Mediator; conciliator.

Avenimiento. Compromise; settlement.

Avenir. To conciliate; to solve a dispute.

Avería. Average; harm or damage to a vessel.

Averías gruesas. General average.

Averías particulares. Particular average.

Averiguación. Inquiry.

Avisos. Legal notice.

Avocación. Assumption of jurisdiction by a higher court of a matter pending in an inferior court.

Ayuntamiento. Government of a municipality.

B

Balance. Balance; statement; one of the books that merchants are required to keep.

Balanza comercial. Balance of trade.

Banca. Banking institution; banking.

Bancario. Pertaining to a bank.

Bancarrota. Bankruptcy; insolvency.

Banco cobrador. Collecting bank.

Banco colector. *See* banco cobrador.

Banco confirmante. Confirming bank.

Banco que avisa o notifica. Advising bank.

Banco que confirma. *See* banco confirmante.

Banda. Crime organization; gang.

Bandera. Flag.

Banquero. Banker.

Barra. Bar association.

Base imposible. Figure that forms the basis for income taxation.

Bastantear. Examination of a power of attorney to test its sufficiency.

Bastanteo. Note written by a lawyer on a power of attorney declaring it sufficient for its purposes.

Bastantero. One in charge of examining powers of attorney authorizing lawyers to represent individuals in law suits.

Beligerancia. Belligerancy.

Beligerante. Belligerant.

Beneficiario. Beneficary.

Beneficio. Benefit; advantage.

Beneficio de competencia. Right of a debtor whose assets have been seized to receive a sum for his support, payable from the value of the assets seized, if he has no other means of support and is unable to work.

Beneficio de división. Right or benefit of division.

Beneficio de excusión. Right or benefit of discussion.

Beneficio de inventario. Benefit of inventory.

Beneficio de pobreza. *See* declaratoria de pobreza.

Beneficio de separación. Right of the creditors of the decedent to have the succession property separated from the property of the heirs of the decedent, so that they may exercise their rights against the decedent's estate.

Bicameral. Bicameral.

Bien común. The common good.

Bien de familia. Assets that are free from seizure, including the right of homestead, because they are basic to the support of a family.

Bienes. Assets; goods; things; property.

Bienes comunes. Community property; assets owned in indivision by the spouses.

Bienes consumibles. Consumable things.

Bienes corporales. Corporeal things; material things.

Bienes de dominio del poder público. Things of the public domain of the state.

Bienes de dominio privado del estado. Things of the state's private domain.

Bienes de propiedad de particulares. Private property; assets belonging to a private individual.

Bienes de uso común. State property destined to be used by all.
Bienes dotales. Dotal assets, dowry.
Bienes embargables. Things subject to seizure.
Bienes fungibles. Fungible things.
Bienes futuros. Future things.
Bienes gananciales. Community property; assets that belong to the community of gains in a community property regime.
Bienes hereditarios. Inherited things.
Bienes hipotecables. Things that may be mortgaged.
Bienes incorporales. Incorporeal things.
Bienes indivisos. Things owned in indivision.
Bienes inembargables. Things not subject to seizure.
Bienes inmuebles. Immovables; real estate.
Bienes litigiosos. Litigious rights; things that are the object of litigation.
Bienes mostrencos. Lost or abandoned things the owner of which is unknown.
Bienes muebles. Personal property; movable property.
Bienes no consumibles. Nonconsumable things.
Bienes parafernales. Paraphernal property; separate property of the wife in a community property regime.
Bienes raíces. Real property; immovable property; real estate; immovables.
Bienes relictos. *See* caudal relicto.
Bienes semovientes. Animals (as property).
Bien público. The public good.
Bigamia. Bigamy.
Bilateral. Bilateral.
Billete de banco. Bank bill; paper currency.
Billete de lotería. Lottery ticket.
Bloqueo. Blockade; temporary freezing of a person's assets.
Boicot. Boycott.
Boicotear. To boycott.
Boleto. Ticket.
Bolsa de valores. Stock exchange; stock market.
Bolsista. Stock broker.
Bono. Bond.
Bono de ahorro. Savings bond; savings certificate; certificate of deposit.
Bono de prenda. Pledge warehouse receipt.
Bono financiero. Type of security issued by a financial institution with a specific guarantee.
Bono hipotecario. Mortgage bond; credit instrument issued by a mortgage credit institution.
Buenas costumbres. Good morals.
Buenos oficios. Good offices; type of mediation.

Buen padre de familia. Prudent administrator.
Bufete. Law office.
Buque mercante. Merchant vessel.

C

Cabezalero. *See* albacea.
Cabildear. To lobby.
Cabildeo. *See* cabildear.
Cabildo. *See* ayuntamiento.
Cabotaje. Coastwise trade; navigation between the ports of a given state.
Cadalso. Gallows; place of execution.
Caducidad. Prescription; peremption; running of the statute of limitations.
Caducidad de la instancia. Peremption of the action.
Calce. Foot of a document.
Calendario. Calendar.
Calificación de grado. Determination of jurisdiction or justiciability without deciding on the merits.
Cámara. Chamber.
Cámara alta. High chamber (senate).
Cámara baja. Lower chamber (house of representatives).
Cámara de diputados. Chamber of deputies.
Cámara de senadores The senate.
Cambial. Bill of exchange.
Cambio. Exchange.
Camino. Road.
Cancelación. Cancellation; extinguishment.
Cancelar. To cancel; annul.
Canciller. Foreign relations minister or secretary.
Cancillería. Office of the foreign relations minister; function of the foreign relations minister.
Canje. Exchange; interchange (as of diplomatic notes or prisoners of war).
Canjear. *See* canje.
Canon. Rule or precept ; price of a rural lease.
Canonista. Canon law expert.
Cañada. Servitude of passage.
Capacidad. Capacity.
Capacidad jurídica. Capacity to make juridical acts.
Capacidad procesal. Procedural capacity.
Capaz. Capable.
Capciosa. *See* pregunta capciosa.
Capitación. Capitation.
Capital. Capital.
Capital contal. A corporation's paid-in capital minus accumulated losses.
Capital social. Paid-in capital.
Capitán de buque. Captain of a vessel.
Capitulación. Capitulation.
Capitulaciones matrimoniales. Matrimonial contract; contractual matrimonial regime.
Captura. Capture; arrest.

Capturar. To capture; to arrest.
Cárcel. Jail; prison; detention center.
Carcelero. Jailer.
Careo. Cross-examination.
Carga. Cargo; burden; obligation.
Carga de la contestación. Burden of answering interrogatories.
Carga de la prueba. Burden of proof.
Carga de notificarse. Duty of going to court to take notice of the court's decision on pending matters.
Cargador. Carrier; one who undertakes to transport things pursuant to a contract of carriage.
Carga procesal. Procedural burden.
Cargo. Filing certificate placed on pleadings by the clerk of court; office or position; function; charge (criminal).
Carnet. Identification card.
Carrera. Career.
Carrera judicial. Organization of the judicial profession.
Carta acordada. Official notification of a judicial decision rendered by a higher court.
Carta credencial. Credentials.
Carta de crédito. Letter of credit.
Carta de marca. Letter of marque.
Carta de naturaleza. Citizenship or naturalization certificate.
Carta de pago. Receipt.
Carta de porte. Bill of lading.
Carta misiva. Private writing of a litigant to a third party. Statements contained therein are inadmissible in evidence.
Carta poder. Written power of attorney.
Carta rogatoria. Letters rogatory.
Casación. Appeal of last restort; appeal limited to legal issues.
Casa de tolerancia. House or establishment where prostitution is practiced.
Casamiento. Marriage.
Casar. To overrule a judgment on grounds of error of law; to overrule.
Casillero criminal. Registry of criminal records.
Caso. Case.
Caso furtuito. Fortuitous event.
Castigar. To punish.
Castigo. Punishment or sanction.
Catastro. Land register; statistical record of immovable property in a particular jurisdiction.
Catear. To search a dwelling or other private place.
Cateo. Search of a dwelling or other private place.
Caución. Security; guarantee; bond.

Caucionero. Surety; guarantor.

Caudal relicto. The assets of a succession.

Causa. Cause; consideration; judicial proceeding.

Causa de menor cuantía. Small claim.

Causahabiente. One who acquires rights or things from another. *See* causante.

Causante. Decedent; predecessor in title; one from whom a right is derived.

Causa pública. Public interest.

Causar estado. Said of a judgment that has attained the status of *Res judicata.*

Causas de almirantazgo. Admiralty cases.

Cedente. Assignor.

Cédula. Citation; summons; subpoena.

Cedulón. Notification of a judicial decision.

Celibato. Civil status of one who has not contracted marriage; celibacy.

Célibe. One who has not contracted marriage; single; celibate.

Censo de población. Population census.

Certificación. Certification; assertion; attestation; written declaration that may be given by some functionaries in lieu of testimony in court.

Certificado. Certificate.

Certificado de Aportación. Certificate of contribution given by cooperative associations to their members.

Certificado de buena conducta. Certificate of good conduct.

Certificado de depósito. Certificate of deposit.

Certificado de depósito bancario. Certificate of deposit.

Certificado de invención. Patent.

Certificado de navegabilidad. Certificate of fitness issued to an aircraft or vessel.

Certificado de origen. Certificate of origin.

Certificado de trabajo. Time and wages certificate.

Cesión. Assignment.

Cesionario. Assignee.

Cesión de bienes. Assignment of a debtor's assets for the benefit of his creditors.

Cesión de créditos. *See* cessión de derechos.

Cesión de derechos. Assignment of rights.

Cesión en pago. Giving in payment; assignment in payment.

Ciencia del derecho Jurisprudence; scientific study of the law.

Circunstancias modificativas. Factors that affect sentencing.

Citación. Citation; summons.

Citación a conciliación. Citation or summoning a party

to attend a conciliation or settlement hearing.

Citación de evicción. Call in warranty of the buyer against the seller in eviction proceedings; suit by the buyer calling the seller to defend eviction action filed by a third party.

Citación para sentencia. Submission of the case for a decision; a court's determination that the procedural activity of the parties has terminated and that the case is now ripe for judgment on the merits.

Citar. Serve with process; give notice; to cite legal authority.

Citas. Citations of authority.

Ciudadano. Citizen.

Civilista. Civilian; civil law expert.

Clandestino. Clandestine; hidden.

Cláusula. Clause.

Cláusula compromisoria. Clause providing for binding arbitration; arbitration clause.

Cláusula de nación más favorecida. Most favored nation clause.

Cláusula "Franco a Bordo". F.O.B clause.

Cláusula limitativa de responsabilidad. Limitation of liability clause.

Cláusula penal. Stipulated damages clause; penal clause.

Cliente. Client.

Coacción. Coercion; compulsion.

Coafianzamiento. Joint suretyship.

Coalición. Coalition; unification.

Coartada. Alibi; giving an alibi.

Coartar. Placing illegal obstacles on the performance of lawful activities.

Coaseguro. Coinsurance; coverage of the same risk by two or more insurers.

Coautor. Co-author.

Cobertura. Collateral; things that guarantee a financial or commercial venture.

Cobro. Collection of a sum owed.

Codelincuencia. Crime committed by two or more defendants.

Codelincuente. Coparticipant in a criminal act.

Codeudor. Codebtor.

Codicilo. Codicil.

Codificación. Codification.

Codificar. To codify.

Código. Code.

Código civil. Civil code.

Código de comercio. Commercial code.

Código de familia. Family code.

Código de menores. Juvenile code.

Código de minas. Mineral code.

Código de procedimiento civil. Code of civil procedure.

Código de procedimiento penal. Code of criminal procedure.

Código de señales. Rules of the road (navigation).
Código de trabajo. Labor code.
Código minero. *See* Código de minas.
Código penal. Criminal code.
Código uniforme de comercio. Uniform Commercial Code.
Coerción. Coercion.
Cofiador. Cosurety; cowarrantor.
Cognación. Cognation; blood kindred.
Cognado. Cognate.
Cognaticio. Relative to blood kindred.
Cohabitar. To cohabitate; to live in concubinage.
Cohechar. To bribe a public official.
Cohecho. To solicit or receive a bribe.
Coheredar. To coinherit.
Coheredero. Coheir.
Colaterales. Collaterals; persons related on the collateral line; kin.
Colegatario. Co-legatee.
Colegio electoral. Electoral college.
Colitigante. Coparty.
Colonato. Lease of rural property.
Colonia. Lease of rural property.
Colono. Lessee of rural property.
Colusión. Collision.
Comandita. Partnership *in commendam* or limited partnership; contribution to the partnership of each of the partners *in commendam* or limited partners.
Comanditado. General partner in a partnership *in commendam* or limited partnership.
Comanditario. Partner *in commendam* or limited partner.
Comerciante matriculado. Merchant registered in the commercial registry.
Comerciar. To perform an act of commerce.
Comercio. Commerce.
Comisario. Corporate officer or group in charge of vigilance of corporate employees.
Comisión. Commission; board.
Comisión mercantil. Commercial agency; mandate applied to acts of commerce.
Comisión rogatoria. Letters rogatory.
Comiso. Forfeiture proceeding.
Comodante. Lender in a loan for use.
Comodatario. Borrower in a loan for use.
Comodato. *See* contrato de comodato.
Compañía. Company; association; corporation; enterprise.
Comparecencia. Court appearance.
Comparecer. Appear in court.
Compareciente. Person who makes a court appearance.

Comparendo. Judicial decree ordering a defendant to appear in court; hearing.
Compeler. To compel.
Compensable. Compensable.
Compensación. Compensation.
Compensador. One who compensates.
Compensar. To compensate.
Competencia. Subject matter jurisdiction; competence.
Competencia desleal. Unfair trade practice.
Compentencia ilícita. Unfair trade practice; unlawful trade practice.
Cómplice. Accomplice.
Complot. Conspiracy; plot.
Comprador. Buyer.
Comprador de buena fe. Good faith purchaser; *bona fide* purchaser.
Compraventa. Sale.
Compraventa al contado. Cash sale.
Compraventa con reserva de dominio. Conditional sale; sale with reservation of ownership.
Compraventa contra documentos. Sale made with stipulation of payment against documents.
Compraventa en abonos. Installment sale.
Compraventa L.A.B. o F.O.B. F.O.B. sale.
Compraventa mercantil. Commercial sale.
Compraventa por peso o medida. Sale by weight or measure.
Compraventa sobre calidades. Sale by description of the characteristics of the thing.
Compraventa sobre muestras. Sale by sample.
Comprobación de letras. Handwriting examination.
Compromiso. Agreement to arbitrate; compromise.
Compulsión. Compulsion; coercion; mandatory injunction.
Comuna. Municipality; township.
Comunero. Co-owner in indivision.
Comunidad. Co-ownership.
Concebido. Conceived.
Concejal. Councilman.
Concejo. Council; *see* ayuntamiento.
Concentración. Principle calling for promptness of and economy in judicial proceedings.
Concesión administrativa. Administrative concession; license.
Concesionario. Concessionary; holder of a concession; licensee.
Conciliación. Conciliation.
Concordato. Treaty between the Vatican and another state; agreement between the creditors and the bankrupt.
Concubina. Concubine.
Concubinario. Man who has a concubine.
Concubinato. Concubinage.

Concurrencia desleal. Unfair competition; unfair trade practices.
Concursado. Bankrupt; debtor in insolvency proceedings.
Concurso. Bankruptcy; insolvency proceedings.
Concurso civil. Bankrupty; meeting of the creditors.
Concurso necesario. Involuntary bankruptcy.
Concurso voluntario. Voluntary bankruptcy.
Concusión. Extorsion by a public official; undue payment demand made by a public official.
Concusionario. Public official that solicits undue payments.
Condena. Judgment; sentence.
Condena condicional. Conditional sentence; sentence subject to parole restrictions.
Condenar. Convict.
Condición. Condition.
Condicional. Conditional.
Condición ilícita. Unlawful condition.
Condición imposible. Impossible condition.
Condición potestativa. Potestative condition.
Condición resolutoria. Resolutory condition.
Condición suspensiva. Suspensive condition.
Condominio. Co-ownership; joint ownership; condominium.
Condómino. Co-owner.
Condonación. Remission; gratuitous liberation of a debt.
Condonación de la deuda. Remission of the debt.
Condonante. One who gratuitously liberates another from a debt.
Condueño. Co-owner.
Confederación. Confederation.
Confesante. One who makes an admission or confession.
Confesión. Admission; confession.
Confesión de parte. Admission by a party to the litigation; judicial admission; confession.
Confesión extrajudicial. Admission or confession made out of court.
Confesión judicial. Judicial confession; admission in open court.
Confesión tácita. Tacit admission; tacit confession.
Confeso. One who has admitted the factual assertions made in the plaintiff's complaint or is taken to have admitted them for failure to answer.
Confirmación. Confirmation; upholding; sustaining.
Confiscación. Confiscation; impoundment; forfeiture.
Conflicto. Conflict.
Conflicto de leyes. Conflict of laws.
Conflicto de trabajo. Labor conflict; labor friction.

Confrontación. Confrontation; method of identification of suspects.
Confusión. Confusion.
Confusión de derechos. *See* confusión.
Congelación de precios. Price freeze.
Congelación de rentas. Rent freeze.
Congreso. Congress; legislature.
Congreso general. (Mexican) Federal congress.
Conjetura. Inference; circumstantial evidence; indirect evidence; conjecture.
Conjeturar. Argument or decison based on circumstantial or indirect evidence.
Conjuez. Attorney at law temporarily appointed to serve as a judge.
Conmoriencia. Presumption of simultaneous death arising when several persons have perished in the same accident.
Conmutación de las penas. Commutation of sentence.
Conmutar. To commute a sentence.
Conmutativo. Commutative.
Conocer el litigio. Hear the case; take jurisdiction over the case.
Conocer una causa. To hear a case; to exercise jurisdiction over a case.
Conocimiento. Bill of lading; cognizance; notice.
Conocimiento de embarque. Bill of lading.
Consanguíneo. Consanguineous; kindred.
Consanguinidad. Consanguinity.
Consejo. Council; advice.
Consejo de administración. Officers of a corporation.
Consejo de estado. Council of state.
Consejo de familia. Family meeting; family council; family advisory committee.
Consejo de guerra. Court martial.
Consenso. Consensus.
Consensual. Consensual.
Consentido. Acquiesced; by consent.
Consentimiento. Consent.
Consentir. To consent; to grant.
Considerando. Whereas; considering.
Consignación. Consignment.
Consignante. Consignor.
Consignatario. Consignee; person who acts as depositary or bailee pursuant to court decree.
Consorcio. Partnership; joint venture; consortium.
Conspiración. Conspiracy.
Constitución. Constitution.
Constitucional. Constitutional.
Constitucionalidad. Constitutionality.
Constitución otorgada. Constitution enacted by the will

of a monarch who renounces to absolute authority thereby.

Constituir en mora. Put in default.

Constituyente. Member of a constitutional assembly.

Cónsul. Consul.

Consulta. Legal opinion; consultation.

Contador. Accountant.

Contención. Dispute; contention; issue.

Contencioso. Controverted; litigious; in contention.

Contencioso administrativo. Administrative law litigation; body of law regulating litigation in which an administrative agency is a party to a case arising from actions taken by the agency in the exercise of its functions.

Contestación. Answer; reply.

Contestación absolutamente negativa. Answer importing a general denial.

Conteste. Corroborating witness.

Contienda. Controversy; dispute.

Contienda de competencia. Dispute concerning propriety of jurisdiction or venue.

Continencia de la causa. Joinder of actions.

Contrademanda. Counterclaim; reconventional demand.

Contradocumento. Counterletter; counterdeed.

Contraescritura. Notarial act made with the intent of nullifying a prior notarial act.

Contraestadía. Demurrage.

Contraestipulación. Counterletter.

Contrainformación. Opposition to an *ex parte* evidentiary hearing. *See* información sumaria.

Contralor. Administrative officer who monitors administrative acts for compliance with the requirements of the law.

Contraloría. Office of the contralor; *see* contralor.

Contraprotesto. Maker's notation on a bill of exchange asserting that it has been paid.

Contraprueba. Rebuttal; presentation of proof by the defendant.

Contrata. Public work or service agreement contracted by a government agency; private contract for the performance of services or construction.

Contratista. Contractor, especially in the construction industry.

Contrato. Contract.

Contrato aleatorio. Aleatory contract.

Contrato colectivo de trabajo. Collective bargaining agreement.

Contrato complejo. *See* contrato mixto.

Contrato conmutativo. Commutative contract.

Contrato consensual. Contract that is perfected by the mere consent of the parties.

Contrato de adhesión. Adhesion contract.

Contrato de agencia. Agency.

Contrato de aparcería. Sharecropping.

Contrato de arrendamiento. Contract of lease.

Contrato de arriendo. lease.

Contrato de bolsa. Contract involving securities.

Contrato de colonato. Lease of rural property.

Contrato de comodato. Loan for use; loan.

Contrato de depósito. Contract of deposit.

Contrato de edición. Publishing contract.

Contrato de fianza. Suretyship.

Contrato de fletamiento. Charter party; lease of a vessel or part of a vessel.

Contrato de hospedaje. Lodging contract.

Contrato de juego. Betting or wagering contract.

Contrato de mandato. Contract of mandate.

Contrato de mutuo. Loan for consumption.

Contrato de prenda. Contract of pledge.

Contrato de préstamo. Loan.

Contrato de refacción agrícola. Crop lien contract.

Contrato de renta vitalicia. Annuity contract.

Contrato de seguro. Insurance contract.

Contrato de sociedad. Partnership agreement.

Contrato de trabajo. Labor contract.

Contrato de suministro. Supply contract; requirements contract.

Contrato de tracto sucesivo. Contract calling for successive acts of performance.

Contrato de transporte. Transportation contract.

Contrato formal. Formal contract.

Contrato innominado. Innominate contract.

Contrato inscribible. Contract amenable to registry; contract subject to or capable of registry.

Contrato instantáneo. Contract calling for immediate performance or for performance at a date set forth in the agreement.

Contrato judicial. Contract executed by the court, pursuant to law, when a party unjustifiably refuses to sign a deed or other document.

Contrato leonino. Inequitable or lopsided contract; contract wherein there is great disproportion between the performances owed by each party.

Contrato mercantil. Commercial contract.

Contrato mixto. Contract that has elements of several contracts, none of which is dominant.
Contrato oneroso. Onerous contract.
Contrato preparatorio. Preparatory contract; ancillary agreement that precedes principal contract.
Contrato principal. Main or principal contract.
Contrato real. Real contract.
Contrato sinalagmático. Synalagmatic contract.
Contrato solemne. Contract the validity of which depends upon the observance of certain formal requirements.
Contrato unilateral. Unilateral contract.
Contrato verbal. Oral contract.
Contravención. Violation; contravention.
Contribución. Contribution; tax.
Contribución inmobiliaria. Real estate tax.
Contribuyente. Tax payer; contributor.
Control jurisdiccional. Judicial review.
Contumacia. Failure to answer within the legal deadline; default.
Contumaz. Defaulting party; *see* contumacia.
Convalidación. Confirmation; validation.
Convalidar. To confirm; to ratify.
Convención. Treaty; convention.
Convenio. Agreement; contract; pact.
Conversión. Transformation of an annullable transaction into a valid one.
Convicto. One convicted of a crime.
Conyugal. Legal relationship existing between spouses.
Cónyuge. Spouse.
Cónyuge supérstite. Surviving spouse.
Coobligado. Coobligor.
Copia. Copy.
Copia auténtica. True copy; authenticated copy.
Copias de escrituras públicas. Copies of authentic acts; copies of notarial acts.
Copropiedad. Coownership.
Corporación. Corporation.
Correal. Solidary or joint and several obligation.
Correalidad. Solidarity; bond uniting joint and several obligors or obligees.
Corrección. Sanction(usually for a misdemeanor); correction.
Corredor de comercio. Agent; broker.
Correduría. Agency; agency on commission; brokerage.
Correo. Codebtor; coobligor.
Correspondencia. Correspondence.
Corretaje. Remuneration or fees received by the corredor de comercio.
Corrupción de menores. Corruption of minors; con-

tributing to the delinquency of a juvenile.

Corsario. Corsaire; type of pirate.

Corte. Court; tribunal.

Corte Internacional de Justicia. International Court of Justice.

Cortes. The Spanish parliament; courts.

Corte suprema. Supreme Court.

Cosa. Thing.

Cosa accesoria. Accessory thing.

Cosa consumible. Consumable thing.

Cosa divisible. Divisible thing.

Cosa fruto. Fruits or products of a thing.

Cosa fuera del comercio. Thing outside of commerce.

Cosa futura. Future thing.

Cosa indivisible. Indivisible thing.

Cosa juzgada. *Res judicata*; a matter that has acquired the authority of the thing adjudged.

Cosa no consumible. Nonconsumable.

Cosa sagrada. Holy object; religous object.

Cosas comunes. Common things.

Costas. Court costs.

Costos. Litigation expenses.

Costumbre. Custom; usage.

Costumbre de la tierra. Custom of the region; local usage.

Costumbre internacional. International custom.

Cotización. Price quotation.

Crédito. Credit right; credit.

Crédito anotable. Credit that may be registered.

Crédito confirmado. Confirmed credit.

Crédito de habilitación o avío. Special loan or credit line agreement whereby the borrower commits itself to use the funds received for specified purposes essential to the enterprise involved.

Crédito hipotecario. Loan or credit line secured by a mortgage.

Culpa "in contrahendo". Fault in the formation of a contract.

Crédito irrevocable. Irrevocable credit.

Crédito revocable. Revocable credit.

Crimen. Crime.

Criminal. Criminal.

Criminología. Criminology.

Cuantía. Amount in dispute.

Cuasicontrato. Quasicontract.

Cuasidelito. Tort; quasidelict.

Cuasi usufructo. Usufruct of consumables; imperfect usufruct.

Cuatrero. Livestock thief.

Cuatrerismo. *See* abigeato.

Cuenta. Account.

Cuenta en participación. Limited partnership in which the identity of the limited partners is not revealed to third parties.

Cuerda. Symbolic unifying thread uniting judicial proceedings of a single case.

Cuerpo cierto. Determinate thing.

Cuerpo del delito. Corpus delicti ("body" of the crime).

Cuerpo diplomático. Diplomatic corps.

Cuestión. Issue; matter in controversy.

Cuestión previa. Prior question.

Culpa. Fault; negligence.

Culpa contractual. Contractual fault.

Culpa grave. Gross negligence.

Culpa leve. Slight negligence.

Cúmplase. Court order of compliance with a judgment or disposition.

Cuota. Quota; portion; part.

Cura. Cure.

Curador. Curator.

Curador ad litem. curator ad litem (representative of a minor or other incompetent as plaintiff or defendant in a law suit).

Curador de la herencia. Special administrator of the decedent's estate.

Curatela. Curatorship.

Curia. The legal profession.

Curial. Attorney at law; person engaged professionally in the practice of law before a court or tribunal.

Curso legal (moneda de). Legal tender; legal currency.

Custodia. Custody.

Ch

Chantaje. Blackmail

Chantajista. Blackmailer.

Cheque. Check.

Cheque a la orden. Check made to order.

Cheque al portador. Check made to bearer.

Cheque certificado. Certified check.

Cheque cruzado. Check that can be presented for payment by a credit institution.

Cheque de caja. Cashier's check.

Cheque de viajero. Traveler's check.

Cheque sin fondos. Check made with insufficient funds to cover it.

D

Dación. Giving; giving in payment.

Dación de arras. Giving of earnest money.

Dación en pago. Giving in payment.

Dádiva. Present; gift.

Dador. Issuer; Issuer of a negotiable instrument or a letter of credit.

Dañar. To harm; to cause prejudice; to misuse a thing.

Daño. Damage; injury.

Daño emergente. Loss; damages.
Daño fortuito. Loss caused by a fortuitous event.
Daño irreparable. Irreparable injury.
Daño moral. Nonpecuniary damages; moral damages.
Daños y perjuicios. Damages.
Data. Indication of the time and place in a document.
Debate. Debate.
Debentures. Debentures.
Deber. Duty.
Debido proceso legal. Due process of law.
Débito Money debt.
Decadencia. *See* caducidad.
Decisión. Decision.
Declaración. Statement; deposition; declaration.
Declaración de ausencia. Declaration of absentee.
Declaración de derechos. Bill of rights; declaration of rights.
Declaración de guerra. Declaration of war.
Declaración de incapacidad. Declaration of lack of capacity; declaration of incompetence.
Declaración de los términos. Statement of terms.
Declaración de pobreza. *See* beneficio de pobreza.
Declaración de voluntad. Expression of the will which produces legal effects.
Declaración en rebeldía. Declaration of default.
Declaración indagatoria. A suspect's statement given upon interrogation by the judge during the investigative phase of the proceedings.
Declaración jurada. Statement under oath.
Declaración preparatoria. Preliminary hearing in criminal proceedings.
Declarante. One who makes a statement.
Declarar sin lugar. Order of dismissal; decree of no cause of action; declaration of no right.
Declaratoria de herederos. Judgment of probate or succession proceeding determining who is called to share in the estate or inheritance.
Declaratoria de pobreza. Judicial resolution authorizing a person to litigate without paying costs due to poverty or lack of means.
Declinatoria (excepción). Declinatory exception; motion to dismiss for lack of jurisdiction or venue.
Decomisar. Forfeiture.
Decretero. Minute book; book wherein the resolutions of the court are recorded in chronological order.
Decreto. Decree; executive order.
Decreto-ley. Decree-law; executive order authorized by the legislature.
De cuyus. Person whose succession is involved.

De derecho. In accordance with law; as a matter of law.
Defectos ocultos. Hidden defects.
Defensa. Plea; defense.
Defensa legítima. *See* legítima defensa.
Defensor. Attorney; counsel; defender.
Defensor de ausentes. Curator of absentees.
Defensor de oficio. Public defender; curator of absentee.
Defensor de pobres. Attorney (usually court appointed) who represents indigent parties.
Defensoría de oficio. Public defender's office.
Deferir. Defer; to concede.
Definitiva. *See* sentencia definitiva.
Defraudación. Fraud.
Defraudar. To defraud.
Delación. Accusation; calling someone to tutorship.
Delación de tutela. Calling to serve as tutor.
Delatar. To accuse; to call someone to tutorship.
Delegación. Delegation; substitution; representation.
Deliberación. Deliberation.
Deliberante. One who deliberates.
Deliberar. Deliberate.
Delictivo. Criminal act.
Delictuoso. *See* delictivo.
Delincuente. Criminal; offender.
Delincuente habitual. Habitual offender; professional criminal.
Delinquir. To commit a crime.
Delito. Crime; illicit act.
Delito agotado. Completed crime.
Delito civil. Tort; offense.
Delito consumado. Consumated crime.
Delito contra el estado. Crime against the state.
Delito contra la persona. Crimes against the person.
Delito contra la propiedad. Crime against property.
Delito contra la salud pública. Public health violation.
Delito culposo. Crime involving criminal negligence.
Delito de imprudencia. *See* delito culposo.
Delito doloso. Intentional crime.
Delito flagrante. Crime in which the perpetrator is caught in the act.
Delito penal. Crime.
Delito político. Political crime.
Delito privado. Crime that can not be prosecuted except by petition of the victim.
Demanda. Complaint; petition; law suit; demand.
Demandado. Defendant (in a law suit).
Demanda documentaria para pago. Documentary demand for payment.
Demandante. Plaintiff.
Demente. Insane.

Demolición. Demolition.
Demora. Delay; default; faulty delay in the performance of an obligation.
Denegación de apelación. Denial of appeal; refusal by the trial judge to sign an order of appeal when he considers it inappropriate.
Denegación de justicia. Denial of justice.
Denegación o retardo de justicia. Special writ of review from trial court's failure to render a judgment within the legal delays.
Denuncia. Accusation; report.
Denuncia calumniosa. Baseless accusation.
Denuncia del intestato. Petition to be put in possession by the heir of an intestate decedent.
Denuncia de obra nueva. Report that constructions are being made on land that infringe upon the rights of the owner of the immovable or the owner of a real right.
Denunciado. Accused; person as to whom an adverse report has been made.
Denuncia falsa. False accusation.
De oficio. Sua sponte; ex officio; on its own initiative.
Dependiente. Employee; dependant.
De pleno derecho. By operation of law.
Deportación. Deportation.
Deposición. Testimony of a witness; deposition.
Depositante. Depositor; bailor.
Depositario. Depositary; bailee.
Depositario judicial. Receiver.
Depósito. Deposit; bailment.
Depósito bancario. Bank deposit.
Depósito de ahorro. Savings deposit.
Depósito en cuenta de cheques. Deposit in checking account.
Depósito mercantil Commercial deposit.
Depósito miserable. Deposit made on the occasion of an emergency or catastrophic event, such as a fire, flood, etc.
Depósito necesario. Deposit made pursuant to a legal obligation or on the occasion of an emergency or catastrophic event.
Depósito regular. Regular deposit or bailment.
Depósito voluntario. Contractual deposit or bailment.
Derecho. Law; right.
Derecho absoluto. Right that is good against the world; real right.
Derecho accesorio. Accessory right.
Derecho adjetivo. Procedural law.
Derecho administrativo. Administrative law.

Derecho adquirido. Vested right.
Derecho aeronáutico. Aviation law; aeronautics law.
Derecho agrario. Agrarian law; agricultural law.
Derecho a la propia imagen. A person's right to publish his own picture and to prevent others from doing it without his authorization.
Derecho a la vida. Right to life.
Derecho ambiental. Environmental law.
Derecho autoral. Copyright law.
Derecho canónico. Canon law.
Derecho civil. Civil law.
Derecho comercial. Commercial law.
Derecho comparado. Comparative law.
Derecho común. General law; common legislation; usually refers to the law of the civil code.
Derecho constitucional. Constitutional law.
Derecho consuetudinario. Customary law.
Derecho de acrecer. *See* acrecimiento.
Derecho de asilo. Right of assylum.
Derecho de autor. *See* derecho autoral.
Derecho de familia. Family law; domestic relations law.
Derecho de gentes. Law of nations; international law.
Derecho de habitación. Right of habitation.
Derecho del tanto. Right of first refusal.
Derecho del trabajo. Labor law.
Derecho de obligaciones. Law of obligations; contract law.
Derecho de petición. Right of petition.
Derecho de propiedad. Property law.
Derecho de representación. Representation in successions law.
Derecho de retención. Right of retention; lien.
Derecho de reunión. Right of assembly.
Derecho de sufragio. Right to vote.
Derecho de superficie. Right of superficies.
Derecho de uso. Right of use; right of use servitude.
Derecho fiscal. Tax law.
Derecho foral. Regional law (Spain).
Derechohabiente. Person who has certain rights derived from another.
Derecho hereditario. Successions law.
Derecho hipotecario. Mortgage law; branch of the law dealing with recordation of rights in real or immovable property and the effects thereof.
Derecho inmobiliario. Immovable or real property law.

Derecho internacional. International law.
Derecho internacional privado. Private international law; conflict of laws.
Derecho internacional público. Public international law.
Derecho interno. The national or internal law of a particular country.
Derecho judicial. Law of court organization and functioning.
Derecho laboral. Labor law.
Derecho marítimo. Admiralty; maritime law.
Derecho mercantil. Commercial law.
Derecho municipal. Municipal law.
Derecho natural. Natural law.
Derecho notarial. Notarial law.
Derecho objetivo. Objective law.
Derecho penal. Criminal law.
Derecho personal. Personal right; credit right; personal law (private international law).
Derecho político. Constitutional law.
Derecho positivo. Positive law.
Derecho preferente. Better right; preferred right; right of priority.
Derecho privado. Private law.
Derecho procesal. Procedural law.
Derecho público. Public law.
Derecho real. Real right; right or interest in a thing.
Derecho registral. Registry laws; public records law; public records.
Derechos del hombre. Human rights.
Derechos de personalidad. Individual rights; fundamental rights.
Derechos humanos. Human rights.
Derechos indisponibles. Rights which due to a disposition of the law may not be exercised by their holders.
Derechos litigiosos. Litigious rights.
Derechos patrimoniales. Patrimonial rights.
Derechos potestativos. Potestative rights.
Derechos renunciables. Waivable rights.
Derecho subjetivo. Subjective law.
Derecho substantivo. Substantive law.
Derecho sucesorio. Successions law; law of descent and distribution.
Derecho supletorio. Suppletive law.
Derogación. Repeal.
Derogar. Repeal; abrogate.
Desacato. Contempt.

Desaforar. To disbar; to withdraw a privilege or special right.
Desafuero. Violent act contrary to law.
Desahuciar. To evict a tenant.
Desahucio. Eviction of a tenant.
Desalojo. *See* desahucio.
Desapoderamiento. Effect of a judgment decreeing bankruptcy whereby a person is deprived of the right to administer or alienate his assets.
Descalificar. Disqualify.
Descargo. Discharge; defense; extinction (of a debt); release.
Descendencia. Descent.
Descendiente. Descendant.
Desconocimiento de la paternidad. Disavowal of paternity.
Descontante. *See* acreditante.
Descontatario. *See* acreditado.
Descuento. Discount.
Desembargo. Order lifting or terminating an attachment or seizure.
Deserción. Abandonment of an action; desertion.
Desertor. Deserter.
Desfalcar. To embezzle.
Desfalco. Embezzlement.
Desheredación. Disinheritance.
Desistimiento. Abandonment of a right, claim, thing, or position; waiver of a claim or defense made during the course of litigation.
Desistimiento de la acción. *See* abandono de la acción.
Desistimiento de instancia. Voluntary dismissal.
Desistimiento de recurso. Voluntary dismissal.
Desistir del pleito. *See* desistimiento de instancia.
Deslindar. Boundary action.
Deslinde. Setting of the boundaries of an immovable.
Desnacionalización. Loss of nationality.
Despacho. Office; law office; dispatch; clearance (at customs); dismissal; discharge.
Despido. Employment dismissal.
Despojo. Violent or unlawful dispossession; possessory action.
Desposar. To marry.
Desposeer. Dispossess.
Déspota. Despot.
Despótico. Absolute; tyrannical; despotic.
Desterrar. To exile.
Destierro. Exile.
Destitución. Dismissal (from office).
Desuetudo. Disuse.
Desuso. Disuse.
Desviación de poder. Misuse or abuse of authority.
Detector de mentiras. Lie detector.
Detención. Arrest; detention.
Detención ilegal. Illegal arrest.

Detener. To arrest; to detain.
Detenido. Arrestee; one who has been arrested or detained.
Detentación. Possession of a thing that belongs to another.
Detentar. To possess a thing that belongs to another.
Deuda. Debt; obligation.
Deuda exigible. Accrued obligation.
Deuda líquida. Liquid obligation or debt.
Deuda pública. Public debt.
Deudas mortuorias. Debts derived from funeral charges and expenses of last illness.
Deudor. Debtor; obligor.
Deudor solidario. Solidary obligor.
Devolución. Return; devolution.
Día feriado. Legal holiday.
Día hábil. Working day; day that may be counted in a limitations period or a term.
Día inhábil. Holiday; day that may not be counted in a limitations period or a term.
Día laborable o laboral. Working day.
Diario oficial. Official journal.
Dictador. Dictator.
Dictadura. Dictatorship.
Dictamen. Decree; order; judgment; legal opinion; advisory opinion.
Dictatorial. Dictatorial.
Dieta. Fee; per diem; honorarium.
Difamación. Defamation.
Diferencia. Difference.
Difunto. Deceased.
Dilación. Continuance; term.
Dilapidación. Squandering.
Dilatoria (excepción). Motion to dismiss for improprieties that may be cured by the plaintiff; exception that tends to delay or suspend the litigation; dilatory exception.
Diligencia. Entry; annotation; proceeding; step in judicial proceedings; diligence; due care.
Diligenciamiento. Action and effect of doing procedural acts; step or action in judicial proceeding.
Diligencia preparatoria. Preparatory or introductory matter in a judicial proceeding.
Diligencias para mejor proveer. Measures that allow a more appropriate resolution of a dispute; additional proof adduced by order of the court.
Diligencias preparatorias de la demanda. Procedural measures in support of his rights taken by the plaintiff before filing the complaint.
Diligente padre de familia. Prudent administrator.
Dimisión. Resignation.
Diplomacia. Diplomacy.
Diplomático. Diplomat.
Diputado. Representative; normally a member of the lower chamber.
Dique. Dry dock; dam.
Dirimente. Impediment or obstacle to marriage.

Dirimir. To resolve a conflict or dispute.
Disceptación. Argument.
Disceptar. To argue.
Discernimiento del cargo. Court appointment (as curator, tutor etc.).
Disciplina. Discipline.
Discordia. Dissenting opinion; dissenting vote.
Discrecional. Discretionary.
Discusión. Argument; discussion.
Disenso. Dissent; discrepancy between two expressions of the will which prevents the formation of a juridical act.
Disentimiento. Dissent.
Disentir. Dissent.
Disidencia. Dissenting opinion; dissent.
Dispensa. Dispensation; waiver.
Disposición. Disposition; order.
Disposición reglamentaria. Regulation; regulatory disposition.
Disposición testamentaria. Testamentary disposition.
Disposición transitoria. Transitional provision; temporary disposition; temporary statute; law of limited duration.
Dispositivo. Dispositive; part of a document wherein rights and obligations are created, modified, or extinguished.
Distancia. Distance.
Dividendo. Dividend.
División. (Benefit of) division.
División de poderes. Separation of powers.
Divorcio. Divorce.
Doctrina. Doctrine.
Doctrina jurídica. Juridical doctrine; legal doctrine.
Documentar. To prove by document; to introduce a document into the record.
Documento. Document.
Documento de resguardo. Document of title.
Documento en tránsito. Document in transit.
Documento privado. Private writing.
Documento público. Public act (for example, a notarial act).
Dogmática jurídica. Science of the law; jurisprudence; systematic exposition of the law.
Dolo. Bad faith; fraud.
Dolo civil. Fraud; bad faith.
Dolo penal. Fraud.
Dolo procesal. Abuse of process; malicious prosecution.
Domicilio. domicile; residence.
Domicilio conyugal. Matrimonial domicile.
Domicilio de origen. Domicile of origin.
Domicilio legal. The situs of a person's domicile fixed by law.
Dominio. Ownership; fee simple.

Dominio eminente. Eminent domain.
Dominio privado del estado. Private domain of the state.
Donación. Donation; gift.
Donación antenupcial. Prenuptial donation or gift.
Donación condicional. Conditional donation or gift.
Donación inoficiosa. Donation subject to attack.
Donación onerosa. Onerous donation.
Donación pura. Unconditional donation.
Donación remunerativa. Remunerative donation.
Donante. Donor.
Donatario. donee.
Dote. Dowry.
Duelo. Duel.
Dueño. Owner.
Dueño útil. Beneficiary owner.
Dúplica. Reply; rejoinder.
Duplicado. Duplicate of a document.

E

Ebriedad. Drunkenness.
Ebriedad consuetudinaria. Chronic drunkenness.
Economía procesal. Judicial economy.
Edad. Age.
Edicto. Notice; public announcement of a judicial resolution; notice of judgment.
Edil. Councilman.
Efecto devolutivo. Devolutive effect (of an appeal).
Efecto retroactivo. Retroactive effect.
Efectos "de pleno derecho". *See* pleno derecho.
Efecto suspensivo. Suspensive effect (of an appeal).
Ejecución. Execution; enforcement.
Ejecución del fallo. Execution of judgment.
Ejecución de sentencia. Execution of judgment.
Ejecutoria. A public document bearing a definitive judgment.
Ejecutoriada. Judgment that is no longer subject to revision.
Elección. Election; selection.
Electo. One who has been elected or selected.
Elector. Elector.
Elevación (del proceso) al superior. Transmission of the record of a judicial proceeding to a higher court.
Emancipación. Emancipation.
Emancipado. Emancipated.
Embajada. Embassy.
Embajador. Ambassador.
Embargado. One whose assets have been seized.
Embargante. The sheriff or other officer who effects a seizure.

Embargo. Seizure; attachment.

Embargo precautorio. Provisional seizure.

Embargo preventivo. Provisional seizure; precautionary seizure; sequestration (of the debtor's property).

Emigración. Migration; immigration.

Emigrantes. Migrants; immigrants.

Emigrar. To migrate; to immigrate.

Emisión de títulos. Issuance of securities; offering of stocks or bonds to the public.

Emisor. Issuer.

Emitente. Issuer.

Emplazamiento. Service of process; summons.

Empleado. Employee.

Empleador. Employer.

Empleo. Employment.

Empresa. Enterprise; company.

Empresa marítima. Maritime company; maritime enterprise.

Empresa mercantil. Commercial enterprise.

Empresario. Entrepreneur; the owner of an enterprise.

Empréstito. Loan.

Enajenable. Alienable.

Enajenación. Alienation; transfer.

Enajenación forzosa. Expropriation; forced alienation; forced transfer.

Encarcelamiento. Imprisonment.

Encarcelar. To imprison.

Encargado de negocios. Chargé d'affaires; diplomatic agent in charge of a state's affairs in the absence of an ambassador.

Encausar. Prosecute.

Enclave. Enclave.

En cuanto haya lugar. Judicial declaration, made in *ex parte* proceedings, of a provisional nature.

Encubridor. Accessory after the fact.

Encubrimiento. To lend assistance to the perpetrator of a crime as an accessory after the fact.

Endosable. instrument susceptible of endorsement.

Endosatario. Beneficiary of an endorsement.

Endoso. Endorsement.

Endoso en blanco. Endorsement in blank.

Endoso en garantía. Endorsement of an instrument as collateral.

Endoso en prenda. *See* endoso en garantía.

Endoso en procuración. Endorsement of an instrument to enable an agent to collect or protest the instrument on behalf of his principal.

Endoso en propiedad. Endorsement whereby ownership of the instrument is conveyed to the beneficiary of the endorsement.

Enfermedad de trabajo. Occupational disease.

Enfiteusis. Emphytheusis.
Enfiteuta. Person with the beneficial ownership of an emphytheusis.
Enjuiciado. One that has been subjected to a judicial proceeding.
Enjuiciamiento. *See* procedimiento.
Enjuiciamiento civil. Civil procedure.
Enjuiciamiento criminal. Criminal procedure.
Enjuiciamiento penal. Criminal procedure.
Enmienda. Amendment.
Enriquecimiento injusto. *See* enriquecimiento sin causa.
Enriquecimiento sin causa. Unjust enrichment.
Ensañamiento. Criminal act whereby the perpetrator intends to produce great harm or injury to the victim.
Entidad. Entity.
Entrega de autos. Delivery of the record.
Entrega de la cosa. Delivery of the thing; summary proceeding whereby a party to a commutative contract who has fulfilled his performance may demand the forced execution of the other party's counterperformance.
Entrega efectiva de la herencia. Putting the heir in possession.
Entrerrenglonaduras. Interlineations.
Epiqueya. *See* equidad.
Equidad. Equity.
Equitativo. Equitable.
Erario. Treasury.
Error. Error; mistake.
Error in judicando. Error committed by the trial judge in evaluating the evidence or applying the law.
Error in procedendo. Judicial error on a procedural matter.
Escalamiento. Burglary; unauthorized entry.
Esclavitud. Slavery.
Esclavo. Slave.
Escolio. Concise exposition on a legal subject.
Escolista. Legal commentator.
Escriba. Scribe; one who devotes himself to the study, exposition, and the practice of law.
Escribano. Notary public; minute clerk.
Escrito. Writing; written.
Escritos judiciales. Briefs.
Escritura. Deed; act; notarial act; writing; document.
Escritura matriz. Original of a document; original of a notarial act.
Escritura privada. Private writing.
Escritura pública. Notarial act; public act; public writing; authentic act.
Escrutinio. Scrutiny; vote recount.
Escuela de derecho. Law school.
Esfera de influencia. Sphere of influence.

Especie. Specie.
Especulación. Speculation.
Espera. Respite.
Espía. Spy.
Espionaje. Espionage.
Esponsales. Promise of marriage made in writing.
Esposa. Wife.
Esposo. Husband.
Establecimiento de un crédito. Establishment of credit.
Establecimiento mercantil. Commercial establishment.
Estado. State; status.
Estado civil. Civil status; status.
Estado constitucional. *See* estado de derecho.
Estado de derecho. State in which power and authority is based on the rule of law.
Estado de guerra. State of war.
Estado de necesidad. Situation or state of necessity.
Estado de quiebra. Legal status of one who has been declared bankrupt.
Estado de sitio. State of siege.
Estado federal. Federal state.
Estado peligroso. Status of one who has a propensity to commit crimes.
Estado soberano. Sovereign state.
Estafa. Theft by fraud.
Estancia. Rural property; farm.
Estanco. State monopoly, usually for fiscal purposes.
Estar a derecho. Response required of one served with a citation of a complaint.
Estatismo. Excessive intervention in the affairs of its citizens by the state, characteristic of totalitarian regimes.
Estatuir. To order, determine, establish, legislate.
Estatutario. In accordance with an "estatuto" or "estatutos".
Estatuto. Legal rule; legislation.
Estatuto personal. Personal law.
Estatutos. Charter of a corporation or association.
Estelionato. Sale of stolen property; fraudulent dealing in another's property; fraudulent representation of ownership of property belonging to another.
Estimación. Appraisal; assessment.
Estipulación. Stipulation; clause.
Estipulación por tercero. Third party beneficiary clause.
Estirpe. Stirpes; root and trunk of a family.
Estrados. Judicial bench.
Estuprador. One who commits the crime of estupro.
Estupro. Carnal knowledge of a juvenile who is also a virgin; seduction of a minor female virgin.
Evasión. Criminal escape; accessory after the fact.

Evasivas. Evasive answers.
Evicción. Eviction.
Evidencia. Evidence.
Examen. Examination.
Excarcelación. Freeing of a person from incarceration pursuant to court order.
Excarcelar. *See* excarcelación.
Excepción. Exception; demurrer; motion to dismiss.
Excepción declinatoria. Declinatory exception; motion to dismiss for lack of jurisdiction or venue.
Excepción de falta de personería. Exception claiming lack of capacity in the representative to sue on behalf of the principal.
Excepción de incompetencia. Exception of lack of jurisdiction or improper venue.
Excepción dilatoria. Dilatory exception; motion to dismiss for improprieties that may be cured by the plaintiff; exceptions that tend to delay or suspend the litigation.
Excepción perentoria. Peremptory exception; motion to dismiss on peremptory grounds; demurrer.
Exclusión. Exclusion.
Exculpación. Declaration of innocence concerning one who has been accused of a crime.
Excusación. Recusation; excuse.
Exégesis. Exegesis.
Exégeta. Interpreter of a legal text.
Exegético. Relating to exegesis.
Exención. Exemption.
Exención contributiva. Tax exemption.
Exención de impuestos. Tax exemption.
Exequatur. Judicial approval of a foreign judgment for execution.
Exhibición. Exhibition.
Exhorto. Letters rogatory.
Exilio. Exile.
Exoneración. Dismissal; exoneration.
Expectativa. Hope based on the acquistion of a thing or a right.
Expediente. Record; proceedings.
Experiencia jurídica. Legal experience.
Expiración. Expiration; termination.
Explicación de sentencia. Court's explanation of a judgment.
Exposición. Statement; complaint.
Exposición de motivos. Exposé des motifs; explanation of the contents and motives of a given body of legislation.
Expresión de agravios. Assignment of errors in an appeal.
Expromisión. Offer by a third party to assume the debt of an obligor.
Expropiación. Expropriation.
Expropiar. To expropriate.

Extinción. Extinction.
Extinción de la obligación. Extinction of the obligation.
Extorsión. Extorsion.
Extradición. Extradition.
Extrajudicial. Extrajudicial.
Extranjería. Immigration law; legal status of a foreigner.
Extranjero. Foreigner.
Extraterritorial. Outside of the territory of a state.
Extraterritorialidad. Extraterritoriality.

F

Facción. Faction; war activity.
Facería. Coownership of pasture lands.
Factor. General manager of a commercial enterprise; high ranking administrator of a business.
Factores del delito. Elements of a crime; causative factors of a crime.
Factura. Bill; statement.
Facultad. Faculty; legal possibility.
Facultad de derecho. Law school; law faculty.
Facultad procesal. Judicial authority over the litigation; procedural rights.
Facultar. To authorize.
Facultativo. Optional; one who is authorized to do something.
Falencia. Bankruptcy; insolvency; failure.
Falsario. One who commits a "falsedad".
Falsedad. False representation; forgery; falsehood.
Falsificación. Forgery.
Falso testimonio. Perjury; false swearing; perjured testimony.
Falta. Misdemeanor; fault.
Falta de acción. No cause of action.
Falta de capacidad legal. Lack of legal capacity.
Falta de capacidad procesal. Lack of procedural capacity.
Falta de méritos. Lack of probable cause.
Falta de personería (excepción de). Dilatory exception claiming lack of capacity in the representative to sue on behalf of the principal.
Falta de poder. Lack of authority.
Faltar. To commit a misdemeanor.
Fallar. To pronounce judgment.
Fallar por expediente. Appeal decided on the record.
Fallecimiento. Death.
Fallido. Bankrupt; insolvent debtor.
Fallo. Judgment; decision.
Familia. Family.

Familia adoptiva. Adoptive family.
Familiar. Corresponding or relating to the family.
Fatal. Peremptive character of a term; fatal.
Fatricida. One who kills a sibling.
Fatricidio. The killing of a sibling.
Fe. Faith.
Fecha. Date.
Fedatario. One who attests, usually a notary public.
Fedatario judicial. Attesting clerk of court or minute clerk.
Federación. Federation.
Federal. Federal.
Federalismo. Federalism.
Federalista. Federalist.
Federativo. Pertaining to the federation.
Fe de vida. Certification that someone is alive.
Fehaciente. Attesting; authentic; bearing evidence.
Felón. Traitor; one who commits an act of disloyalty.
Felonía. Treason; disloyalty.
Fe pública. Authority of certain officers, such as notary publics, to attest documents; authentic character of certain documents due to attestation of a public officer.
Feriado. Legal holiday.
Feticidio. Killing of a fetus.
Fiado. One on whose behalf a person serves as a surety.
Fiador. Surety.
Fianza. Suretyship.
Fianza convencional. Conventional suretyship.
Fianza de arraigo. Security for costs.
Fianza de judicatum solui. *See* fianza de arraigo.
Fianza de rato et grato. Security that must be paid by the representative whose authority is questionable.
Fianza judicial. Suretyship decreed by a court of law.
Fianza legal. Legal suretyship.
Fianza procesal. Bond; bail.
Ficción. Fiction.
Fidedigno. Creditable.
Fideicomisario. Trust beneficiary.
Fideicomiso. Trust; fideicomissum.
Fideicomitente. Settlor.
Fiduciario. Trustee; fiduciary.
Filiación. Filiation.
Filiación adoptiva. Filiation by adoption.
Filiación matrimonal. Filiation by marriage; legitimate filiation.
Filiación no matrimonial. Extramarital or illegitimate filiation.
Filiación por naturaleza. Natural filiation.
Filial. Filial; pertaining to the child or children.
Filicida. One who violently kills his child.
Filicidio. Violent killing of a child by a parent.

Filosofía del derecho. Jurisprudence; philosophy of law.
Finalización del plazo. End of term; accrual; maturity (as of a debt).
Finca. Real estate; piece of real estate or immovable property; farm.
Finca habitación. Dwelling.
Finiquitar. Payment of an obligation.
Finiquito de una deuda. Payment of a debt.
Firma. Firm; enterprise; business; signature.
Firma a ruego. Signing of a person's name by a third party due to the inability to sign of the person whose name is being signed.
Firma de letrado. Signature of attorney (as in a pleading).
Firma social. Corporate name; firm name.
Fiscal. Prosecutor; state attorney; district attorney; having to do with the treasury.
Fiscalía. Prosecutor's office.
Fisco. Treasury.
Fletador. One who charters or hires an entire vessel, or a part thereof, for the transportation of persons or merchandise.
Fletamento. Charter party or lease of a vessel for the transportation of persons or merchandise.
Fletar. To charter or hire a vessel.
Flete. Price of a charter party or lease of a vessel or part thereof; price for the transport of merchandise.
Flota. Fleet.
Foja. Page.
Folio. Page.
Fondo de comercio. Commercial establishment; commercial enterprise.
Forense. Pertaining to the bar; pertaining to the forum.
Formalidad. Requirement (as of a particular form); formality.
Formalizar. To satisfy a formality.
Fórmula. Form; formulary; form book.
Foro. Bar; forum.
Fortuito. Fortuitous.
Fortuna de mar. *See* abandono de buque.
Franquicia. Tax exemption; franchise.
Fraude. Fraud.
Fraude de ley. In fraud of the law; *in fraudem legis;* unlawful or inappropriate exercise of a right.
Fraudulento. Fraudulent.
Frontera. Border.
Frutos. Fruits; products.
Frutos pendientes. Pendent fruits.
Fuentes del derecho. Sources of the law.
Fuentes secundarias. Secondary sources.
Fuero. Special law; subject matter jurisdiction; forum.
Fuero de atracción. Jurisdiction over all suits

instituted against the debtor (as that of the judge presiding over bankruptcy proceedings).
Fuerza de ley. Force or effect of law.
Fuerza ejecutiva. Efficacy of a document giving a party the right to use executory process.
Fuerza ejecutoria. Efficacy of a document giving a party the right to the "apremio" (a very summary executory proceeding).
Fuerza irresistible. Irresistible force.
Fuerza mayor. Force majeure; irresistible force.
Fuerza probatoria. Evidentiary value; probative strength.
Funcionario. One who performs a public function; government agent.
Funcionario público. Public official.
Función jurisdiccional. Judicial function; adjudicatory function.
Función pública. Public function.
Función tuitiva. Parental duty of custody and care.
Fundación. Foundation; endowment; trust.
Fundamentos de la sentencia. Reasons for judgment.
Fundo. An immovable by nature.
Fungibles. *See* bienes fungibles.
Fusión de sociedades mercantiles. Corporate merger.

G

Gabela. Tax or contribution.
Gabinete. Cabinet.
Ganancia. Earnings.
Gananciales. *See* bienes gananciales.
Ganzúa. Burglary tool; item used in the perpetration of a burglary.
Garante. Surety; guarantor.
Garantía. Suretyship; guaranty; warranty; protection of rights; collateral.
Garantías constitucionales. Constitutional guarantees; rights and liberties protected by the constitution.
Garantías del acusado. Constitutional rights of the accused.
Gastos de puro lujo. Expenses made for the embellishment of a thing which do not increase its value.
Gastos necesarios. Necessary expenses; expenses made for the preservation of a thing.
Gastos procesales. Court costs; litigation expenses.
Gastos útiles. Useful expenses; expenses that increase the value of a thing.

Gastos voluntarios. Expenses made for the embellishment of a thing or for the pleasure or comfort of the possessor of the thing.

Generales de la ley. General questions asked of witnesses, such as name, nationality, domicile, etc.

Genocidio. Genocide.

Gerencia. Management; office of the manager.

Gestión. Negotiation; action; handling.

Gestión de negocios. Voluntary managment of another's affairs.

Gestor. Volunteer; voluntary manager of another's affairs.

Gestor administrativo. Professional who handles the affairs of others in administrative agencies.

Gestor de negocios ajenos. *See* gestor.

Girado. Payee of a bill of exchange.

Girador. Maker of a bill of exchange.

Giro. Transfer of funds from a person's account to another person's account; draft; line of business.

Giro bancario. Money order; bank draft.

Giro documentario. Documentary draft.

Gobernador. Governor.

Gobernante. One who governs; designation of the head of state.

Gobierno de facto. *De facto* government.

Gobierno de hecho. *See* gobierno de facto.

Gobierno parlamentario. Parliamentary government.

Goce pacífico (de un derecho). Peaceful possession; peaceful exercise of a right.

Gracia. Grace; clemency.

Grado de parentesco. Degree of relationship.

Graduación de créditos. Ranking of liens (or privileges).

Graduación de la culpa. Degrees or classification of negligence or fault.

Gravado. Burdened person or thing.

Gravamen. Charge; encumbrance; burden.

Gravar. Burden (as by a mortgage, privilege, lien, etc.); encumber.

Gravedad (del acto). Severity of the act; seriousness of the offense; seriousness of the crime.

Guardador. Generic name given to a person in charge of the custody and administration of the assets of another, such as curators, tutors, and guardians.

Gubernamental. Governmental.

Guerra civil. Civil war.

H

Haber. To have a thing or right; asset(s).
Haber hereditario. Succession assets; portion of the inheritance falling to each heir.
Habilitación. Validation; removal of impediments.
Habilitación de día. Judicial resolution authorizing the performance of a particular act on a legal holiday.
Habilitación de hora. Judicial resolution authorizing the performance of a particular act at a time beyond regular hours.
Habitación. Habitation.
Habitacionista. One who has a right of habitation.
Hacer deshonor. Dishonor.
Hacienda. Patrimony; balance of assets and liabilities; treasury; property.
Hacienda mercantil. Patrimony of a commercial enterprise.
Hacienda pública. Treasury; totality of the assets belonging to the state.
Hecho jurídico. Fact that creates, modifies, or extinguishes rights.
Hecho notorio. Generally known fact; fact of which a court may take judicial notice.
Hecho procesal. Fact that creates, modifies, or extinguishes procedural rights.
Hecho punible. Punishable act, punishable offense.
Heredad. Estate.
Heredero. Heir.
Heredero aparente. Heir apparent.
Heredero beneficiario. Beneficiary heir; heir that accepts the decedent's succession under benefit of inventory.
Hereditario. Hereditary.
Herencia. Inheritance.
Herencia adida. Inheritance or succession the heir of which has expressed his intention to accept.
Herencia indeferida. Inheritance subject to a suspensive condition.
Herencia legítima. Legal succession.
Herencia testamentaria. testamentary succession.
Herencia yacente. Succession that has not been accepted by the heirs.
Hermana política. Sister in law.
Hermanastra. Half sister.
Hermanastro. Half brother.
Hermano político. Brother in law.
Hijo adulterino. Child born of an adulterous relationship.
Hijo de familia. Minor child under parental authority.
Hijo ilegítimo. Illegitimate child.
Hijo incestuoso. Child born of an incestuous relationship.
Hijo legitimado. Legitimated child.
Hijo legítimo. Legitimate child.

Hijo natural. Natural child.
Hijo reconocido. Acknowledged child.
Hijuela. Part of an inheritance falling to one of the heirs; part of the deed of partition where the succession assets falling to each of the heirs is set forth.
Hipoteca. Mortgage.
Hipoteca abstracta. Mortgage wherein there exists no registry relationship between the credit and the security.
Hipoteca de responsabilidad limitada. *In rem* mortgage; mortgage wherein the mortgagor's liability is limited to the proceeds of the sale of the property mortgaged.
Hipoteca dotal. Mortgage by virtue of dowry; dotal mortgage.
Hipoteca legal. Legal mortgage; judicial mortgage.
Hipoteca naval. Ship mortgage.
Hipoteca necesaria. Legal mortgage that some persons must give because of the assets they administer or to guarantee the obligation owed to certain creditors.
Hipotecar. To mortgage.
Hipoteca voluntaria. Conventional mortgage.
Hitar. *See* amojonamiento.
Hito. *See* mojón.
Homicida. Perpetrator of a homicide; one who kills a human being.
Homicidio. Homicide; murder.
Homicidio con alevosía. Homicide committed with malice; homicide committed with specific intent to kill.
Homicidio inintencional. Involuntary manslaughter; negligent homicide.
Homologación. Homologation.
Honorario(s). Fee (especially of an attorney).
Horario judicial. Court hours.
Honrar. To honor.
Hospedaje. Lodging.
Huelga. Strike.
Hurto. Theft.

I

Identidad de causa. Procedural situation occurring when the same claim has been asserted in another suit.
Identidad de objeto. *See* Identidad de causa.
Identificación. Identification.
Ignorancia del derecho. Ignorance of the law.
Iguala. Retainer fee; agreement whereby an attorney is retained on the basis of a percentage of the economic benefit to be derived from the litigation; contingency fee.
Igualdad ante la ley. Equal protection of the law.

Igualdad del salario. Equal pay for equal work.
Igualdad procesal. Procedural equality (of the parties).
Ilegítimo. Illegitimate.
Ilícito. Unlawful; illicit.
Impedimento. Impediment; legal cause for recusation or impeachment.
Impedimento dispensable. Impediment subject to waiver.
Impensas. Expenses.
Imperio. Authority; power.
Imperio de la ley. The rule of law; the authority of law.
Implicancia. Absolute impediment; cause for recusation or impediment that cannot be cured.
Importancia del asunto. Amount in dispute; importance of the matter.
Imprescriptibilidad. Not subject to prescription.
Imprescriptible. A right that is not subject to prescription.
Imprevisible. Unforeseeable; *see* also imprevisión.
Imprevisión. Unforeseeable; force majeure; frustration of purpose.
Improcedencia de la vía. Dilatory exception of inappropriate type of procedure.
Improcedente. Without right; inappropriate.
Improrrogabilidad. A term that is not subject to extension.
Improrrogable. Not subject to continuance; that which cannot be delayed.
Imprudencia. Imprudence; fault; negligence.
Impúber. Person who has not reached puberty.
Impuesto. Tax; assessment.
Impugnación. Attack; appeal; refute.
Impulso procesal. Process of expediting an action to judgment.
Impunidad. Impunity.
Imputabilidad. Legal capacity to commit a crime.
Imputación. Imputation; attribution.
Imputación de pagos. Imputation of payments.
Imputado. Accused; defendant in a criminal case.
Imputador. One who accuses.
Imputar. To impute; attribute; accuse.
Inalienable. Inalienable.
Inamovible. Nonremovable character of certain public employees.
Inamovilidad judicial. Nonremovability of judges.
Inapelabilidad. Not subject to appeal.
Inapelable. Unappealable.
Incapacidad. Lack of capacity.
Incapacidad legal. Lack of legal capacity; lack of capacity to sue or be sued.
Incapacidad procesal. Lack of procedural capacity.
Incautación. Seizure; confiscation.

Incautar. To confiscate; taking disputed assets into the custody of the court.

Incestuoso. Incestuous.

Incidente. Incident; ancillary matter.

Incidente de no contestar. Interposition of dilatory exceptions prior to filing the answer.

Incidente de previo y especial pronunciamiento. Prior matter that must be resolved before the matter in dispute can be tried on the merits.

Incidente de tachas. Procedure for rebuttal of witness testimony.

Inciso. Section, paragraph (as of a statute, etc.).

Incomparecencia. Failure of a person to appear before a judicial or administrative officer.

Incompatibilidad. Incompatibility.

Incompetencia. Incompetence; lack of jurisdiction; improper venue.

Incompetencia absoluta. Lack of jurisdiction, lack of venue, or incompetence which cannot be waived by agreement.

Incompetencia manifiesta. *See* incompetencia absoluta.

Incompetencia notoria. Notorious incompetence.

Incompetencia relativa. Waivable incompetence or lack of jurisdiction or venue.

Inconstitucional. Unconstitutional.

Inconstitucionalidad. Unconstitutionality.

Inculpado. Accused; convict; defendant.

Incumplimiento. Breach.

Indagatoria. Interrogation of the defendant or a witness by the judge during the investigative phase of the proceedings.

Indemnización. Payment of damages; compensation; indemnification.

Independencia judicial. Independence of the judiciary.

Indice. Index; index of records in clerk of court's office.

Indicio. Evidentiary indicia.

Indignidad. Unworthiness of heirs to inherit.

Indisponibles. Rights that are not subject to alienation.

Individualización de la pena. Tailoring of the sentence to the circumstances of the case.

Indivisibilidad de la confesión. Principle that prohibits the introduction into evidence of only the unfavorable part of a confession.

Indivisible. Indivisible.

Indivisión. Indivision; status of joint ownership; undivided interest.

Indiviso. Status of joint ownership of a thing or a right.

Inducción. Incitement or instigation to commit a crime.

Inductor. One who incites or instigates another to commit a crime.

Indulto. Pardon.

Inembargabilidad. Not subject to attachment or seizure.
Inenajenabilidad. Inalienability.
Ineptitud. Incompetence.
Inexistencia. Lack of existence of a juridical act for lack of a formal requirement.
Infamia. Infamy.
Infancia. Infancy.
Infanticidio. Killing of a child, especially shortly after its birth.
Infidelidad. Disloyalty.
Infidelidad conyugal. Lack of fidelity in the marriage.
Información sumaria. Summary evidentary hearing usually conducted *ex parte*.
Informe "in voce". Oral report.
Infracción. Infraction; violation.
Inhabilidad. One who lacks a legal requirement to perform a particular juridical act.
Inhabilitación. Loss of certain rights concomitant with the sentence in a criminal case; disqualification; impediment.
Inhibición. Recusation; court's *sua sponte* declaration of lack of jurisdiction or venue; prohibition.
Injuria. Offensive remark; insult.
Inmatriculación. Registration in the public records.
Inmigrado. Immigrant status; an immigrant that acquires permanent resident status.
Inmueble. Immovable.
Inmune. Immune; a person who has the right of immunity.
Inmunidad. Immunity.
Inmunidad de jurisdicción. Immunity; immunity from prosecution or civil suit.
Inmunidad diplomática. Diplomatic immunity.
Inmunidad parlamentaria. Parliamentary immunity.
Innovación. Proceeding to prevent the trial court from issuing further orders after the action is on appeal.
Inoponibilidad. Ineffectiveness as to a certain party.
Inquilinato. Lease of a dwelling.
Inquilino. Lessee of a dwelling.
Insaculación. Type of voting by choosing a paper ballot from among several.
Inscribible. Amenable to registry; subject to or capable of registry.
Inscripción. Registry; inscription.
Inscripción hipotecaria. Mortgage recordation; mortgage inscription; entry in mortgage records.
Inscripción preventiva. Precautionary recordation; preventive recordation; preventive inscription.
Insolvencia. Insolvency; bankruptcy.
Insolvencia fraudulenta. Fraudulent insolvency.
Insolvente. Insolvent; bankrupt.

Inspección. Inspection; examination of the evidence by the trial judge.
Instancia. The prosecution of the trial from the filing of the law suit to judicial decision on the merits; instance; level in court hierarchy.
Instancia de parte. At the request of a party in interest.
Instigador. One who incites or instigates another to commit a crime.
Institución. Institution; company.
Institucional. Institutional; relating to institutions.
Institución de crédito. Credit institution.
Institución de fianzas. Bonding or surety company.
Institución de heredero. Designation by the testator of the universal heir.
Institución de seguros. Insurance company or agency.
Institución fiduciaria. Trust institution; fiduciary institution.
Instrucción. Investigative phase of criminal proceedings.
Instrumento público. Public document; authentic act; notarized document.
Insubordinación. Insubordination.
Insurrección. Insurrection.
Integración de tribunal. Sitting of required number of judges that make up the panel involved.
Intención. Intention.
Intencional. Intentional.
Interdicción. Interdiction; prohibition.
Interdicción general de bienes. Order prohibiting a debtor from disposing of his assets in fraud of creditors' rights.
Interdicto. Order; decree; interdict.
Interdicto de recuperar. Action to recover possession by one who has been wrongfully dispossessed.
Interdicto de retener. Action by one whose possession has been disturbed against the person causing the disturbance.
Interés. Interest.
Interesado. Interested party; real party in interest.
Interés privado. Private interest.
Interés público. Public interest.
Interfecto. A person who has been killed by violent means.
Intermediario. Intermediary.
Interpósita persona. Agent that acts for an undisclosed party. Generally the undisclosed party is one who cannot enter a particular transaction.
Interpretación. Interpretation.
Interpretación doctrinal. Interpretation of the law made by legal commentators.
Interpretación evolutiva. Interpretation of the law in a way not contemplated by the

law maker, but in tune with contemporary reality.

Interpretación extensiva. Broad interpretation of a statute or legislative text.

Interpretación restrictiva. Narrow interpretation.

Intérprete. Interpreter; one who interprets legislation or a juridical act.

Interrogatorio. Examination of a witness; interrogatory.

Intervalo lúcido. Lucid interval.

Intervención. Intervention.

Intervenir. Audit; inspect; supervise; intervene.

Interventor. Auditor; inspector; superintendent; supervisor; intervenor.

Intestado. Decedent who died without leaving a will; intestate; intestate succession.

Intimidación. Intimidation.

Invalidación. Annulment; invalidation.

Inventario. Inventory.

Investigación del derecho. Legal research.

Inviolabilidad. Immunity; inviolability.

Irracional disenso. Proceeding by a child to obtain judicial dispensation to the age requirements for marriage when the parents unreasonably deny him the necessary approval.

Irresponsable. One who need not respond for a certain act or situation.

Irretroactividad. Nonretroactivity.

Irrevocabilidad. Irrevocability

J

Jefe de Estado. Chief of state.

Jerarquía. Hierarchy.

Jornal. Wages; salary.

Jornalero. Wage earner.

Jubilación. Retirement; pension.

Jubilado. Retiree; one who receives a pension.

Judicatura. The judiciary.

Judicial. Judicial; relative or pertaining to the administration of justice.

Juez. Judge.

Juez árbitro. Arbitrator.

Juez competente. Judge or court with jurisdiction and proper venue.

Juez de instrucción. *See* juez instructor.

Juez de letras. District judge.

Juez de lo civil. Civil court judge.

Juez de menores. Juvenile court judge; judge with jurisdiction over minors.

Juez de paz. Justice of the peace.

Juez incompetente. Judge or court without jurisdiction or of improper venue.

Juez instructor. Investigating judge. Judge in charge of investigating the commission of a crime and ascertaining the existence of the *corpus delicti.*

Juez suplente. Substitute judge.

Juicio. Trial; hearing; judgment; decision; process.

Juicio arbitral. Arbitration proceedings.

Juicio civil. Civil proceedings; civil trial.

Juicio criminal. Criminal proceedings; criminal trial.

Juicio de alimentos. Alimony or child support hearing; alimony or child support rule.

Juicio de árbitros. Arbitration; trial before arbitration panel.

Juicio de incompetencia (promover). Action to dismiss or transfer suit on grounds of lack of jurisdiction or improper venue.

Juicio de responsabilidad. Proceedings against a judge for malfeasance in office.

Juicio escrito. Judicial proceedings wherein pleadings, proof, and argument are all submitted in writing.

Juicio extraordinario. Extraordinary proceedings.

Juicio oral. Oral proceedings.

Juicio ordinario. Ordinary proceedings.

Juicio penal. Criminal proceedings.

Juicio petitorio. Petition; petitory action.

Juicio posesorio. Possessory action.

Juicio sumario. Summary proceedings.

Juicio verbal. *See* juicio oral.

Junta. Commission; meeting.

Jurado. Jury; juror.

Juramento. Oath.

Juramento decisorio. Defendant's oath concerning the veracity of the assertions made in the petition.

Juramento estimatorio. Appraisal oath.

Jurídico. Judicial; legal.

Jurisconsulto. Legal scholar; jurisconsult; lawyer.

Jurisdicción. Jurisdiction.

Jurisdicción contenciosa. Contradictory proceedings; jurisdiction to hear ordinary or contradictory proceedings.

Jurisdicción convencional. Jurisdiction by consent of the parties.

Jurisdicción legal. Jurisdiction as provided by law.

Jurisdicción mercantil. Commercial jurisdiction.

Jurisdicción voluntaria. *Ex parte* proceedings; jurisdiction to hear *ex parte* proceedings.

Juris et de jure. Non-rebuttable presumption.

Jurisprudencia. Case law; jurisprudence.

Juris tantum. Rebuttable presumption.

Justicia. Justice; administration of justice; proceedings.
Justificación. Justification.
Justificado. Justified; appropriate; reasonable.
Justificar. To justify.
Justipreciar. Appraisal.
Justiprecio. Fair market value; just price.
Justiprecio de peritos. Assessment of fair market value by experts.
Juzgado. Court; tribunal; decided; adjudged.
Juzgador. Judge; trier of fact.
Juzgamiento. Trial.
Juzgar. To adjudge; to try a case.

L

Ladrón. One who commits a theft or robbery.
Lagunas de la ley. Hiatus in the legislation.
Lanzamiento. Eviction; ouster.
Latifundio. Large tract of land.
Latrocinio. Theft.
Laudo. Arbitral award.
Laudo arbitral. *See* laudo.
Legación. Legation.
Legado. Legacy.
Legado alternativo. Legacy wherein the legatee is called to choose between two or more things.
Legado causal. Legacy wherein the testator expresses the reason for making the legacy.
Legado de cantidad. Legacy of a sum of money.
Legado de cosa específica. Legacy of an individualized thing.
Legado de cosa indeterminada. Legacy of a thing defined by gender only.
Legado de crédito. Legacy of a credit that the testator has against a third party.
Legado de deuda. Legacy of remission of the debt owed by the legatee to the testator.
Legado de educación. Legacy of the means to earn a professional degree or to learn a trade.
Legado puro. Unconditional legacy.
Legal. Legal.
Legalidad. Legality; lawfulness.
Legalización. Authentication; notarization; legalization.
Legalizar. To legalize.
Legalmente. Legally.
Legar. To leave someone a legacy.
Legatario. Legatee.
Legislación. Legislation.
Legislación civil. Civil legislation; civil law.
Legislación común. General law; common legislation; usually refers to the law of the civil code.

Legislación foral. Special law; law of a region having authority to legislate (Sp.).
Legislador. Legislator; legislature; law making body.
Legislar. To legislate.
Legislativo. Legislative.
Legista. Lawyer; expert on legislation.
Legítima. Legitime; legitimate portion.
Legitimación. Legitimation.
Legitimación procesal. Procedural interest; right of action; competence to sue.
Legítima defensa. Self defense; defense of others.
Legitimado. Legitimated.
Legítimo. Legitimate; in accordance with law.
Leguleyo. One who, having a superficial knowledge of the law, pretends to be a lawyer.
Lesión. Injury; lesion.
Letra de cambio. Draft; bill of exchange.
Letra de resaca. Bill of exchange drawn to recover the amount owed on an unpaid bill of exchange.
Letrado. *See* abogado.
Letra pagadera a la vista. Sight draft.
Levantamiento de embargo. Release of attachment or seizure.
Ley. Legislation; law; statute; act.
Ley de propiedad horizontal. Condominium law; horizontal property law.
Ley hipotecaria. Mortgage law; mortgage laws.
Ley imperativa. Imperative law; mandatory law, not subject to change by agreement.
Ley irrenunciable. A law the dispositions of which are not subject to change by agreement.
Ley marcial. Martial law.
Ley nacional. National law.
Ley orgánica. Organic law; a law that sets up an institution or a public service.
Ley orgánica del poder judicial. Statute or code setting forth the organization and jurisdiction of courts, as well as administrative matters concerning the courts, judges, and court auxiliary personnel.
Ley permisiva. A law that authorizes or tolerates certain acts.
Ley prohibitiva. Prohibitory law.
Ley renunciable. A law the dispositions of which may be changed by agreement.
Libelo. Defamatory writing; petition.
Liberación. Liberation.
Liberalidad. Liberality; gift.
Libertad. Liberty.
Libertad de asociación. Freeedom of association.
Libertad de los mares. Freedom of navigation; freedom of the seas.
Libertad de opinión. Freedom of speech.
Libertad de prensa. Freedom of the press.

Libertad de religión o libertad religiosa. Freedom of religion.
Libertad de reunión. Right of assembly.
Libertades individuales. Individual rights.
Libertades políticas. Political liberties.
Libertades públicas. Individual rights.
Libertad preparatoria. Parol of convicts for good conduct.
Libertad provisional. Provisional release of an accused pending trial, either after giving security or on his own recognizance.
Libertad vigilada. Probation; parol.
Librado(da). Drawee bank, credit institution, or person.
Librador. Drawer of a draft or bill of exchange.
Libramiento. Order of payment.
Libranza. Draft; bill of exchange.
Librar. Draw (draft); liberate; set forth.
Libre albedrío. Freedom of choice.
Libre convicción. Judidical discretion in assessment of the evidence in certain cases; freedom of evaluation.
Libro de acuerdos. Case reporter; book wherein decisions of appellate courts are recorded.
Libro de archivo. Case register.
Libro de conocimientos. Register of proceedings.
Libro de discordias. Compilation of dissenting opinions of an appellate court.
Libro de embargos. Register of attachments and seizures.
Libro de entradas. Chronological register of actions.
Libro de oficios. Register of judicial orders.
Libros administratorios. Books of administration, such as merchants' books.
Libros de comercio. Merchants' books.
Licencia. Leave; license, permit.
Licenciado. Professional who has a university degree; one who holds a license.
Licitación. Auction sale.
Licitador. Bidder at an auction sale.
Licitante. *See* licitador.
Licitar. To bid at an auction sale.
Lícito. Licit; lawful.
Licitud. Lawfulness; licit character of.
Ligamen. Legal relationship.
Ligereza culpable. Abuse of process; fault; negligence.
Liquidación. Liquidation.
Liquidación de sentencia. Proceeding to determine with specificity the sum to be paid by the debtor; execution of judgment.
Liquidación de sociedades mercantiles. Liquidation of a corporation.

Liquidez. Liquidity of a credit or obligation.
Litigante. Party to a law suit; litigator; litigant.
Litigante temerario. One who knowingly abuses the litigation process.
Litigar con malicia temeraria. Abuse of process; malicious prosecution.
Litigio. Law suit; litigation.
Litigioso. Litigious; controverted.
Litis. Litigation; law suit.
Litisconsorcio. Status of coparties in a judicial proceeding.
Litisexpensas. Contribution to the expenses of litigation.
Litis pendencia. *Lis pendens*; procedural situation arising when there are two or more suits between the same parties on the same cause of action.
Locación. Lease.
Locación de bienes muebles. Lease of personal or movable property; bailment.
Locación de cosas. Lease of things.
Locación de fundos rústicos. Lease of rural property.
Locación de fundos urbanos. Lease of urban property.
Locador. Lessor.
Locatario. Lessee.
Lógica jurídica. Legal reasoning; legal logic.
Lucro cesante. Lost profits as an element of damages.
Lugar público. Public place.

Ll

Llamada en garantía. Call in warranty.
Llamamiento. Summons; citation.
Llamamiento del tercero pretendiente. Joinder by the defendant of a third party claimant.

M

Madre política. Mother in law.
Magistrado. Judge; magistrate.
Magistrado ponente. Judge or justice who delivers the opinion of the court.
Mala fama. Bad reputation.
Mala fe. Bad faith.
Mala fe procesal. Abuse of process; malicious prosecution.
Malicia. Malice; bad faith.
Malos tratos. Ill treatment.
Malversación. Embezzlement.
Malversador. Embezzler.
Malversar. To embezzle.
Mancomunidad. Coownership.
Mandamiento. Order; injunction.
Mandamiento de cancelación. Cancellation order.

Mandamiento de detención. Arrest warrant; arrest order.
Mandamiento judicial. Order; mandamus; injunction.
Mandante. Principal (in an agency or mandate relationship).
Mandatario. Agent; mandatary; attorney-in-fact.
Mandato. Agency; mandate; power of attorney.
Mandato judicial. Judicial order; decree.
Mando. Command.
Marca. Trademark.
Marca registrada. (Registered) trademark.
Marido. Husband.
Mar libre. Part of the sea outside a state's territorial waters.
Mar territorial. Territorial sea.
Martillador. Auctioneer.
Martillero. Auctioneer.
Martillo. (by) auction.
Masa. Totality of the assets owned by a person.
Masa de la quiebra. Totality of the assets belonging to a bankrupt estate.
Matrícula. Registry.
Matrimonio. Marriage.
Matrimonio civil. Civil marriage.
Matrimonio por poder. Marriage by procuration.
Matrimonio rato. Unconsumated marriage.
Matriz. Original of a document.
Máxima. Maxim.
Mayor cuantía. Cases wherein the amount in dispute exceeds a certain sum; higher amount in dispute.
Mayoría de edad. Age of majority; full age.
Media firma. Signature consisting of only the surname and the paraph or flourish.
Medianería. Coownership of partition walls and fences; sharecropping.
Medicina legal. Legal medicine.
Médico legalista. Court physician.
Medidas cautelares. Precautionary proceedings; precautionary measures.
Medidas de seguridad. Security measures.
Mejora. Improvement.
Mejora de embargo. Expansion of attachment or seizure to cover additional assets belonging to the debtor.
Mejoras. Improvements.
Mejoras útiles. Useful improvements.
Mejor derecho. Better right.
Mejor postor. Highest bidder.
Menor. Minor.
Menor cuantía. Amount in dispute for courts of limited jurisdiction; lesser amount than.
Menor de edad. Minor; person who has not attained the full age of majority.
Menor habilitado. Minor legally authorized to litigate in

proper person or through a curator *ad litem*.

Mensura. Measurement of immovable property.

Mera tenencia. Tenancy at sufferance; occupancy of immovable property without title or right with no intent of possessing as owner.

Mercader. Merchant.

Mercadería. Merchandise.

Mercado. Market.

Mérito. Merits; grounds; rationale.

Ministerio. Ministry.

Ministerio fiscal. Attorney general's office; government attorneys; prosecuting attorney.

Ministerio público. *See* ministerio fiscal.

Ministro. Minister; supreme court justice.

Minuta. Statement of legal fees.

Misión en posesión. Putting in possession.

Moción. Motion.

Mojón. Landmark; boundary mark.

Monarca. Monarch.

Monarquía. Monarchy.

Monocrático. A court with only one judge.

Monopolio. Monopoly

Mora. Default; delay.

Moral. Moral; morals.

Morar. To habitate a dwelling.

Moratoria. A moratorium.

Motivación de sentencia. Reasons for judgment.

Motivo. Motive.

Muebles. Movables; personal property.

Muerte civil. Civil death.

Multa. Fine; penalty; stipulated damages.

Mutua petición. Counterclaim; reconventional demand.

Mutuo. Loan for consumption.

Mutuo disenso. Agreement to dissolve a contract.

N

Nación. Nation.

Nacional. National; citizen.

Nacionalidad. Nationality.

Nacionalización. Naturalization; nationalization.

Naciones Unidas. United Nations.

Narcoanálisis. Confession produced by giving the confessor a truth serum.

Nativo. Native.

Nave. Vessel.

Navegación. Navigation.

Naviero. Owner of a maritime enterprise.

Navío. Vessel.

Negación. Denial.

Negligencia. Negligence; fault.

Negociabilidad. Negotiability.

Negociable. Negotiable.

Negociación. Negotiation.

Negociante. Participant in a transaction; merchant.
Negociar. Negotiate.
Negocio. Affair; business; matter in contention; issue; transaction; juridical act.
Negocio contencioso. Litigated issue; matters in litigation.
Negocio judicial. *Ex parte* or controverted matter submitted to the judicial process for resolution.
Negocio jurídico. Juridical act; subject matter.
Negocio jurídico abstracto. Transaction that need not have a cause or consideration to be valid.
Negocio jurídico causal. Transaction that needs a cause or consideration to be valid.
Neutral. Neutral.
Neutralidad. Neutrality.
Neutralización. Neutralization.
Nexo contractual. Contractual bond.
No beligerancia. Nonbelligerancy.
No inmigrante. Nonimmigrant.
No intervención. Nonintervention.
Nombre comercial. Commercial name; corporate name.
Norma jurídica. Legal norm; rule of law.
Nota. Note; annotation; notice.
Nota marginal. Annotation at the margin (as of a deed, document, conveyance, etc.).
Notario. Notary; notary public.
Notario público. Notary public; notary.
Notificación. Notice; notification; service of process; summons.
Notificación personal. Personal service of process; personal notification.
Notificación por cedulón. Service of process by leaving summons at the door of the defendant's domicile.
Notificación por publicación. Notice by publication.
Novación. Novation.
Nudo propietario. Naked owner; owner of a thing burdened by a usufruct or an equivalent real right.
Nulidad. Nullity.
Nulidad absoluta. Absolute nullity.
Nulidad notoria. Extraordinary writ on grounds of nullity.
Nulidad relativa. Relative nullity.
Nulo. Null.
Numerario. Currency; legal tender.
Nuncupativo. Nuncupative.

O

Obediencia. Obedience.
Objeto. Object.
Oblación. Offer to pay made to the creditor by the debtor; deposit on the purchase price made by the purchaser at an auction sale.
Obligación. Obligation; duty.
Obligación accesoria. Accessory obligation.
Obligación alternativa. Alternative obligation.
Obligación a plazo. Obligation subject to a term.
Obligación condicional. Conditional obligation.
Obligación conjuntiva. Conjunctive obligation.
Obligación consensual. An obligation the validity of which depends on the consent of the parties.
Obligación de dar. Obligation to give.
Obligación de hacer. Obligation to do.
Obligación de no hacer. Obligation not to do.
Obligación divisible. Divisible obligation.
Obligaciones recíprocas. Reciprocal obligations.
Obligación facultativa. Facultative obligation.
Obligación genérica. Generic obligation.
Obligación indivisible. Indivisible obligation.
Obligacionista. Obligee; creditor.
Obligación mancomunada. Joint obligation.
Obligación mercantil. An obligation that has a commercial performance as its object.
Obligación natural. Natural obligation.
Obligación negativa. An obligation of not doing something.
Obligación principal. Principal obligation.
Obligación pura. An obligation that is not subject to a condition or term.
Obligado. Obligor.
Obligatoriedad. Obligatory nature of.
Obligatorio. Obligatory.
Obra ruinosa. Building in ruins.
Ocultación. Concealment.
Ocupación. Occupancy; occupation.
Oferente. Offeror.
Oferta. Offer.
Ofertante. *See* oferente.
Oficial. Official; officer.
Oficial de justicia. Marshal; sheriff.
Oficio. Notification; action taken by the court *sua sponte*; office.
Ofrecimiento. Debtor's offer to pay creditor which precedes payment by consignation.
Ofrecimiento de prueba. Offer to prove made in a pleading.

Ofrenda. Donation made in gratitude.
Oídas, de. Hearsay.
Oir. Hear (a trial, proceeding, etc.).
Ológrafo. Olographic will.
Omisión. Ommission; nonfeasance.
Oneroso. Onerous.
Opción. Option.
Operación. Negotiation; transaction; operation.
Operación de bolsa. Stock market transaction.
Opinión. Opinion.
Oponibilidad. Effectiveness of a right, act, document, or defense against another.
Oposición. Opposition.
Oralidad. Oral proceedings.
Orden. Order.
Ordenamiento jurídico. Juridical order; law.
Ordenanza. Administrative regulation; ordinance; an agent of the administration.
Ordenanza municipal. Municipal ordinance; municipal regulation.
Ordenanzas de necesidad. Emergency executive orders.
Orden del día. Agenda.
Orden de suceder. Order of succession.
Orden jurídico. The legal order of a given state; the totality of a state's laws.
Orden público. Public policy; public order.
Organización de los tribunales. Organization of the courts.
Organizaciones auxiliares de crédito. Nonbank credit institutions.
Original. Original.
Otorgamiento. Grant; execution.
Otorgar. Grant; authorize; execute.
Otrosi. Also; in addition.

P

Pabellón. The official flag of a state.
Pacto. Pact; contract.
Pacto comisorio. Contractual clause in a sale whereby it is stipulated that if the price is not paid within a certain period of time the sale will be dissolved; agreement whereby the pledgee acquires ownership of the thing pledged if the pledgor fails to pay the debt within a stipulated term.
Pacto de no concurrencia. Agreement in restraint of trade.
Pacto de preferencia. Right of first refusal.
Pacto de retraer. Right of redemption.
Pacto de retroventa. Sale with the right of redemption.
Pacto de reventa. Sale with the right of return; sale and return.
Padrasto. Stepfather.

Padre político. Father in law.
Pagar. To pay.
Pagaré. Promissory note.
Pagaré a la orden. Promissory note payable to order.
Pagaré al portador. Promissory note payable to bearer.
Pago. Payment.
Pago de lo indebido. Payment of a thing not due.
Pago por consignación. Tender of payment and deposit.
Pandilla. Gang.
Papel de actuaciones. Ordinary paper used as a substitute for sealed paper.
Papeles domésticos. Private papers; private documents.
Papel sellado. Stamped paper; paper bearing the official seal of a country.
Parafernales. Paraphernal assets; separate property of the wife in a community property regime.
Paralización del expediente. Interruption or suspension of judicial proceedings.
Parentesco. Relationship by blood or marriage.
Parientes. Relatives by blood or marriage.
Parlamentarismo. Parliamentary system.
Parlamento. Parliament.
Paro. Lockout.
Parricidio. Killing of a parent.
Parte. Party to a contract or law suit.
Parte civil. Victim of a crime or tort as a party in criminal proceedings instituted against the offender.
Parte principal. Plantiff or defendant in a law suit.
Partición. Partition.
Partición de herencia. Partition of the succession or inheritance.
Partición extrajudicial. Partition by agreement.
Partición judicial. Judicial partition.
Partida. Certificate.
Partida de bautizo. Baptismal certificate.
Partida de defunción. Death certificate.
Partida de matrimonio. Marriage certificate.
Partida de nacimiento. Birth certificate.
Partido político. Political party.
Partidor. Succession administrator; one who divides a patrimonial mass.
Pasante. Student trainee; law clerk.
Pasaporte. Passport.
Pasaporte diplomatico. Diplomatic passport.
Pasivo(el). The debts or liabilities of a person or entity.
Patentar. To grant or obtain a patent.
Patente. Patent.
Patente de navegación. Certificate authorizing a merchant vessel to sail.
Paternidad. Paternity.

Paterno. Paternal.
Patria. Fatherland.
Patria potestad. Paternal authority; custody (over children).
Patrimonial. Patrimonial.
Patrimonio. Patrimony.
Patrocinio. Legal defense or representation on behalf of an individual.
Patrón. Employer; master; standard.
Peculio. Peculium.
Pedimento. Petition.
Peligrosidad. Conduct that presents a danger to society.
Pena. Sentence; punishment; penalty.
Penable. Punishable conduct.
Pena capital. Capital punishment.
Pena corporal. Punishment of incarceration or death.
Pena de muerte. Capital punishment.
Pena de privación de libertad. Jail sentence.
Penado. One who has been sentenced.
Penalidad. Punishment for the violation of a criminal statute.
Penalista. Criminal lawyer.
Pena pecuniaria. Pecuniary punishment.
Penitenciaría. Penitentiary; jail.
Pensión. Pension; alimony; child support.
Pensión alimenticia. Alimony; child support.
Pensionista. One entitled to receive a pension; one entitled to receive alimony or child support.
Perdón. Pardon; remission of a debt.
Perención. Peremption.
Perención de la instancia. Abandonment of the cause of action; lapse of the cause of action.
Perentoria (excepción). Peremptory exception; motion to dismiss on peremptory grounds.
Perentorio. Peremptory.
Pericia. Testimony or report of an expert; skill.
Peritaje. *See* pericia.
Perito. Expert.
Perjudicado. One who has sustained damages.
Perjuicio. Damage; injury.
Perjurar. To commit perjury.
Perjurio. Perjury.
Perjuro. One who commits perjury.
Permiso. Authorization.
Permuta. Exchange.
Permutante. A party to a contract of exchange.
Persecución. Prosecution; persecution.
Persona. Person.
Persona física. Physical person.
Persona jurídica. Juridical person; legal person; juristic person.
Personalidad. Personality.
Persona moral. Juridical person.

Personería. Capacity to sue as representative.
Perturbación de hecho. Factual interference with a property right; trespass.
Pesquisa. Investigation; search.
Petición. Petition; prayer.
Peticionario. Petitioner.
Petición de herencia. Petition to be put in possession of the decedent's estate as heir.
Pieza. Part of the record of a judicial proceeding.
Pieza de autos. Main part of the record of a judicial proceeding.
Pieza separada. Ancillary part of the record of a judicial proceeding.
Pignorar. To pledge; to hypothecate.
Pignorativo. Relating to a pledge or hypothecation.
Pirata. Pirate.
Piratería. Piracy.
Plagiar. To plagiarize.
Plagiario. One who commits plagiarism.
Plagio. Plagiarism.
Planilla de distancias. Official computation of the distance between municipalities.
Plano. Survey; plan.
Plazo. Term.
Plebiscito. Referendum; plebiscite.
Pleito. Litigation; law suit.
Plena fe. Full proof.
Plena prueba. *See* plena fe.
Plenario. Part of civil proceedings during which the parties have ample opportunity to file pleadings and introduce evidence. In criminal proceedings, the actual prosecution and defense following the investigative part of the proceedings.
Plenipotenciario. Plenipotentiary.
Pleno derecho. By operation of the law; undisputable right.
Plenos poderes. Extraordinary powers.
Plica. Sealed envelope containing a will or other document the contents of which are not to be made public until a certain time or event transpires.
Pliego. Sheet or group of sheets of a pleading; pleading.
Pliego de posiciones. Pleading containing factual allegations.
Poder. Power of attorney; authority; proxy; mandate.
Poderdante. Principal; person who grants a power of attorney.
Poder de abogado. Power of attorney.
Poderes del Estado. The branches of government; the powers of the state.
Poderes extraordinarios. Extraordinary powers or faculties.
Poder especial. Special power of attorney.
Poderes públicos. Branches of government.
Poder general. General power of attorney.
Poder habiente. One who holds a power of attorney.

Poder judicial. Judiciary; the judicial power; power of attorney; power of attorney to prosecute actions through the courts.
Poder legislativo. The legislative branch.
Poder público. A state's authority; governmental power.
Policía. Police.
Policitación. Pollicitation; offer.
Poligamia. Polygamy.
Polígrafo. Polygraph.
Política. Politics; policy.
Política legislativa. Legislative policy; legislative intent.
Ponencia. Judgment; resolution; report; motion.
Ponente. Proponent of a bill; party who sends a request for admissions to his adversary; mover; judge that delivers the opinion of the court; the author of a resolution or report.
Portador. Bearer.
Porte. Freight; price in a contract of carriage; transportation costs.
Porteador. Carrier.
Portear. To carry a thing from one place to another for a price.
Poseedor. Possessor.
Poseedor de buena fe. Good faith possessor.
Poseedor de mala fe. Possessor in bad faith.
Poseer. To possess.
Posesión. Possession.
Posesión arrendaticia. Possession as lessee.
Posesión civilísima. Heir's possession over succession assets.
Posesión continua. Possession that has not been interrupted or suspended.
Posesión de estado. Family and social situation of a person (of importance in proving filiation).
Posesión natural. Natural possession.
Posesión pacífica. Peaceful possession.
Posesión precaria. Precarious possession; possession or tenancy at the sufferance of the landowner.
Posesión pública. Open and notorious possession.
Posiciones. Request for admissions; positions.
Postor. Bidder at an auction sale.
Postulante. One who requests or solicits something; a candidate.
Postular. To solicit; to request; to be a candidate.
Póstumo. Posthomous.
Postura. Bid; posture.
Potencia. Sovereign state; power.
Potestad. Authority; power.
Potestad discrecional. Discretionary authority.
Potestativo. Potestative.
Práctica. Practice.
Práctica forense. Court procedure; court rules.

Preaviso. Notice; lessor's notice of termination in a month to month lease.
Precaria. Tenancy at the mercy or will of the owner of the real estate or immovable property.
Precarista. Tenant at the mercy or will of the owner of the real estate or immovable property.
Precepto. Law; norm; precept; legal disposition.
Precepto jurídico. Legal precept; norm; law.
Precio. Price.
Precio alzado. Lump price.
Preclusión. Loss or extinction of a right; foreclosure.
Precontrato. Preparatory agreement; promise to enter into a particular contract.
Predial. Predial.
Predio. Estate; a particular immovable.
Predio dominante. Dominant estate.
Predio rural. Rural property.
Predio rústico. Rural property.
Predio sirviente. Servient estate.
Pregunta capciosa. A question that attempts to induce a mistake from the person to whom it is directed.
Pregunta sugestiva. Leading question.
Prejudicialidad. Preliminary matter that must be resolved prior to the decision on the merits.
Prejuzgamiento. Prejudging.
Prejuzgar. Prejudge.
Prelación de créditos. Ranking of liens; ranking of credit rights.
Prelegado. A legacy made to a person who is also an heir to the testator.
Premeditación. Deliberation; premeditation.
Premorencia. A death that occurs prior to another death.
Prenda. Pledge.
Prenda mercantil. Commercial pledge.
Prender. To imprison.
Presa Marítima. Prize (maritime).
Prescribir. Prescribe.
Prescripción. Prescription; limitations period.
Prescriptible. Prescriptible.
Presentación. Filing for registry; presentation.
Presentación de documentos. Introduction of documentary proof.
Presentación de testigos. List of witnesses that a party intends to call to testify.
Presentación de una letra de cambio. Presentment of a draft; presentment of a bill of exchange.
Presentante. Presenter.
Presidencia. Presidency.
Presidente. President.
Presidente del tribunal. Presiding judge; chief justice of the supreme court; chief judge of an appellate court.
Presidio. Prison.

Preso. Imprisoned; incarcerated.
Prestación. Performance; consideration.
Prestación imposible. Impossible performance.
Prestamista. Lender.
Préstamo. Loan.
Presunción. Presumption.
Presunción de inocencia. Presumption of innocense.
Presunción de muerte. Presumption of death.
Presunción judicial. *See* presunción.
Presunción juris et de jure. Irrebuttable presumption.
Presunción juris tantum. Rebuttable presumption.
Presunción legal. Presumption; legal presumption.
Presunción legal absoluta. Irrebuttable presumption.
Presunción legal relativa. *See* presunción legal simple.
Presunción legal simple. Rebuttable presumption.
Presupuesto. Requirement; budget; presupposition.
Presupuesto de la quiebra. Requirements for a declaration of bankruptcy.
Presupuesto del Estado. National or state budget.
Presupuesto procesal. (Procedural) presupposition.
Presupuestos procesales. Procedural requirements.
Pretender. To claim; to request.
Pretendiente. Claimant; one who makes a request.
Pretensión. Claim; request.
Pretensor. Claimant.
Preterisión. Omission of a forced heir in a person's will.
Prevaricato. Prevarication; breach of faith by an attorney or judge.
Prevención. Warning; exercise of jurisdiction by a court having concurrent jurisdiction over the action.
Prima. Insurance policy premium.
Primera instancia. First instance.
Principal. Principal.
Principio. Principle.
Principio de prueba. Partial proof.
Principio de prueba por escrito. Partial written proof.
Prisión. Imprisonment; prison.
Prisionero. Prisoner.
Privación de libertad (pena de). Jail sentence.
Privilegio. Privilege; grant.
Probanza. Evidence; method of proof.
Probatorio. Probative.
Proceder. To proceed.
Procedimiento. Procedure.
Procedimiento civil. Civil procedure.
Procedimiento criminal. Criminal procedure.
Procedimiento judicial. Law suit; judicial process.
Procedimiento ordinario. Ordinary proceedings.
Procedimiento penal. Criminal procedure.

Procedimiento sumario. Summary proceedings.
Procesal. Procedural.
Procesalista. Procedure expert.
Proceso. Proceedings; litigation; trial; process.
Proceso dispositivo. Proceedings that must be started and pursued by the parties.
Proceso inquisitorio. Inquisitorial proceedings.
Proclama. Political declaration.
Proclamación. Proclamation.
Proclamar. To publish.
Procura. Power of attorney.
Procuración. To grant a power of attorney; procuration.
Procurador. Agent with authority to appear in judicial proceedings on behalf of another; agent; mandatary.
Procurador general. Attorney general.
Procurador judicial. Agent with authority to appear in judicial proceedings on behalf of another.
Prodigalidad. Prodigality.
Pródigo. Prodigal.
Producción de pruebas. Introduction of evidence into the record; production of evidence.
Producto. Product; produce.
Profesión. Profession.
Proindivisión. Indivision; status of a mass of assets prior to partition.
Promesa. Promise.
Promesa de compra. Promise of purchase; contract to buy; option.
Promesa de compraventa. Contract to sell; promise of sale; option.
Promesa de contrato. Preparatory contract; promise to enter into a contract.
Promisorio. Promissory.
Promitente. Promissor.
Promotor. Promoter.
Promulgar. Promulgate; putting legislation in force.
Pronunciar sentencia. Render judgment; sentence.
Propiedad. Property; ownership.
Propiedad comercial. The assets of a commercial establishment; commercial property.
Propiedad en condominio. Condominium; coownership.
Propiedad horizontal. Condominium property; condominium; horizontal property.
Propiedad intelectual. Copyright; intellectual property.
Propiedad particular. Private property.
Propiedad privada. Private property.
Propietario. Property owner.
Proposición. Offer; proposition.
Propuesta. Offer.
Propuesta verbal de negocio. Oral offer.
Prorrata. Prorata.
Prorratear. To prorate.
Prórroga. Extension; continuance.

Prorrogación voluntaria. Waiver of improper venue.
Prórroga de competencia. Waiver of a court's lack of jurisdiction or venue.
Prórroga de término. Extension of a term or limitation period.
Proscribir. To proscribe; expulsion of a person from his home country.
Proscriptor. One who proscribes; one who expells another from his home or country.
Proscrito. Proscript; one who has been expelled from his home or country.
Prostitución. Prostitution.
Protesta. Protest; promise to perform well the duties of an office.
Protesto. Notarial protest.
Protocolo. Protocol.
Protocolo notarial. Notarial register; register of documents passed before a notary.
Protutor. Undertutor.
Proveer. To decide.
Proveído. Decided.
Providencia. Judicial decision; order; decree.
Providencia de oficio. Order, decree, or issue raised by the court on its own initiative (*sua sponte*).
Providencia judicial. Judicial order; judicial decision; judicial decree.
Provincia. Province.
Proyecto de ley. Bill (of projected legislation).
Prudencia. Prudence.
Prueba. Proof; evidence.
Prueba documental. Documentary evidence; demonstrative evidence; real evidence.
Prueba impertinente. Irrelevant evidence.
Prueba inadmisible. Inadmissible evidence.
Prueba instrumental. Documentary evidence.
Prueba oral. Oral evidence; testimony.
Prueba plena. Full proof; conclusive evidence.
Prueba preconstituída. Evidence existing prior to trial.
Prueba semiplena. Inconclusive evidence; evidence that is insufficient by itself to prove the matter at issue.
Prueba testifical. Testimonial proof; witness' testimony.
Prueba testimonial. Testimonial proof.
Púber. One who has attained the age of puberty.
Pubertad. Puberty.
Publicación. Publication.
Público. Public.
Puerto de base. Home port of a vessel.
Pujar. To offer a higher bid in an auction sale.
Punible. Punishable.
Punición. Punishment.
Punir. To punish.
Punitivo. Punitive.
Pupilar. Relative to the ward or minor subject to tutorship.
Pupilo. Ward.

Purgación de la mora. Cure or waiver of default.
Putativo. Putative.

Q

Quasidelito. *See* cuasidelito.
Quebrado. Bankrupt.
Quebrado fraudulento. Fraudulent bankruptcy.
Quebrantamiento. Violation of the law; violation of a promise.
Quebrantamiento de sanción. Escape.
Quebrar. To fall into a state of bankruptcy or insolvency.
Queja. Complaint; special writ for denial of justice.
Queja por denegación de apelación. Writ for denial of appeal.
Queja por denegación o retardo de justicia. Writ for denial or delay of justice.
Querella. Complaint; accusation; dispute.
Querellado. Accused.
Querellante. One who has filed a criminal accusation or complaint.
Quiebra. Bankruptcy.
Quiebra culpable. Guilty bankruptcy; bankruptcy wherein the debtor has committed fraud or bad faith.
Quiebra fortuita. Ordinary bankruptcy; bankruptcy wherein the bankrupt is not guilty of fraud or misconduct.
Quiebra fraudulenta. Fraud committed by the bankrupt, as by hiding assets.
Quirografario. Unsecured creditor; creditor without preference or privilege; unsecured credit.
Quirógrafo. Unsecured credit or debt.
Quita. Remission of the debt; release.
Quitanza. Liberation or release of a debt; payment receipt.
Quita y espera. Request of a bankrupt or insolvent person for a remission of the debts or a respite.

R

Radicar. To establish a domicile; to file a pleading.
Rapto. Abduction; kidnapping; rape.
Raptor. Abductor; kidnapper; rapist.
Ratería. Petty theft.
Ratero. Petty thief.
Razón de sus dichos. Basis or foundation for the testimony of a witness.
Razón social. Firm name; corporate name.
Reaseguro. Reinsurance.

Rebelde. Defendant in default for failure to answer.
Rebeldía. Default; failure of a party to file responsive pleadings or make an appearance within the time provided by law.
Recambio. *See* resaca.
Recaudo. Care; precaution; security.
Receptación. To assist another in hiding stolen things.
Receptador. Accessory after the fact; one who assists another in hiding stolen things, tools, or weapons used in the commisison of a crime.
Receptor. Tax collector; receiver; bailiff; officer commissioned by the court to record the testimony of a witness.
Receptoría. Tax collector's office.
Recibir a prueba. (Period for) introducing evidence.
Recibo. Receipt.
Reciprocidad internacional. International reciprocity.
Reclusión. Imprisonment.
Recluso. Prisoner; one who is serving a jail sentence.
Recomendatario. Co-drawee of a bill of exchange; one from whom the payee of a bill of exchange or draft may demand acceptance or payment of the bill.
Reconducción. Reconduction (of lease); renewal (of lease).
Reconocimiento. Identification; acknowledgment; register; recognition.
Reconocimiento de beligerancia. Recognition of belligerancy,
Reconocimiento de deuda. Acknowledgment of the debt.
Reconocimiento de firma. A person's acknowledgment of a signature as his own.
Reconocimiento de gobierno. Recognition of a government.
Reconvención. Reconventional demand; counterclaim.
Reconvenir. To file a reconventional demand; to counterclaim; to recriminate.
Rectificación. Correction.
Rectificación de partida. *Ex parte* proceeding to correct errors in the civil status registry.
Recurrente. Appellant; applicant of a writ of review.
Recurso. Appeal; writ of review.
Recurso de aclaración. *See* aclaración de sentencia.
Recurso de ampliación. *See* ampliación de sentencia.
Recurso de apelación. Appeal.
Recurso de nulidad. *See* nulidad.
Recusación. Recusation.
Recusante. Person who has pursued the recusation of a judge or a court official.
Recusar. To recuse.
Redención. Redemption; extinquishment of a debt or burden.
Redhibición. Redhibition; dissolution of a sale on account

of breach of warranty of hidden defects.

Redhibir. To dissolve a sale on account of hidden defects in the thing sold.

Redhibitoria. Redhibitory action; action to dissolve a sale on account of hidden defects.

Redhibitorio. Redhibitory defect; hidden defect in the thing sold.

Réditos. Proceeds; civil fruits; interest.

Redituar. To yield periodically rent, interest, or benefit.

Reembolso. Reimbursement.

Reenvío. Remand; renvoi.

Referendum. Referendum.

Reforma agraria. Agrarian reform.

Reformar la demanda. Amendment of the petition or complaint.

Refrendación. *See* refrendo.

Refrendar. To grant a refrendo.

Refrendata. *See* refrendo.

Refrendo. Cosignature or approval of an executive act by a cabinet minister or secretary.

Regalía. Royalty; additional compensation that public employees may receive in addition to their salaries; privilege.

Regente. Regent.

Registro. Registry; public registry; registration.

Registro de la propiedad. Land register; public records.

Registro público. Public registry; public records.

Registros parroquiales. Parish registries; church registries.

Regulación de honorarios. Decree fixing professional fees.

Regulador de honorarios. Officer who fixes professional fees.

Rehabilitación. Rehabilitation (of a debtor in bankrupty or insolvency proceedings).

Reincidencia. Second and subsequent criminal acts by the same defendant.

Reincidente. Second offender.

Reiteración. Commission of a crime by one who has a prior conviction.

Reivindicación. Reivindication; replevin.

Reivindicar. Action by the owner of a thing to obtain possession.

Relación. Report; relation; abbreviated form of appeal.

Relación jurídica. Legal relationship; juridical relation.

Rematador. Auctioneer.

Remate. Sale by public auction.

Remedio. Appeal; remedy.

Remisión. Remission of a debt.

Remoción. Removal of a public official.

Rendición de cuentas. Rendering of accounts.

Rendir pruebas. Give evidence; offer proof.

Renta. Rent.

Rentas públicas. State revenues.

Renta vitalicia. Annuity.
Renuncia. Waiver; abandonment; resignation.
Renunciable. Waivable; subject to contrary agreement.
Renunciación. Waiver.
Renunciamiento. *See* renuncia.
Renunciante. One who makes a waiver.
Renunciatario. Beneficiary of a waiver.
Reo. Defendant.
Reparación de perjuicios. Payment of damages.
Repartición. Partition.
Repetición. Recovery; action to recover.
Repetir. Action to recover.
Reporto. A contract whereby a party obtains securities for another in exchange for a promise of delivering securities of the same kind, plus a premium, within a stipulated time.
Reposición. Modification or amendment of a judgment; writ of error.
Representación. Representation; agency.
Representado. One who is represented by another.
Representante común. Co-party that represents the interest of other co-parties in a civil proceeding.
Representante diplomático. Diplomat.
República. Republic.
Repudiación anticipada. Anticipatory repudiation.
Repudiación de herencia. Renunciation of a succession or estate.
Requerimiento. Order; injunction; notice.
Requisición. Requisition.
Resaca. Procedure authorizing the holder of an unpaid draft to draw a second draft on the drawee or on one of the endorsers of the original draft.
Rescisión. Rescission.
Reserva legal. Corporate reserves.
Reservatario. One who is entitled to the reservation of certain assets for his use and benefit.
Reservista. One who must reserve certain assets for the benefit of another.
Resguardo. Collateral security; writing wherein a person asserts to have received a document for safekeeping or as notice.
Residencia. Residence; domicile.
Resolución. Decision; judgment; dissolution; resolution.
Resolución firme. Final resolution; firm resolution.
Responsabilidad. Liability; responsibility.
Responsabilidad civil. Tort or contractual liability; civil liability.
Responsabilidad concurrente. Comparative negligence; comparative fault.

Responsabilidad contractual. Liability for breach or faulty performance of a contract.
Responsabilidad judicial. Judicial liability for malfeasance in office.
Responsabilidad objetiva. Strict liability; liability without fault.
Responsabilidad subjetiva. Liability arising from fault or intentional conduct.
Responsable civil en el proceso. Person civilly liable for a criminal act which he has not committed.
Restitución. Restitution.
Restituir. To make restitution.
Resultandos. Part of the judgment setting forth the proven facts.
Retardo de justicia. Unjustifiable delay in the administration of justice.
Retasa. Reevaluation or reassessment of a thing offered for sale at public auction after an unsuccessful auction; reappraisal.
Retención. Right of retention; lien.
Retorsión. Retortion; retaliation.
Retracto. Redemption; alienation of rights; *i.e.*, sale with right of redemption.
Retracto convencional. Contractual redemption; alienation of rights; *i.e.*, sale with right of redemption.
Retracto legal. Legal redemption.
Retraer. To exercise the right of redemption.
Retribución. Retribution; compensation.
Retroactividad. Retroactivity.
Retroactivo. Retroactive.
Retrocesión. Retrocession; return of a thing or right.
Reunión. Meeting; reunion.
Reversión. Reversion.
Revisión. Revision.
Revocabilidad. Susceptibility to revocation; revocability.
Revocación. Revocation; reversal (of a lower court judgment).
Revocar. To revoke.
Riesgo. Risk.
Riesgo asegurable. Insurable risk.
Riesgo de trabajo. Work risk; accident or disease to which a worker is exposed by reason of his employment.
Riesgo imprevisible. Unforeseeable risk.
Robo. Robbery.
Rogatorio. Letters rogatory.
Rubricar. Paraph; affix signature.
Rueda de presos. Lineup (criminal law).

S

Sabotaje. Sabotage.
Sabotear. To commit sabotage.
Saca de autos. Request made by the clerk of court for the return of a record.
Sala. Courtroom; section or division of a court.
Salario. Salary; wages.
Salario efectivo. Salary or wages paid in money.
Salario igual. Equal pay for equal work.
Salario mínimo. Minimum wages.
Saldo. Remaining part of a debt or merchandise; payment or performance of an obligation.
Salvoconducto. Safe conduct.
Sanción. Sanction.
Saneamiento. Warranty; to make good.
Sanear. Warrant title; warrant against hidden defects.
Secretario. Secretary; clerk.
Secreto profesional. Confidentiality told to a professional.
Secuela. Sequel.
Secuestro. Sequestration; preventive custody; kidnapping.
Sede. Headquarters.
Sede de gobierno. Seat of government.
Sedición. Sedition.
Sedicioso. One who commits the crime of sedition; an act of sedition.
Seducción. Seduction.
Seductor. One who commits a seduction.
Segregación de fincas. Subdivision of an immovable into smaller tracts.
Segunda instancia. Appeal; second instance.
Seguro. Contract of insurance.
Sello. Seal; stamp.
Semovientes. Animals (as property).
Senado. Senate.
Senador. Senator.
Sentar doctrina. Establish doctrine; statement on the law made in the course of a judicial opinion.
Sentencia. Judgment; verdict; sentence.
Sentencia absolutoria. Verdict of acquittal; judgment for the defendant.
Sentencia arbitral. Award or judgment of an arbitration panel.
Sentencia cautelar. Judgment concerning the validity of a precautionary proceeding.
Sentencia condenatoria. Guilty verdict (from a court or jury); sentence.
Sentencia confirmatoria. Appellate decision affirming a lower court judgment.
Sentencia constitutiva. Judgment establishing or modifying a legal or juridical status.
Sentencia declarativa. Declaratory judgment; judgment that merely declares rights or facts.

Sentencia de condena. Judgment ordering a party to pay damages or to do or not to do something.
Sentencia definitiva. Final judgment.
Sentencia ejecutoriada. *See* sentencia firme.
Sentencia firme. Definitive judgment.
Sentencia ilíquida. Judgment that issues a decree without quantifying the sum to be paid by the party cast.
Sentencia interlocutoria. Interlocutory judgment.
Sentencia líquida. Judgment for a determinate or ascertainable sum or performance.
Sentencia mere declarativa. *See* sentencia declarativa.
Sentencia revocatoria. Appellate court judgment of reversal.
Señal. Earnest money; indication; signal.
Separación de bienes. Separation of property.
Separación de cuerpos. Legal separation; separation from bed and board.
Separación de poderes. Separation of powers.
Servidumbre. Servitude; easement.
Servidumbre aparente. Apparent servitude.
Servidumbre continua. Continuous servitude.
Servidumbre discontinua. Disontinuous servitude.
Servidumbre no aparente. Nonapparent servitude.
Servidumbre personal. Personal servitude.
Servidumbre real. Predial servitude.
Sevicia. Extremely cruel act.
Signatario. Signing; person who signs a document.
Signo. Sign.
Simulación. Simulation.
Sinalagmático. Bilateral contract.
Sindicado. Member of a union.
Sindicalismo. Unionism.
Sindicato. Labor union; employers' union.
Síndico. Trustee; receiver.
Sirviente. Servant; servient estate.
Sistema penal acusatorio. Accusatory penal system.
Sistema penal inquisitivo. Inquisitive penal system.
Sistema penal mixto. Penal system conbining the accusatory and inquisitive systems.
Soberanía. Sovereignty.
Soberanía territorial. Territorial sovereignty.
Soberano. Sovereign.
Soborno. Bribe.
Sobreestadía. Demurrage; undue delay.
Sobregiro. Overdraft.
Sobreprima. Supplementary premium.
Sobreseimiento. Dismissal of judicial proceedings before judgment.

Sobresueldo. Additional remuneration paid an employee as compensation for additional risks assumed or for higher cost of living in the locality where the place of employment is situated.

Sociedad. Partnership; association.

Sociedad abierta. Publicly held corporation.

Sociedad anónima. Corporation.

Sociedad cerrada. Closely held corporation.

Sociedad civil. Civil partnership or corporation.

Sociedad comercial. Commercial partnership.

Sociedad conyugal. Community or partnership of gains in a community property system.

Sociedad cooperativa. Cooperative.

Sociedad de capital variable. Corporation with varying capital.

Sociedad de gananciales. Community of gains; the legal regime in a community property system.

Sociedad de hecho. *See* sociedad irregular.

Sociedad de las Naciones. League of Nations.

Sociedad de responsabilidad limitada. Corporation.

Sociedad en comandita. Partnership *in commendam* ; limited partnership.

Sociedad extranjera. Foreign corporation or partnership.

Sociedad irregular. Unregistered partnership or corporation; oral partnership.

Socio. Partner; member of an association.

Socio capilalista. Partner or associate who contributes capital to the partnership or association.

Socio comanditado. General partner in a partnership *in commendam* or limited partnership.

Socio industrial. Partner or associate who contributes his labor, rather than capital, to the partnership or association.

Solemne. An act in authentic form that has complied with all legally prescribed formalities.

Solemnidad. Formal requirement; solemnity.

Soltero. Single.

Sorteo. Drawing lots; raffle.

Standar jurídico. Reasonable man standard.

Subarrendamiento. Sublease.

Subarrendar. To sublease.

Subarriendo. Sublease.

Subasta. *See* remate.

Súbdito. Subject.

Subfiador. Surety or guarantor of the surety.

Sublocación. Sublease.

Subrogación. Subrogation.

Subsanar. Remedy; to correct (an impropriety).

Suceder. To inherit; to succeed, either universally or by universal or particular title.
Suceder a título singular. To succeed by particular title.
Sucesión. Decedent's estate; succession; descent and distribution.
Sucesión legítima. Legal or legitimate succession.
Sucesión por cabeza. Succession by heads.
Sucesión por estirpe. Succession by stirpes.
Sucesión testamentaria. Testamentary succession.
Sucesor. Successor.
Sucesor testamentario singular. Legatee.
Sucesor universal. Universal successor.
Sueldo. *See* salario.
Sufragio. Vote; suffrage.
Sufragio universal. Universal suffrage.
Sujeto de derecho. Subject of the law; person.
Sumario. Preliminary stages of a criminal proceeding; summary proceedings.
Sumariamente. Summarily.
Sumisión. Waiver of jurisdiction or venue.
Superintendencia. Supervision.
Suposición. Criminal imposture.
Suposición de cualidad. Unauthorized practice of a profession by one who, without the proper certification, pretends to be an authorized member of the profession.
Suposición de nombre. Unauthorized use of a name.
Suprema corte de justicia. Supreme court.
Suspensión. Suspension.
Suspensión de ejecución. Suspension of execution.
Suspensión de garantías. Suspension of constitutional guarantees.
Suspensión de pagos. Suspension of payments.
Sustanciación. Conduct of trial by the court so as to give each party an opportunity to prove its case.
Sustitución. Substitution.
Sustitución de heredero. Substitute or replacement legacies.
Sustitución procesal. Right of a creditor to exercise his debtor's action in certain cases; oblique action.
Sustracción. Theft; robbery.

T

Tabelión. Notary public.
Tacha. Impeachment; refutation; impediment; defect.
Tacha absoluta. Absolute impediment.
Tachar. To impeach a witness.

Tacha relativa. Impediment as to a particular proceeding.
Tácita reconducción. Tacit reconduction.
Tahúr. Habitual gambler.
Tahurería. Gambling house.
Talón. Order of payment against a bank; check.
Tantear. Exercise of the right of first refusal.
Tanteo. Right of first refusal.
Tanto. Quantity of a thing; commission; testimony concerning a proceeding.
Tanto de culpa. Testimony from the record of a proceeding which is indicative of criminal liability.
Tarifa. Tariff.
Tarjeta de identidad. Identity card.
Tasa. Rate; ceiling price.
Tasación. Assessment; evaluation; regulation; appraisal.
Tasación de costas. Assessment of court costs.
Tasa de interés. Interest rate.
Tasador. One who makes an appraisal.
Tasar. To appraise.
Temibilidad. *See* peligrosidad.
Tenedor. Holder.
Tenedor legítimo. Holder in due course.
Tenencia. Possession of a thing; precarious possession.
Tenencia de armas. Possession of illegal weapons.
Tenuta. Possession of the fruits, rents, or benefit in litigation, until their ownership is determined.
Teoría de la imprevisión. Frustration of purpose; impracticability of performance.
Teoría del derecho. Legal theory; jurisprudence.
Teoría general del derecho. General theory of law; jurisprudence.
Teoría pura del derecho. Pure theory of law.
Tercera instancia. Third instance; appellate proceedings following the conclusion of the first appeal.
Tercería. Third party practice.
Tercería coadyuvante. Intervention with a posture coinciding with that of the plaintiff or of the defendant.
Tercería de dominio. Intervention whereby the intervenor prays to be declared the owner of the property that has been the subject of the dispute in the main action.
Tercería de mejor derecho. Intervention whereby the intervenor claims to have a better right to the property in dispute than the litigants in the main demand.
Terecería excluyente. Intervention whereby the intervenor takes a position that is contrary to that of the litigants in the main demand.
Tercerista. Third party; intervenor.
Tercero. Third party; intervenor.

Tercero adquirente, Third possessor; third party acquiring ownership or other interest in a thing.
Tercero beneficiario. Third party beneficiary.
Tercero en discordia. Additional person appointed to resolve the differences or to help form a majority when the experts or arbitrators cannot agree.
Término. Term; period.
Término de gracia. Grace period.
Término extraordinario de prueba. Extraordinary term for introduction of evidence.
Término improrrogable de medianoche. Midnight deadline.
Término judicial. Court fixed term.
Término legal. Term fixed by law.
Terna. List of persons from whom a candidate for a position is to be selected.
Terrateniente. Land owner.
Territorialidad. Territoriality.
Tesoro. Treasure.
Tesoro nacional. Public treasury.
Tesoro público. The state's assets; public treasury.
Testado. Decedent who leaves a valid will.
Testador. Testator.
Testaduras. Erasures made in a writing.
Testaferro. Straw man; person interposed as a party who in reality has no interest in the transaction involved.
Testamentaría. Succession proceedings; succession.
Testamentario. Testamentary.
Testamentifacción. The capacity of making a will.
Testamento. Testament; will.
Testamento abierto. Testament in which the testator manifests his last will in front of witnesses.
Testamento cerrado. Closed will; testment not made in front of witnesses.
Testamento común. Ordinary will.
Testamento especial. Special will.
Testamento marítimo. Testament made during a sea voyage.
Testamento militar. Testament made by a soldier during a campaign or by a prisoner of war.
Testamento místico. Mystic will.
Testamento nuncupativo. Nuncupative will; will by oral statement.
Testamento ológrafo. Olographic will.
Testamento público. Will made before a public functionary or a notary public.
Testar. To testate; to make a will; to give by will.

Testifacción. To give testimony.
Testigo. Witness.
Testigo de actuación. Witness to a juridical act (such as the signing of a document).
Testigo de cargo. Witness for the prosecution in a criminal case.
Testigo de conocimineto. Witness who knows the identity of a person.
Testigo de descargo. Defense witness in a criminal case.
Testigo de oídas. Witness who gives hearsay testimony.
Testigo falso. Witness who intentionally fails to declare the truth.
Testigo hábil. Competent witness.
Testigo idóneo. Appropriate witness; competent witness.
Testigo instrumental. Witness to a written instrument.
Testigo ocular. Eyewitness.
Testigo singular. Only witness.
Testimonio. Testimony.
Timbre. Stamp.
Titularidad. Ownership; title bearing.
Título. Title; right.
Título ejecutivo. Instrument allowing the bearer or beneficiary to proceed by executory process (by *via executiva*).
Título lucrativo. Donative title; gift.
Título negociable. Negotiable instrument.
Título oneroso. Onerous title; for a consideration.
Título particular. Particular title.
Título traslativo de dominio. Deed transfering real or immovable property; deed or title capable of transferring real or immovable property.
Título universal. Universal title.
Título valor. Negotiable instrument.
Traba de embargo. Attachment or seizure pursuant to court order.
Tradición. Delivery; tradition.
Trámite. Proceedings; part or step in the proceedings.
Transacción. Transaction; compromise; settlement.
Transacción garantizada. Secured transaction.
Transigir. Settle; compromise.
Traslado. Service of a pleading on a party; notification of the contents of a document.
Traspaso. Transfer (as of ownership, rights, etc.).
Tratado. Treaty; treatise.
Tribunal. Court; tribunal.
Tribunal común. Ordinary court; court of first instance.
Tribunal de apelaciones. Court of appeal.
Tribunal de excepción. Special court established to hear a particular class of cases.

Tribunal de lo contencioso administrativo. Court with appellate jurisdiction over decisions of administrative agencies.
Tribunal supremo. Supreme court.
Tributo judicial. Filing fees; fees owed to the court by the litigants.
Tripulación. Crew of a vessel.
Trueque. Exchange.
Tutela. Tutorship; protection of rights.
Tutelado. Ward; person under tutorship.
Tutor. Tutor.

U

Ultrapetita. Judgment that goes beyond the prayer or object of the dispute.
Unilateral. Unilateral.
Urgencia. Urgency; emergency.
Uso bancario. Banking usage.
Usucapión. Acquisitive prescription.
Usufructo. Usufruct.
Usufructo legal. Legal usufruct.
Usura. Usury.
Utilidad. Utility; usefulness; rate of return.

V

Vacante. Vacant; without owner.
Vago. Vague.
Vale. Promissory note.
Valor. Negotiable instrument; security; value.
Vencimiento. Accrual; maturity.
Vencimiento del plazo. Accrual of the term; maturity (as of a debt).
Vencimiento de término. Accrual of term.
Vendedor. Seller.
Venia. Permission; license; authorization.
Venta. Sale.
Venta al gusto. Sale *ad gustum*; sale subject to buyer's subjective approval; sale on approval; sale on trial.
Venta a precio alzado. Sale by lump; sale at lump sum price.
Venta forzosa. Forced sale; expropriation.
Venta por ensayo. Sale with reservation of view and trial.
Venta por prueba. Sale with reservation of view and trial.
Ventas en martillo. Auction sale.
Ventilar. Disposition of legal or factual issues, as in a hearing or judgment; bring to trial; litigate.
Verificación de créditos. Proof of claims in bankruptcy.

Vía. Procedure; manner of proceeding.
Vía de apremio. *See* apremio.
Vicios ocultos. Hidden defects; hidden vices.
Vigencia de la ley. Effectiveness of the law; time when legislation becomes effective.
Violación. Rape; violation.
Vista. Hearing; trial.
Vista de ojos. Visual inspection.
Vistos. Seen.
Votación. voting.
Voto. Vote.

Part II English - Spanish

Parte II Inglés - Español

A

Abandon. Abandonar; renunciar.
Abandoned property. Propiedad abandonada; bienes abandonados.
Abandonment. Abondono; desamparo; abandono de hogar.
Abandonment of action. Caducidad de la instancia.
Abandon property. Abandonar o desamparar bienes.
Abandon ship. Abandonar la nave.
Abate. Terminar; suspender; aminorar.
Abate an attachment. Desembargar.
Abatement. Reducción; disminución; supresión.
Abatement of a nuisance. Remediar o eliminar una incomodidad o una actividad perjudicial.
Abdicate. Abdicar.
Abduct. Secuestrar; raptar.
Abduction. Secuestro; rapto.
Abet. Incitar; instigar.
Abettor. Incitador; instigador; cómplice.
Abeyance. En suspenso.
Abide. Atenerse; cumplir.
Ab initio. Desde el principio.
Ab intestate. Abintestato.
Ab intestato. Abintestato; intestado(a).
Abjuration. Renuncia; abjuración.
Abode. Domicilio; residencia.
Abolish. Abolir; revocar; derogar.
Aborticide. Aborto; homicidio del feto dentro del útero.
Abortion. Aborto.
Abrogate. Abrogar.
Abrogation. Abrogación; rescisión.
Abscond. Fugarse; ocultarse.
Absentee. Ausente.
Absolute incapacity. Incapacidad absoluta.
Absolute liability. Responsabilidad objetiva; responsabilidad absoluta; responsabilidad sin culpa.
Absolute nullity. Nulidad absoluta; nulidad insubsanable.
Absolute possession. Posesión permanente; posesión absoluta.
Absolute right. Derecho absoluto.
Absolute simulation. Simulación absoluta.
Absolve. Absolver; declarar inocente.
Absque injuria. *Véase* damnun absque injuria.
Abstention, doctrine of. Doctrina de la abstención. Llámase así a la práctica de los tribunales federales de los E E. U U. de abstenerse de resolver problemas de orden constitucional en ciertos casos.
Abstract. Resumen; sumario; *véase* abstract of title.
Abstract of title. Resumen o extracto de título.
Abuse. Abuso.
Abuse of authority. Abuso de autoridad.

Abuse of discretion. Abuso de discreción (usualmente de los tribunales de primera instancia).

Abuse of process. Uso abusivo del proceso.

Abuse of rights. Abuso del derecho.

Abuttals. Linderos.

Abutting. Lindante.

Abutting property. Propiedad colindante.

Accelerated maturity. Vencimiento acelerado.

Acceleration clause. Cláusula de vencimiento anticipado.

Accept. Aceptar.

Accept a draft. Aceptar un giro.

Acceptance. Aceptación.

Acceptance by performance. Aceptación por cumplimiento.

Acceptance by promise. Aceptación por promesa.

Acceptance by silence. Aceptación tácita; aceptación en silencio.

Acceptance of an inheritance. Aceptación de la herencia.

Acceptance of goods. Aceptación de mercancías.

Acceptance of the succession. Aceptación de la herencia.

Acceptance under benefit of inventory. Aceptación a beneficio de inventario.

Acceptor. Aceptante.

Accession. Accesión.

Accession in relation to immovables. Accesión respecto a los inmuebles.

Accession in relation to movables. Accesión respecto a los bienes muebles.

Accessory. Accesorio; cómplice; encumbridor.

Accessory after the fact. Encubridor (criminal).

Accessory contract. Contrato accesorio; contrato subsidiario.

Accessory things. Bienes accesorios.

Accidental death. *Véase* death by accidental means.

Accomodation. Aval.

Accomodation bill. Letra o pagaré de favor o de acomodación.

Accomodation endorsement. Avalar; endoso de favor.

Accomodation endorser. Avalista de favor.

Accomodation paper. Valor de acomodación; valor de favor o cortesía.

Accomodation party. Parte por acomodar; avalista.

Accomplice. Cómplice.

Accord. Convenio; acuerdo.

Accord and satisfaction. Transacción; arreglo sobre una deuda cuyo monto se disputa.

According to law. De derecho; conforme a derecho.

Account. Rendir cuenta; cuenta.

Accountability. Responsabilidad.

Accountable. Responsable.

Account, joint. Cuenta mancomunada.
Account, on. A cuenta.
Account, on open. En cuenta corriente.
Accounts receivable. Cuentas a cobrar.
Account stated. Cuenta acordada; cuenta convenida.
Accredit. Acreditar; dar credenciales.
Accretion. Derecho de acrecer; acrecencia; accesión.
Accrual. Acumulación.
Accrual of the cause of action. Surgimiento de la acción.
Accrue. Acumular; acrecer.
Accrued dividends. Dividendos devengados o acumulados.
Accumulation of actions. Acumulación de acciones.
Accusation. Acusación.
Accuse. Acusar.
Accused. Acusado; inculpado.
Accuser. Acusador.
Acknowledgment. Reconocimiento.
Acknowledgment of debt. Reconocimiento de deuda.
Acquets. Bienes gananciales.
Acquiesce. Allanarse; aceptar; convenir.
Acquire. Adquirir.
Acquisition of possession. Adquisición de posesión.
Acquisitive prescription. Usucapión; prescripción adquisitiva de dominio.
Acquit. Absolver; exonerar.
Acquittal. Absolución; sentencia absolutoria.
Acquittance. Recibo; descargo; finiquito.
Act. Ley; acto.
Act in pais. Hecho realizado fuera del tribunal y que no consta en el expediente.
Action. Acción.
Actionable. Procesable; actuable.
Action at law. Acción fundamentada en el derecho.
Action for damages. Acción por daños.
Action in disavowal. Acción de impugnación de la paternidad.
Action in equity. Acción fundamentada en la equidad.
Action of ejectment. Acción posesoria.
Act of bankruptcy. Acción del deudor que puede producir la quiebra involuntaria.
Act of commerce. Acto de comercio.
Act of God. Caso fortuito; fuerza mayor.
Act of indemnity. Ley que exime de responsabilidad a ciertas personas.
Act of ownership. Acto dominical; acto de disposición.
Act of preservation. Acto de preservación.
Act of state. Acto de soberanía; acto de Estado.
Actual force. Fuerza propinada a la víctima de un robo por el acusado que obligó a

la víctima a ceder el objeto que, consecuentemente, fue robado.

Actual fraud. Dolo; fraude.

Actual service. Emplazamiento al demandado en persona.

Act under private signature. Escritura privada.

Additional servitude. Uso diferente de aquel para el cuál se efectuó la expropiación.

Additur. Aumento; aumento en el monto de la indemnización de la sentencia o veredicto del jurado.

Ademption. Revocación de legado implícita por los actos del testador.

Adequacy of consideration. Suficiencia de la causa; suficiencia de la consideración; idoneidad de la causa; idoneidad de la consideración.

Adequate remedy. Remedio adecuado. Llámase así al remedio legal apropiado a las peculiaridades del caso.

Adequate remedy at law. Remedio adecuado en derecho. Cuando existe un remedio adecuado en el derecho (law) es improcedente recurrir a los remedios de la "equity" o equidad; *véase* equity.

Adhesion contract. Contrato de adhesión.

Adit. Paso lateral a una mina, casi siempre horizontal.

Adjective law. Derecho adjetivo; derecho procesal.

Adjoining property. Propiedad colindante.

Adjourn. Suspender una sesión o junta.

Adjournment. Aplazamiento.

Adjudge. Adjudicar; juzgar.

Adjudgment. Adjudicación.

Adjudicate. Adjudicar.

Adjudication. Adjudicación; fallo; sentencia.

Adjust. Ajustar; componer; transar.

Adjuster. Ajustador; tasador.

Adjustment. Arreglo; ajuste; tasación.

Ad litem. En el proceso; para el propósito del proceso.

Admeasurement. Medida; arqueo.

Administer. Administrar.

Administer an estate. Administrar un patrimonio.

Administer an oath. Tomar juramento.

Administer a trust. Administrar un fideicomiso.

Administer justice. Impartir justicia.

Administer the estate. Administrar la herencia.

Administration. Administración; gerencia.

Administration of a succession. Albaceazgo.

Administration of property Administración de los bienes.

Administrative court. Tribunal de lo contencioso administrativo.

Administrative law. Derecho administrativo.

Administrator. Administrador; albacea dativo; gerente.

Administratrix. Administradora; albacea dativo.
Admiralty. Derecho marítimo; almirantazgo.
Admiralty bond. Fianza marítima.
Admiralty court. Tribunal marítimo o de almirantazgo.
Admiralty jurisdiction. Jurisdicción marítima; jurisdicción de almirantazgo.
Admiralty law. Derecho marítimo.
Admiralty rules. Normas procesales de Derecho marítimo.
Admissibility of evidence. Admisibilidad de la prueba.
Admissible. Admisible; lícito; permisible.
Admissible evidence. Prueba admisible; prueba procedente.
Admission. Confesión; admisión.
Admission against interest. Confesión o admisión contra el interés propio.
Admit to bail. Señalar fianza para libertad provisional.
Admonish. Amonestar; prevenir; advertir.
Admonition. Amonestación; advertencia.
Adopt. Adoptar.
Adoption. Adopción.
Adulterer. Adúltero.
Adulterine. Adulterino.
Adulterous child. Hijo adulterino.
Adultery. Adulterio.
Ad valorem. Basado en el valor.
Ad valorem tax. Impuesto por avalúo.
Adventitious property. Bienes adventicios.
Advent of hostilities. Advenimiento de hostilidades.
Adversary proceeding. Proceso entre dos partes adversarias.
Adverse claim. Pretensión contraria; pretensión de tercero.
Adverse party. Parte contraria.
Adverse possession. Posesión de un inmueble de mala fe; posesión por quién no es dueño que puede conducir a la usucapión.
Advertise. Anunciar; avisar.
Advertisement. Anuncio; aviso.
Advice. Consejo; notificación; aviso.
Advise. Asesorar; notificar; informar; recomendar.
Advisory jury. Jurado asesor.
Advisory opinion. Opinión consultiva.
Advocacy. Abogar por una causa.
Advocate. Abogado; defensor.
Aequitas. Equidad.
Aequitas agit in personam. La equidad (equity) actúa sobre la persona. De acuerdo con esta doctrina, la orden de un tribunal de "equity" obliga a la persona del demandado pero no afecta su propiedad.
Aequitas est quasi aequalitas. La equidad es como si fuera la igualdad.

Aequitas sequitur legem. La equidad actúa en consecuencia con el derecho; por tanto, un tribunal de "equity" o equidad no puede alterar los derechos de las partes si los mismos están claramente definidos por la ley.

Aequum et bonum. Bueno y equitativo.

Affiance. Esponsales; dar en prenda.

Affiant. Declarante bajo juramento.

Affidavit. Declaración jurada.

Affiliated company. Compañía afiliada o subsidiaria.

Affiliation. *Véase* filation.

Affinity. Afinidad.

Affirm. Confirmar; afirmar; convalidar.

Affirmation. Declaración; aseveración; afirmación.

Affirmative defense. Defensa específica; defensa afirmativa; defensa a los alegatos de la demanda.

Affirmative pregnant. Alegato ambiguo; afirmación ambigua.

Affirmative relief. Resarcimiento positivo, usualmente a favor del demando.

Affirmitive servitude. Servidumbre positiva.

Affirm the judgment. Confirmar la sentencia.

Affirm under oath. Declarar bajo juramento.

Affix the seal. Fijar el sello.

Affreight. Fletar.

Affreightment. Contrato de transporte marítimo; fletamento.

Aforethought. Premeditación.

A fortiori. Por mayor razón; a fortiori.

After-acquired property. *Véase* after-acquired title.

After-acquired title. Dominio subsiguientemente adquirido.

Against acceptance. Contra aceptación.

Agency. Mandato; agencia.

Agenda. Orden del día; agenda.

Agent. Mandatario; agente.

Agent for service of process. Mandatario o agente para emplazamientos.

Agent, universal. *Véase* universal agent.

Age of majority. Mayoría de edad.

Aggravated assault. Agresión con agravante; agresión con objeto peligroso.

Aggravating circumstances. Circumstancias agravantes.

Aggravation. Agravante.

Aggregatio mentium. Compenetración de las mentes.

Aggression. Agresión.

Aggressor. Asaltante; agresor.

Aggrieve. Agraviar.

Aggrieved. Agraviado.

Aggrieved party. Parte agraviada.

Agnate. Agnado.

Agrarian legislation. Legislación agraria.

Agrarian reform. Reforma agraria.

Agree. Acordar; convenir.
Agreement. Acuerdo; convenio.
Agreement of rescission. Acuerdo de disolución.
Agreement to the contrary. Pacto en contrario.
Aid and abet. Coadyuvar en la comisión de un crimen.
Air bill. Conocimiento de embarque aéreo.
Aleatory. Aleatorio.
Aleatory agreement. *Véase* aleatory contract.
Aleatory contract. Contrato aleatorio.
Alibi. Coartada; prueba de ausencia.
Alien. Extranjero.
Alienable. Enajenable.
Alienate. Enajenar.
Alienation. Enajenación.
Alienation of affection. Desproveer cariños o afectos; sustracción de afectos.
Alienee. Persona a quien se han transferido bienes.
Alieni juris. Bajo la autoridad de otro.
Alienor. Enajenante.
Alimentary obligations. Obligación de alimentos.
Alimony. Pensión de alimentos.
Alimony pendente lite. Pensión provisional.
Allegation. Alegato; alegación; argumento; declaración.
Allege. Alegar; argumentar; declarar.
Allegiance. Lealtad, o fidelidad, debida a la patria.
Alleviate. Aliviar; mitigar.
All fours. Acuerdo sustancial entre dos o más casos.
Allodium. Alodio.
Allograph. Documento o firma hecha por persona diferente de la que se supone haya redactado o firmado.
Allonge. Papel adherido a un pagaré o a una letra de cambio en el cuál pueden hacerse endosos.
All risk insurance. Seguro a todo riesgo.
Alluvion. Aluvión.
Alternate jurors. Miembros suplentes del jurado.
Alternative obligations. Obligaciones alternativas.
Alternative performances. Obligaciones alternativas; prestaciones alternativas.
Amalgamation. Fusión de sociedades.
Ambassador. Embajador.
Amendatory. Reformatorio.
Amendatory deed. Escritura de modificación.
Amendment. Enmienda.
Amendment of the pleadings. Enmienda de los alegatos de un proceso.
Amicable action. Proceso amistoso. Llámase así a la demanda presentada por acuerdo de las partes para obtener una opinión consultiva.
Amicable compounder. Amigable componedor.
Amicable demand. Reclamación amistosa.

Amicable settlement. Arreglo amistoso.
Amicus curiae. Memorial de un tercero, que no es parte en el litigio, apoyando la posición de una de las partes.
Amnesty. Amnistía.
Amortization. Amortización.
Amortize. Amortizar.
Ancestor. Ascendiente.
Ancient documents. Documentos antiguos; llámase así a los documentos de no menos de 20 años de antigüedad, a los cuáles se presume genuinos, siempre y cuándo provengan de un lugar donde presumiblemente estarían situados si fuesen genuinos.
Ancient writings. *Véase* ancient documents.
Ancillary. Subsidiario; subordinado.
Ancillary administration. Albaceazgo auxiliar.
Ancillary document. Documento subordinado a otro.
Ancillary jurisdiction. Jurisdicción ancilaria o subordinada.
Ancillary letter of credit. Carta de crédito auxiliar.
Ancillary proceeding. Proceso subordinado.
Animus capiendi. Con intención de coger.
Animus furandi. Con intención de hurtar.
Animus lucrandi. Con intención de lucro.
Animus manendi. Con intención de permanecer.
Animus morandi. Con intención de morar.
Animus revocandi. Con intención de revocar.
Animus testandi. Con intención de testar.
Annotation. Anotación; apunte; nota.
Annuitant. Pensionista; censualista.
Annuity. Pensión; censo; renta.
Annul. Anular; invalidar; cancelar.
Annulment. Anulación; invalidación; cancelación.
Annulment of judgment. Anulación de una sentencia.
Answer. Contestación.
Answerable. Responsable.
Antecedent debt. Deuda anterior.
Antenuptial agreement. Contrato entre los futuros esposos; contrato matrimonial.
Antichresis. Antícresis.
Anticipatory breach (of contract). Incumplimiento de contrato adelantado o anticipado.
Anticipatory repudiation. Incumplimiento anticipado; llámase así al acto por el cual una de las partes declara que no habrá de efectuar su prestación cuando le corresponda hacerlo.
Antigraphy. Duplicado o contrapartida de un documento.
Antitrust law. Derecho antimonopolístico.

Apparent authority. Poder aparente; autorización aparente.
Apparent defects. Defectos aparentes.
Apparent easement. Servidumbre aparente.
Apparent promise. Condición potestativa; promesa aparente; promesa ilusoria.
Apparent servitude. Servidumbre aparente.
Appeal. Apelación; recurso.
Appealable. Apelable.
Appeal, devolutive. *Véase* devolutive appeal.
Appeal, suspensive. *Véase* suspensive appeal.
Appearance. Comparecencia.
Appear in court. Comparecer ante el tribunal.
Appellant. Apelante; recurrente.
Appellate court. Tribunal de apelación.
Appellate judge. Juez o magistrado de un tribunal de apelación.
Appellate jurisdiction. Jurisdicción apelativa.
Appellate procedure. Procedimiento en apelación.
Appellate proceedings. Proceso de apelación.
Appellee. Apelado.
Applicable law. Derecho aplicable.
Applicant of a writ. Recurrente.
Application for a writ. Solicitación de recurso.
Application of payments. Imputación de pagos.
Application, power of. *Véase* power of application.
Appointment. Nombramiento.
Appraisal. Tasación; justiprecio.
Appraise. Valorar; tasar; justipreciar.
Appraiser. Justipreciador; tasador.
Apprehend. Aprehender; prender.
Appropriation. Apropiación; asignación; dotación.
Appropriation law. Ley de presupuestos.
Appurtenance. Pertenencia; accesorio; incidental.
Arbiter. Arbitro.
Arbitrable. Arbitrable.
Arbitrary punishment. Pena discrecional.
Arbitrate. Arbitrar.
Arbitration. Arbitraje.
Arbitration award. Laudo arbitral.
Arbitration procedure. Procedimiento de arbitraje.
Arbitrator. Arbitro.
Argument. Argumento; debate.
Arms length transaction. Acuerdo entre personas de igual conocimiento o poderío económico.
Arraign. Instruir de cargos.
Arraignment. Instrucción de cargos; vista de un preceso penal donde el acusado debe declararse culpable o inocente.
Arrearage. Atrasos; estado de estar atrasado.

Arrest. Arrestar; aprehender; arresto; detención.

Arrest, false. *Véase* false arrest.

Arrest of judgment. Negación del tribunal a dictar sentencia, el fallo o veredicto del jurado no obstante, cuando se ha cometido un error sustancial que vicia la legalidad del proceso, o cuando se hace patente que el demandante no tiene derecho al fallo dictado a su favor.

Arrest of vessel. Embargo de la nave.

Arrest warrant. Orden de arresto.

Arson. Incendio doloso; incendio intencional.

Articles of agreement. Memorial sobre las cláusulas de un contrato; contrato; convenio.

Articles of impeachment. Declaración escrita de los cargos en un proceso de residencia.

Articles of incorporation. Escritura de constitución; carta de constitución; estatutos de una sociedad anónima.

Articles of partnership. Cláusulas de un contrato de sociedad.

Articulo mortis. En el momento de la muerte.

Artificial person. Persona jurídica.

Ascendant. Ascendiente.

Assailant. Asaltante; agresor.

Assasinate. Asesinar.

Assasination. Asesinato.

Assault. Asalto; agresión.

Assault and battery. Agresión violenta con golpes.

Assent. Aprobación; consentimiento.

Assert a claim. Ejercitar una pretensión.

Assessment. Avalúo; tasación.

Assessment of damages. Avalúo del daño; evaluación del daño.

Assessor. Tasador; amillarador.

Asset. Bien; provecho; activo.

Assign. Ceder; traspasar; causa habiente; sucesor.

Assignability. Transferabilidad.

Assignee. Cesionario.

Assignment. Cesión; traspaso.

Assignment of accounts. Cesión de cuentas.

Assignment of rights. Cesión de créditos; cesión de derechos.

Assignor. Cedente; cesionista.

Association. Asociación; compañía; sociedad.

Assumption of liability. Asunción de responsabilidad.

Assumption of mortgage. Asunción de la hipoteca; promesa del comprador de un inmueble gravado por hipoteca de pagar la deuda al acreedor.

Assumption of obligations. Asunción de obligaciones.

Assumption of the risk. Asunción del riesgo; actuar con conocimiento del riesgo.
Assurer. Asegurador.
Asylum. Asilo.
Asylum, political. Asilo político.
Attach. Embargar; decomisar; encautar.
Attachment. Embargo; comiso; secuestro.
Attachment, writ of. *Véase* writ of attachment.
Attainder. Ley que condena a una persona sin procesamiento.
Attempt. Atentado; tentativa de cometer un delito.
Attest. Certificar; dar fe; refrendar.
Attestation. Autenticación; testimonio bajo juramento.
Attorney. Abogado; licenciado; letrado.
Attorney at law. Abogado.
Attorney for the defense. Defensor; abogado de la defensa.
Attorney for the prosecution. Fiscal.
Attorney general. Procurador general; fiscal general.
Attorney-in-fact. Apoderado.
Attorney's fees. Honorarios del abogado.
Attractive nuisance. Condición peligrosa que resulta atractiva para los niños.
Auction. Subasta; venta a martillo; remate.
Auctioneer. Rematador; martillero.
Authentic. Auténtico; fehaciente.
Authentic act. Instrumento público; documento notarizado; documento autenticado.
Authenticate. Autenticar; refrendar; dar fe.
Authentication. Autenticación.
Authority. Facultad; poder; autoridad; autorización; fundamentación legal; precedente.
Authorization. Autorización.
Authorization to charge. Autorización para cargar.
Authorize. Autorizar.
Authorized capital. Capital autorizado.
Autrefois acquit. Defensa de absolución en una vista anterior.
Autre vie. Por, o durante, la vida de otro.
Average. Avería.
Average adjuster. Tasador de averías.
Average bond. Fianza de averías.
Average policy. Póliza de averías.
Average quality. Calidad media; mediana calidad.
A vinculo matrimonii. Del vínculo matrimonial.
Avoid. Anular.
Avoidable. Anulable o cancelable.
Avoidance. Anulación.
Avulsion. Avulsión.
Award. Adjudicación; fallo; laudo.

B

Back letter of credit. Carta de crédito auxiliar.
Bad faith. Mala fe; dolo.
Bail. Fianza carcelera; afianzamiento o caución de libertad.
Bailable. Delito o falta caucionable.
Bail bond. Caución de libertad.
Bailee. Depositario; locatario.
Bailiff. Alguacil del juzgado; oficial de justicia.
Bail jumping. Violación del contrato de afianzamiento o caución de libertad.
Bailment. Depósito; arrendamiento de bienes muebles; libertad bajo fianza.
Bailor. Depositante; locador.
Ballot. Papeleta o boleta electoral.
Balloting. Votación.
Ban. Prohibición; proscripción.
Bank. Banco.
Bank acceptance. Aceptación bancaria.
Bank clearance. Compensación bancaria.
Bank draft. Giro bancario.
Banking usage. Uso bancario.
Bank of issue. Banco emisor.
Bank reserves. Reservas bancarias.
Bankrupt. Quebrado; fallido; concursado.
Bankruptcy. Quiebra; concurso.
Bankruptcy act. Acto de quiebra.
Bankruptcy court. Corte o tribunal de quiebras.
Bankruptcy discharge. Rehabilitación del quebrado.
Bankruptcy trustee. Síndico de la quiebra.
Bankruptcy, voluntary. *Véase* voluntary bankruptcy.
Bar. El foro; el cuerpo de abogados en su totalidad.
Bareboat charter. Carta de fletamento desnudo (sin tripulación ni combustible).
Bargain. Pacto; convenio; contrato; negociación.
Barter. Permuta; trueque.
Base fee. Dominio sujeto a condición resolutoria.
Basis of the bargain. Base del negocio.
Bastard. Hijo ilegítimo.
Battery. Agresión.
Bearer. Portador.
Bearer note. Pagaré al portador.
Bearer paper. Valores al porador.
Bearer shares. Acciones al portador.
Belligerency. Beligerancia.
Belong to. Pertenecer a.
Bench. Tribunal; el poder judicial; la judicatura.
Bench warrant. Orden judicial de arresto.
Beneficiary. Beneficiario.

Beneficiary interest. Interés útil; interés del beneficiario; llámase así al derecho del beneficiario de un fideicomiso (trust) sobre bienes de los cuáles no tiene el título legal.
Beneficiary of a letter of credit. Beneficiario o portador de una carta de crédito.
Benefit of inventory. Beneficio de inventario; derecho de inventario.
Bequeath. Legar; donar.
Bequest. Legado; donación.
Best evidence. Mejor prueba (o evidencia); llámase así a la prueba que provee la mayor certeza sobre el hecho a probar.
Bicameral. Bicameral.
Bid. Proposición; propuesta; puja; postura; oferta.
Bidder. Proponente; pujador; licitador.
Bigamist. Bígamo.
Bigamy. Bigamia.
Bilateral agreement. Acuerdo o convenio bilateral.
Bilateral contract. Contrato bilateral.
Bill. Billete de banco; proyecto de ley; cuenta.
Bill in equity. Demanda ante un tribunal de equidad.
Bill of attainder. *Véase* attainder.
Bill of exceptions. Objeciones a las decisiones del juez de primera instancia.
Bill of exchange. Letra de cambio.
Bill of indictment. Proyecto de acusación para el gran jurado.
Bill of lading. Conocimiento de embarque.
Bill of lading, clean. Conocimiento de embarque limpio; conocimiento de embarque sin tacha; conocimiento de embarque sin anotaciones.
Bill of particulars. Declaración o informe de la fiscalía dónde se le da información adicional al acusado sobre los hechos del delito que se le acusa haber cometido.
Bill of rights. Declaración de derechos; carta de derechos.
Bill of sale. Escritura de compraventa de bienes muebles.
Binder. *Véase* insurance binder.
Blackacre. Nombre ficticio usado para distinguir una heredad de otra; a la otra heredad se le llama usualmente "whiteacre".
Blackmail. Chantaje.
Blockade. Bloqueo.
Blue sky laws. Leyes estatales regulando la emisión de acciones, y el mercado de valores.
Board. Junta; consejo.
Boarder. Pensionista; huésped.
Board inquiry. Junta de investigación.
Board meeting. Sesión del consejo de administración.
Board of appeals. Junta de apelaciones.
Board of directors. Junta o consejo de dirección.

Board of trade. Cámara de comercio.

Bodily injury. Lesión corporal.

Body corporate. Corporación; sociedad anónima.

Body of law. Cuerpo legislativo; colección de leyes.

Body politic. Cuerpo político.

Bona fide. Buena fe.

Bona fide purchaser. Comprador de buena fe; adquirente de buena fe.

Bona fides. Buena fe.

Bona vacantia. Bienes que nadie reclama como suyos.

Bond. Fianza; depósito; vínculo; afianzar; bono.

Bonding contract. Contrato de afianzamiento.

Book value. Valor neto de los bienes de una sociedad; valor contable.

Border. Frontera.

Borrower. Prestatario.

Boss. Empresario; patrón; jefe.

Bottomry. Contrato a la gruesa; hipoteca a la gruesa; préstamo a la gruesa.

Bottomry bond. Contrato de hipoteca a la gruesa; contrato de cambio marítimo.

Bottomry loan. Préstamo a la gruesa.

Boundary. Lindero; límite; frontera.

Boycott. Boicot.

Breach. Incumplimimento; contravención.

Breach of contract. Incumplimiento de contrato.

Breach of duty. Incumplimiento del deber; prevaricación.

Breach of faith. Abuso de confianza; prevaricación.

Breach of promise of marriage. Incumplimiento de la promesa de matrimonio.

Breach of warranty. Incumplimiento de garantía.

Breach, partial. *Véase* partial breach.

Breach, total. *Véase* total breach.

Breaking and entering. Escalamiento.

Bribe. Soborno; sobornar.

Bribery. Soborno.

Brief. Memorial; informe; alegato.

Bring suit. Presentación de una demanda.

Broker. Comisionista; agente de bolsa; corredor de comercio.

Brokerage. Corretaje;comisión.

Broker's contract. Contrato de comisión.

Bulk cargo. Carga a granel.

Bulk sales. Ventas a granel; ventas de negocios.

Bulk transfers. Traspasos a granel; cesiones a granel.

Burden. Gravamen; carga.

Burden of proof. Carga de la prueba.

Burglary. Escalamiento.

Business. Negocio; comercio; tráfico.

Business activity. Actividad comercial.
Business dealing. Transacción comercial; gestión mercantil; negociación mercantil.
Business establishment. Establecimiento mercantil.
But for rule. *Véase* sine qua non.
Buy. Comprar; compra.
Buyer. Comprador.
Bylaws. Estatutos; reglamento de una sociedad anónima.

C

Cabinet. Gabinete.
Caducity. Caducidad.
Calendar. Calendario; lista de casos en proceso en los libros de un tribunal.
Call. Demanda de pago de un pagaré vencido; demanda de pago de acciones no pagadas por la sociedad anónima que las ha vendido.
Callable bonds. Bonos redimibles o retirables.
Callable securities. Valores retirables.
Call in warranty. Notificación al vendedor a que proteja al comprador de la evicción.
Call loan. Préstamo pagadero a solicitud o a la demanda.
Call money. Préstamo con valores como garantía.
Cancel. Cancelar; rescindir; anular; invalidar.
Cancellation Cancelación; rescisión; anulación; invalidación.
Canon. Canon.
Canons of ethics. Cánones de ética; reglas de conducta que gobernaban el ejercicio de la profesión del Derecho en los E E.U U.entre 1908 y 1969.
Capable. Capaz; hábil.
Capacity. Capacidad; competencia.
Capacity to contract. Capacidad para contratar.
Capias. Término genérico de orden judicial, dirigida a un oficial de la autoridad, ordenando el arresto de una persona.
Capias ad audiendum judicium. Orden que se traiga al reo ante el tribunal a oir la sentencia.
Capital. Capital.
Capital assets. Activos; activos capitalizados.
Capital crime. Delito castigable por la pena de muerte.
Capitalization. Capitalización.
Capital offense. *Véase* capital crime.
Capital punishment. Pena capital; pena de muerte.
Capital reserves. Reservas de capital.
Capital stock. Acciones de capital.
Capitation tax. Impuesto de capitación.
Capitulate. Capitular.

Capitulation. Capitulación; rendición.
Captation. Captación.
Caption. Título; encabezamiento; epígrafe.
Capture. Capturar; arrestar.
Care. Cuidado.
Cargo. Cargamento; carga.
Cargo lien, against the ship. Privilegio sobre la nave basado en el cargamento.
Carriage. Porte; transporte.
Carriage of goods. Transporte de mercancías.
Carrier. Cargador.
Carrying a concealed weapon. Portar arma escondida.
Cartel. Cartel.
Case. Caso; causa; asunto.
Casebook. Libro de casos.
Case in point. Precedente; caso análogo.
Case law. Derecho elaborado por los casos.
Case method. Método del caso.
Case of first impression. Caso que presenta un problema de derecho sin precedente jurídico.
Case system. *Véase* case method.
Cash. Dinero en efectivo.
Cash dividend. Distribución de dividendos en efectivo.
Cashier's check. Cheque de administración; cheque de gerencia; talón bancario; cheque de caja.
Cash on delivery. Cóbrese a la entrega; entrega contra reembolso.
Cash proceeds. Producto en efectivo.
Cash sale. Venta al contado.
Cassation. Casación.
Casualty. Accidente; siniestro.
Casus belli. Acto que ocasiona o justifica la guerra.
Causa mortis. Por razón de muerte; en contemplación de muerte.
Causation. Causa.
Cause. Causa.
Cause-in-fact. Causa de hecho.
Cause of action. Derecho de actuar; causa de actuar.
Cause of action, accrual of the. *Véase* accrual of the cause of action.
Cause, sufficient. *Véase* sufficient cause.
Cause, unlawful. *Véase* unlawful cause.
Caveat. Aviso; prevención.
Caveat emptor. Que se cuide el comprador; principio de derecho según el cuál el comprador asume el riesgo de la evicción y vicios ocultos de la cosa vendida a menos que exista garantía explícita o implicita.
Cedent. Cedente.
Censor. Someter a censura; censurar.
Censorship. Censura.
Censorship in advance. Censura previa.
Censure. Censura.
Ceremony. Ceremonia; acto formal.
Certificate. Certificación.

Certificate of birth. Partida de nacimiento.

Certificate of death. Partida de defunción.

Certificate of deposit. Certificado de depósito.

Certificate of encumbrances. Certificación de cargas; certificación de gravámenes.

Certificate of incorporation. Certificado de incorporación de una sociedad anónima.

Certificate of insurance. Certificado de seguro.

Certificate of public convenience and necessity. Certificado de conveniencia pública y necesidad.

Certificate of stock. Certificado de acciones; escrito que sirve de título de propiedad de acciones.

Certificate of title. Título.

Certification. Certificación.

Certification proceeding. Proceso de certificación. Llámase así al proceso administrativo laboral que se sigue para constatar la voluntad de los obreros sobre su representación.

Certified check. Cheque certificado.

Certiorari, writ of. *Véase* writ of certiorari.

Cesset executio. Arresto de ejecución de sentencia.

Cesset processus. Arresto o paro de la instancia.

Cessio bonorum. Cesión de los bienes del deudor para beneficio de sus acreedores.

Cession. Cesión de soberanía sobre un territorio.

Cestui que trust. Beneficiario de un fideicomiso.

Chain of title. Cadena del título; cadena dominical del título.

Chairman of the board. Presidente del consejo de dirección de una sociedad.

Challenge for cause. Impugnación de un miembro del jurado por causa justificada.

Challenge, peremptory. *Véase* peremptory challenge.

Chancellor. Magistrado o juez de un tribunal de equidad (equity).

Chancery. Cancillería; llámase así al tribunal de equidad (equity); equidad (equity).

Change of venue. Traslado de tribunal; traslado de jurisdicción.

Character evidence. Prueba de reputación. Testimonio sobre la reputación de una persona en la comunidad.

Character witness. Testigo de reputación; testigo que declara acerca de la reputación de una persona en la comunidad.

Charge. Gravamen; carga; acusación.

Chargeable. Imputable; acusable.

Charge back. Contracargo; cargar de nuevo en cuenta.

Chargé d'affaires. Encargado de negocios.
Charge to the jury. Instrucciones que el juez da al jurado.
Charitable corporation. Sociedad de beneficencia.
Charitable trust. Fundación; fideicomiso con fines caritativos.
Charter. Estatutos de una sociedad anónima; carta constitutiva.
Charter, bareboat. *Véase* bareboat charter.
Charterer. Fletador.
Charter of the United Nations. Carta constitutiva de las Naciones Unidas.
Charter party. Contrato de fletamento.
Charter, time. *Véase* time charter.
Charter, voyage. *Véase* voyage charter.
Chattel mortgage. Hipoteca de bienes muebles; prenda sin desplazamiento.
Chattel paper. Escritura que evidencia una obligación monetaria y un derecho de garantía o un arrendamiento de bienes muebles.
Chattels. Bienes muebles.
Chattels personal. *Véase* chattels.
Chattels real. Figuras jurídicas, tales como el arrendamiento de inmuebles, las cuáles, sin constituir propiedad inmueble, se relacionan a la propiedad inmobiliaria.
Chattel trust. Fideicomiso mobiliario.
Check. Cheque; talón.
Checking account. Cuenta corriente; cuenta de cheques.
Check payable to bearer. Cheque al portador.
Check payable to order. Cheque a la orden.
Checks and balances. Frenos y contrapesos.
Chief, examination in. Interrogatorio directo.
Chief justice. Magistrado presidente de un tribunal de apelación.
Chief place of business. Centro (o lugar) principal de negocios.
Child. Hijo.
Child support. Alimentos para los hijos; pensión de alimentos para los hijos.
Choice of law rule. Regla de conflicto (der. int. privado).
Chose of action. Pretensión; deuda; obligación.
Circuit. División territorial; división territorial de jurisdicción; circuito.
Circuit court. Tribunal de circuito.
Circuit court of appeals. Tribunal de apelación de circuito (federal).
Circumstantial evidence. Prueba circunstancial; prueba indirecta.
Citation. Citación; emplazamiento.

Citation of authorities. Cita de precedentes de jurisprudencia.
Citizen. Ciudadano.
Citizenship. Ciudadanía.
Civil. Civil.
Civil action. Acción civil.
Civil code. Código civil.
Civil contempt. Desacato civil del tribunal.
Civil effects. Efectos en el estado civil.
Civil effects of marriage. Efectos civiles del matrimonio.
Civil fruits. Frutos civiles.
Civilian. Civilista.
Civil law. Derecho civil.
Civil liberties. *Véase* civil rights.
Civil obligation. Obligación civil; obligación que el derecho da acción para hacerla cumplir.
Civil possession. Posesión civil.
Civil procedure. Procedimiento civil.
Civil registry. Registro civil.
Civil remedy. Remedio civil; resarcimiento o compensación para la víctima de un delito o cuasidelito.
Civil rights. Derechos individuales; derechos civiles; libertades públicas.
Claim. Pretensión; demanda.
Claimant. Demandante.
Claims, priority of. *Véase* priority of claims.
Clandestine possession. Posesión clandestina u oculta.
Class action. Acción de clase; llámase así la acción en que los miembros de un grupo grande de personas--o clase--demandan, o, son demandados, por representación. Este tipo de acción se usa cuando las personas miembros de la clase son muy numerosas, resultando que su acumulación no es factible.
Clause. Cláusula; estipulación.
Clean bill of lading. Conocimiento limpio (sin tacha u observaciones).
Clean hands doctrine. Doctrina de "manos limpias". Llámase así a la regla que exige que el que reclama un derecho haya procedido de buena fe en el asunto de que se trata.
Clear and convincing evidence. Prueba clara y convincente. Este tipo de prueba se requiere en ciertos casos de índole civil.
Clearing corporation. Corporación compensadora.
Clearing house. Casa de liquidación; banco de liquidación; banco o casa de compensación.
Clear title. Dominio libre de gravamen o restricciones; título sano.
Clear title, to. Sanear el título.
Clemency. Clemencia.
Clerk of court. Secretario de administración de un tribunal.

Clerkship (law). Puesto de pasante en un bufete o juzgado.
Client. Cliente.
Close corporation. Sociedad anónima cuyas acciones no se cotizan en bolsa de valores, y por lo general no se venden al público.
Closely held corporation. *Véase* close corporation.
Close the transaction. Concluir la operación; concluir el negocio jurídico.
Closing of an act. Cierre de un documento.
Cloud on the title. Nube sobre el título; imperfección del título causada por pretensión real o posible de tercero.
Coalition. Alianza; coalición.
Coast guard. Guardacostas; prefectura marítima.
Coastwise cargo. Cargamento de cabotaje.
Coastwise navigation. Cabotaje; navegación costera.
Coastwise shipment. Embarque de cabotaje.
Coastwise trade. Cabotaje.
Code. Código.
Codefendant. Coacusado.
Code of civil procedure. Código de procedimento civil.
Code of criminal procedure. Código de procedimiento criminal.
Code of professional responsibility. Código de responsabilidad profesional del abogado.
Codification. Codificación.
Codified law. Ley escrita; ley codificada; derecho escrito; derecho codificado.
Coerce. Coaccionar; forzar.
Cognate. Cognado.
Cognizance. Conocimiento de un asunto; competencia.
Cognovit. Admisión del demandado que no tiene defensa y confesión de sentencia en su contra.
Cognovit note. Pagaré que contiene confesión de sentencia.
Cohabit. Cohabitar.
Coheir. Coheredero.
Collate. Colar bienes.
Collateral. Bienes gravados; garantía.
Collateral agreement. Pacto o acuerdo colateral.
Collateral attack. Impugnación de una sentencia en una acción independiente.
Collateral estoppel. Cosa juzgada sobre hechos disputados; llámase así al efecto de cosa juzgada que impide que los hechos litigados, o que pudieron litigarse, entre las partes, vuelvan a ser litigados.
Collateral facts. Hechos que no tienen conexión directa con el problema en litigio.
Collateral issue. Problema incidental en un juicio.
Collateral line. Línea colateral.
Collateral mortgage. Hipoteca colateral.
Collateral promise. Promesa colateral.

Collateral security. Garantía; resguardo.
Collation. Colación de bienes.
Collect (to). Cobrar.
Collecting bank. Banco cobrador; banco colector.
Collection. Cobro; recaudación.
Collection of taxes. Recaudación de impuestos.
Collective bargaining. Contratación colectiva.
Collective bargaining agreement. Contrato laboral colectivo.
Collision at sea. Abordaje.
Collision, lien for. Privilegio o derecho de retención por abordaje.
Collision with a vessel. Abordaje.
Collusion. Colusión.
Colorable. Acto o situación que aparenta o pretende ser legítima, o con arreglo a derecho, pero que realmente no lo es.
Color of law. Apariencia o pretexto de derecho.
Color of title. Apariencia o pretexto de título o dominio.
Combination in restraint of trade. Convenio que impide el libre funcionamiento del comercio.
Comity. Cortesía.
Commerce clause. La cláusula de comercio (de la constitución de los E E.U U.).
Commercial contract. Contrato comercial.
Commercial court. Juzgado o tribunal de comercio.
Commercial law. Derecho mercantil; Derecho comercial.
Commercial paper. Títulos valores; documentos negociables; obligaciones mercantiles; valores.
Commercial practices. Prácticas comerciales; usos del comercio.
Commercial reasonableness. Razonabilidad mercantil.
Commercial suretyship. Fianza mercantil.
Commercial symbol. Símbolo comercial; seña comercial.
Commercial transaction. Transacción comercial; acto de comercio.
Commercial unit. Unidad comercial.
Commission. Comisión; encargo; encomienda.
Commission agent. Comisionista.
Commissioner. Oficial autorizado a desempañar algunas funciones judiciales.
Commitment. Obligación; encarcelamiento; encierro.
Committing magistrate. Magistrado que dicta auto de encierro o prisión.
Commodatum. Comodato.
Commodity. Mercancía.
Commodity exchange. Bolsa de comercio.
Common carrier. Transporte público; porteador público; cargador.

Common creditor. Acreedor quirografario.

Common law. Derecho común; derecho consuetudinario.

Common law action. Acción basada en el derecho común (common law).

Common law marriage. Unión de hecho reconocida por el derecho como matrimonio especial; concubinato reconocido como matrimonio por el common law.

Common stock. Acciones ordinarias.

Common things. Bienes comunes; bienes que no pertenecen a nadie en particular y que todos pueden usar.

Common wall servitude. Servidumbre de medianería.

Community assets. Bienes gananciales.

Community obligation. Obligación de la sociedad de gananciales.

Community of acquets and gains. *Véase* community of gains.

Community of gains. Sociedad legal de gananciales.

Community property. Bienes gananciales.

Community property law. Derecho de comunidad de bienes en el matrimonio.

Commutation of sentence. Conmutación de la sentencia.

Commutative contract. Contrato conmutativo

Compact. Contrato; contrato formal.

Company. Compañía; sociedad anónima.

Comparative law. Derecho comparado.

Comparative negligence. Negligencia comparativa; negligencia comparada; falta comparativa; falta comparada.

Compensate. Compensar.

Compensation. Compensación; indemnización.

Compensatory damages. Resarcimiento del daño de hecho sufrido. Esta clase de resarcimiento obedece al propósito de compensar a la víctima y no al de castigar al autor del daño.

Competence. Competencia.

Competency. Capacidad de un testigo para atestiguar; cualidad de la prueba que amerita se la tenga en cuenta en la determinación de un pleito.

Competent evidence. Prueba competente; prueba admisible.

Competent witness. Testigo capaz.

Complainant. Demandante.

Complaint. Demanda.

Complicity. Complicidad.

Component part. Parte componente (esp. de propiedad inmueble).

Component parts of an immovable. Partes integrantes de un inmueble.

Composition. Componenda; arreglo entre el deudor y sus acreedores.

Compos mentis. De mente sana.

Compromise. Transacción; arreglo; compromiso.
Compulsion. Coacción; compulsión.
Compulsory counterclaim. *Véase* counterclaim, compulsory.
Compulsory joinder. Unificación compulsiva de acciones o partes.
Compulsory process. Proceso compulsivo. Derecho del demandado a obligar forzosamente la comparecencia de testigos ante el tribunal.
Compulsory sale. Venta forzosa.
Compulsory unit. Unidad minera obligatoria ; *véase* unitization.
Computation of damages. Cómputo del daño.
Concealed weapon. *Véase* carrying a concealed weapon.
Concealment. Ocultación; secreto.
Concession. Licencia; autorización.
Conclusions of law. Conclusiones de derecho.
Conclusive presumption. Presunción juris et de jure; presunción absoluta o irrefutable.
Concordat. Concordato; convención.
Concubinage. Concubinato.
Concurrent jurisdiction. Jurisdicción o competencia concurrente. Esta situación ocurre cuando hay jurisdicción o competencia simultánea de varios tribunales sobre un caso en particular.
Concurrent negligence. Culpa concurrente o compartida. Ocurre cuando la culpa de dos o más personas se combina para producir el daño de que se trata.
Concurrent sentence. Pena que se cumple simultáneamente con otra impuesta por la comisión de otro delito.
Concurring opinion. Opinión concurrente; opinión aparte de un magistrado que coincide con la decisión de la mayoría.
Condemn. Condenar; sentenciar.
Condemnation. Expropiación; condenación.
Condemn land. Expropiar tierra.
Condemn to death. Condenar a muerte.
Condition. Condición.
Conditional. Condicional.
Conditional promise. Promesa condicional; obligación condicional.
Conditional sale. Compraventa con reserva de dominio.
Condition, potestative. Condición potestativa.
Condition precedent. Condición suspensiva.
Condition, resolutory, Condición resolutoria.
Condition subsequent. Condición resolutoria.
Condition, suspensive. Condición suspensiva.
Condonation. Condonación; perdón.

Confederacy. Confederación.
Confession. Confesión.
Confession and avoidance. Escrito en que se admiten ciertos alegatos de la otra parte, pero se evitan las consecuencias de los mismos mediante nuevas aseveraciones.
Confession of judgment. Confesión de sentencia sin proceso.
Confidential communications. Comunicaciones confidenciales.
Confinement. Reclusión; encarcelamiento.
Confirm (to). Ratificar; corroborar; confirmar.
Confirmation. Ratificación; corroboración; confirmación.
Confirmed credit. Crédito confirmado.
Confirming bank. Banco confirmante.
Confiscation. Confiscación; decomiso.
Conflicting decisions. Decisiones opuestas.
Conflict of interests. Intereses opuestos; conflicto de intereses.
Conflict of laws. Derecho internacional privado; conflicto de leyes.
Conforming goods. Mercancías en conformidad con el contrato.
Confrontation. Confrontación.
Confrontation of witnesses (right of). Derecho del acusado en un juicio penal a confrontar a los testigos que declaran en su contra.
Confrontation rights. Derechos de confrontación; derecho a carear testigos.
Confusion. Confusión de derechos.
Congeable. Legal; realizado con permiso.
Congé d'emparler. Permiso para conferenciar con la parte opuesta para tratar de llegar a un arreglo.
Conjoints. Consortes.
Conjugal partnership. Sociedad conyugal.
Conjugal rights. Derechos conyugales; derechos de los cónyuges por su condición de tales.
Connivance. Ayuda o consentimiento de una persona al delito cometido por otro.
Consanguinity. Consanguinidad.
Conscientious objector. Persona que se opone al servicio militar obligatorio por razones de conciencia.
Consecutive sentence. Pena que debe cumplirse después de terminada otra que generalmente es impuesta al mismo tiempo (por la comisión de otro delito).
Consensual contract. Contrato consensual.
Consent. Consentimiento.
Consent decree. *Véase* consent judgment.
Consent judgment. Sentencia dictada en consecuencia con

el acuerdo arribado por las partes.
Consent, vice of. *Véase* vices of consent.
Consequential damages. Daño consecuente; daño consiguiente.
Conservatory acts. Actos de conservación; actos de administración.
Consideration. Causa; consideración.
Consideration, adequacy of. *Véase* adequacy of consideration.
Consideration, valuable. *Véase* valuable consideration.
Consign (to). Consignar; entregar; ceder.
Consignee. Consignatario; destinatario.
Consignment. Consignación; envío.
Consignor. Consignador; remitente.
Consolidation. Fusión de varios litigios separadamente radicados.
Conspiracy. Conspiración; conjura; confabulación.
Conspirator. Conspirador.
Conspire (to). Conspirar.
Constable. Alguacil; guardia.
Constituent. Mandante; elector.
Constituent assembly. Asamblea constituyente.
Constitution. Constitución.
Constitutional. Constitucional.
Constitutional amendment. Enmienda a la constitución.
Constitutional convention. Asamblea constituyente.
Constitutionality of a statute. Constitucionalidad de la ley.
Constitutional law. Derecho constitucional.
Construction. Interpretación.
Construction of a statute. Interpretación de la ley.
Constructive. Implícito de derecho.
Constructive possession. Posesión legal; situación en que, sin tenerse la posesión física, se tiene el derecho y la intención de poseer.
Constructive trust. Fideicomiso legal; fideicomiso implícito por los hechos.
Construe. Interpretar.
Consuetudinary. Consuetudinario.
Consul. Cónsul.
Consul general. Cónsul general.
Consumable things. Bienes consumibles.
Consumer. Consumidor.
Consumer credit protection act. Ley de protección al consumidor en su utilización del crédito.
Consumer goods. Artículos de consumo; bienes de consumo.
Consumer protection laws. Legislación de protección al consumidor.

Consumer transaction. Acto jurídico (o transacción) en la cual una de las partes es un consumidor.
Cosurety. Cofiador.
Contemmer. Persona que ha cometido desacato al tribunal; contumaz.
Contempt. Desacato; contumacia.
Contempt of congress. Desacato al congreso.
Contempt of court. Desacato de tribunal.
Contentious jurisdiction. Jurisdicción contenciosa; jurisdicción para oir pleitos entre litigantes.
Contest. Contestar; impugnar; disputa; contienda.
Contingency. Posibilidad; contingencia.
Contingent fee. Honorarios de abogado basados en el éxito de una causa.
Contingent liability. Responsabilidad contingente.
Contingent remainder. Derecho real futuro condicionado.
Continuance. Prórroga; aplazamiento.
Continuing guaranty. Garantía continua; afianzamiento continuo.
Contraband. Contrabando; comercio ilícito.
Contra bonos mores. Contra las buenas costumbres; contra la moral.
Contract. Contrato; convención.
Contract, accessory. *Véase* accessory contract.
Contract, aleatory. *Véase* aleatory contract.
Contract, bilateral. *Véase* bilateral contract.
Contract calling for repeated performances. Contrato de tracto sucesivo.
Contract clause. Cláusula contractual (o de derechos adquiridos) de la constitución de los E E.U U.
Contract, commutative. *Véase* commutative contract.
Contract for continuous or periodic performance. Contracto de tracto sucesivo.
Contract, formal. *Véase* formal contract.
Contract, for sale. Compraventa; promesa bilateral de venta.
Contract, gratuitous. *Véase* gratuitous contract.
Contract implied in fact. Contrato implícito por virtud de los hechos.
Contract implied in law. Cuasicontrato.
Contract, innominate. *Véase* innominate contract.
Contract, nominate. *Véase* nominate contract.
Contract not to sue. Contrato de no demandar; contrato mediante el cuál el acreedor promete no demandar al deudor por el incumplimiento de determinada obligación.
Contract of affreightment. Contrato de fletamento.

Contract of agency. Mandato; contrato de agencia.
Contract of carriage. Contrato de transporte.
Contract of exchange. Permuta.
Contract of fidelity. Contrato de fianza.
Contract of guarantee. Contrato de garantía.
Contract of insurance. Contrato de seguro.
Contract of lease. Contrato de arrendamiento.
Contract of purchase and sale. Contrato de compraventa.
Contract of sale. Contrato de compraventa.
Contract of sale with right of redemption (or repurchase). Venta con pacto de retro.
Contract, onerous. *Véase* onerous contract.
Contractor. Contratista; contratante.
Contract, principal. *Véase* principal contract.
Contract, requirements. *Véase* requirements contract.
Contract, synallagmatic. *Véase* synallagmatic contract.
Contract to sell. Promesa bilateral de compraventa.
Contractual liability. Responsabilidad contractual.
Contractual presuppositions, doctrine of. Imprevisión; frustración del fin del contrato.
Contractual regime. Régimen económico matrimonial convencional; contrato matrimonial.
Contract, unenforceable. *Véase* unenforceable contract.
Contract, unilateral. *Véase* unilateral contract.
Contract, voidable. *Véase* voidable contract.
Contra proferentem. Contra el proponente.
Contrary to law. Contra la ley; improcedente.
Contribution. Contribución; cuota.
Contributory negligence. Negligencia concurrente; culpa concurrente; negligencia contribuyente; culpa contribuyente.
Controversy. Pleito; litigio; controversia.
Convention. Convención; asamblea; convenio; tratado.
Conventional. Convencional.
Conventional estate. Derecho real surgido de un acto privado de las partes.
Conventional mortgage. Hipoteca convencional.
Conventional obligations. Obligaciones convencionales; obligaciones contractuales.
Conventional subrogation. Subrogación convencional.
Conventional unit. Unidad minera convencional; *véase* unitization.
Conversion. Apropiación ilícita de bienes muebles ajenos.
Convertible bonds. Bonos convertibles en acciones.

Convey (to). Traspasar; ceder.
Conveyance. Transferencia o cesión de derechos reales inmobiliarios; transferencia; cesión.
Conveyance records. Registro de la propiedad inmueble; registro de enajenaciones inmobiliarias.
Conveyor. Vendedor; cedente.
Convict. Convicto; culpable de un delito; reo; condenado; penado.
Conviction. Sentencia de culpabilidad.
Coobligor. Coobligado; obligado de forma mancomunada.
Cooperative association. Cooperativa.
Coowner. Condómino; comunero.
Coownership. Copropiedad.
Coparcency. Herencia indivisa.
Copartner. Socio; copartícipe.
Copartnership. Sociedad; asociación.
Coproprietor. *Véase* coowner.
Copyright. Derecho de autor; derecho de propiedad literaria o intelectual.
Copyright law. *Véase* copyright.
Coram nobis. Ante nosotros.
Corporate affairs. Intereses societarios; intereses sociales.
Corporate capital. Capital social.
Corporate charter. Estatutos de una sociedad anónima.
Corporate director. Director de la sociedad; miembro del consejo de dirección de la sociedad.
Corporate domicile. Domicilio societario; Estado en que está incorporada una sociedad anónima.
Corporate management. Gerencia o administración social.
Corporate organization. Organización societaria.
Corporate purpose. Objetivo societario.
Corporate securities. Valores corporativos; valores societarios.
Corporate stock. Acciones de la sociedad.
Corporate tax. Impuesto a las sociedades anónimas.
Corporation. Corporación; sociedad anónima.
Corporation law. Derecho de sociedades anónimas; derecho societario.
Corporeal immovables. Inmuebles corpóreos.
Corporeal movables. Muebles corpóreos.
Corporeal possession. Posesión material; posesión física.
Corporeals. Bienes corpóreos.
Corporeal things. Bienes corpóreos; bienes materiales.

Corpus delicti. Cuerpo del delito; prueba de que se ha cometido un delito.

Correlative duty. Deber correlativo.

Correlative right. Derecho correlativo.

Correlative rights. Derechos recíprocos (Der. min.).

Correlative rights of owners of common reservoir or deposit. Derechos recíprocos de los dueños de un yacimiento común.

Correspondent. Persona acusada de cometer adulterio con el cónyuge del demandante; corresponsal.

Correspondent bank. Banco corresponsal.

Corroborative evidence. Prueba, generalmente testimonial, que corrobora otra prueba presentada previamente.

Corroborative testimony. Testimonio conteste o corroborativo.

Corroborative witness. Testigo conteste.

Corruption. Corrupción.

Cost & freight (C&F). Costo y flete.

Cost, insurance, and freight (C.I.F.). Costo, seguro, y flete.

Costs. Costas; gastos.

Cosurety. Cofiador.

Counsel. Abogado.

Counselor or counsellor. Abogado.

Count. Cuenta; cargo.

Counteraffidavit. Declaración jurada presentada en contra de otra declaración; contradeclaración.

Counter bond. Fianza dada para indemnizar al fiador que ha prestado fianza a beneficio de una persona.

Counterclaim. Reconvención; contrademanda.

Counterclaim, compulsory. Reconvención obligatoria.

Counterclaim, permissive. Reconvención permisible.

Counter deed. Documento secreto que invalida los efectos de una escritura.

Counterfeiting. Falsificación de moneda; falsificación.

Counterletter. *Véase* counter deed.

Countermand. Contraorden.

Counteroffer. Contraoferta.

Counterplea. Reconvención.

Counterproof. Contraprueba.

Countersecurity. *Véase* counter bond.

Countersign. Contrafirmar; refrendar; visar.

County. Condado; entidad política en que se dividen administrativamente 48 de los 50 estados de la unión norteamericana.

County clerk. Secretario del condado.

County commissioner. Oficiales que desempeñan funciones gubernamentales en un condado.

County court. Tribunal del condado; tribunal distrital del condado.

Course of business. Curso del negocio.

Course of dealing. Curso del comercio; curso del negocio; curso de la gestión.

Course of performance. Curso del cumplimiento; curso de la prestación.

Court. Tribunal; corte; juzgado.

Court costs. Costos; litisexpensas; gastos judiciales.

Court en banc. Tribunal en pleno.

Court martial (to). Consejo de guerra.

Court not of record. Tribunal irregular en el cual no se lleva expediente de los casos que conocen sus jueces.

Court of admiralty. Tribunal de Derecho marítimo; almirantazgo.

Court of appeals. Corte de apelaciones.

Court of arbitration. Tribunal de arbitraje.

Court of claims. Tribunal de reclamación (contra los E E.U U.).

Court of equity. Tribunal de equidad.

Court of first instance. Tribunal de primera instancia.

Court of general jurisdiction. Tribunal de primera instancia de competencia ordinaria.

Court of last resort. El más alto tribunal de apelaciones.

Court of original jurisdiction. Tribunal de primera instancia.

Court of record. Tribunal ordinario.

Court order. Orden del tribunal; mandamiento judicial.

Court proceedings. Vistas; proceso dentro de la sala del tribunal.

Courtroom. Sala del tribunal; sala de justicia.

Court rules. Reglamento procesal del tribunal.

Covenant. Convención; convenio; pacto.

Covenant running with the land. Obligación adherida a la heredad.

Cover. Compra de mercancías para cubrirse. Llámase así a la compra de mercancías por el comprador para cubrir el incumplimiento del vendedor del contrato de compraventa.

Coverture. Situación o estado de la mujer casada.

Credentials. Carta credencial.

Credibility. Credibilidad.

Credit. Crédito.

Creditor. Acreedor.

Creditors' meeting. Concurso o junta de acreedores.

Credit sale. Venta a plazos; venta fiada.

Credits, ranking of. *Véase* ranking of credits.

Credit to. Acreditar.

Crime. Delito; crimen.

Crime against humanity. Crimen contra la humanidad.

Crime against nature. Delito contra la naturaleza.

Criminal. Delincuente; criminal.

Criminal act. Hecho o acto criminal.

Criminal attempt. Atentado; intento de comisión de un delito.

Criminal contempt. Desacato criminal, generalmente de un tribunal.

Criminal court. Tribunal o juzgado de lo criminal.

Criminal intent. Intención dolosa.

Criminality. Criminalidad.

Criminal law. Derecho penal; derecho criminal.

Criminal libel. Difamación criminal.

Criminal neglect of family. Falta criminal de proveer alimentos a sus familiares necesitados por alguien que tiene el deber legal de proveerlos.

Criminal negligence. Negligencia criminal.

Criminal offense. Delito; crimen.

Criminal procedure. Procedimiento criminal; procedimiento penal.

Criminal prosecution. Procesamiento criminal.

Criminal record. Antecedentes penales.

Criminology. Criminología.

Crop lien contract. Contrato de refacción agrícola.

Cross-action. *Véase* counterclaim, cross-claim.

Cross claim. Demanda de un colitigante contra otro.

Cross complaint. *Véase* counterclaim, cross-claim; este término se usa algunas veces para referirse a la reconvención (counterclaim), y otras a la demanda contra la coparte en el litigio (cross-claim).

Cross demand. *Véase* counterclaim, cross-claim; este término se usa algunas veces para referirse a la reconvención (counterclaim), y otras a la demanda contra la coparte en el litigio (cross-claim).

Cross examination. Careo.

Cruel and unusual punishment. Condena cruel y excepcional.

Cryer. Secretario del tribunal cuya función es hacer ciertas proclamas.

Culpability. culpabilidad.

Cumulation. Acumulación.

Cumulation of actions. Acumulación de acciones.

Cumulative. Cumulativo; acumulable.

Cumulative evidence. Prueba que se ofrece para demonstrar algo que ya ha sido probado por otras pruebas, lo que hace que esta última prueba sea supérflua.

Curative act. Ley adoptada para corregir defectos en una ley anterior.

Curator. Curador.
Curatorship. Curatela.
Cure. Saneamiento.
Cure of improper tender or delivery. Saneamiento de entrega impropia, o de oferta de entrega impropia.
Curing title. Saneamiento de título.
Currency. Moneda de curso legal.
Custodia legis, ships in. Nave embargada y bajo custodia de la autoridad.
Custodial parent. Cónyuge que obtiene la patria potestad sobre los hijos del matrimonio tras la separación legal o el divorcio.
Custodian. Custodio; guardián.
Custodian bank. Banco custodio.
Custody. Patria potestad; custodia; cuidado.
Custom. Costumbre; uso.
Customary law. Derecho consuetudinario.
Customs. Aduana.
Customs clearance. Despacho aduanal.
Customs declaration. Declaración de aduana.
Customs duties. Derechos de aduana.
Customs regulations. Reglamento aduanal.

D

Damage. Daño; menoscabo; quebranto; perjuicio.
Damage faisant. *Véase* damage feasant.
Damage feasant. Daño causado por animales en un predio atropeyando pastos, comiendo, o lesionando la cosecha.
Damages. Daños y perjuicios.
Damages, assessment of. *Véase* assessment of damages.
Damages, computation of. *Véase* computation of damages.
Damages, general. *Véase* general damages.
Damages, incidental. *Véase* incidental damages.
Damages, liquidated. *Véase* liquidated damages.
Damages, moral. *Véase* moral damages.
Damages, nonpecuniary. *Véase* nonpecuniary damages.
Damages, punitive. *Véase* punitive damages.
Damages, special. *Véase* special damages.
Damages, stipulated. *Véase* stipulated damagees.
Damnify. Damnificar.
Damnum absque injuria. Daño para el cuál no hay remedio legal.
Dangerous instrumentality. Instrumentos destinados a causar lesión en las personas, tales como las armas.
Dative tutorship. Tutela dativa.

Daughter in law. Hija política.
Day in court. Derecho del individuo de acudir ante los tribunales de justicia y ser oído sobre sus demandas, defensas, o quejas.
Daysman. Juez electo; árbitro.
Deadline. Término; límite.
Deal. Negocio; convenio; trato.
Death by accidental means. Muerte accidental.
Death on the high seas act. Ley sobre muerte en alta mar.
Death penalty. Pena capital; pena de muerte.
Death, presumption of. Presunción de muerte.
Death sentence. Sentencia de muerte; pena capital.
Death warrant. Orden de ejecución.
Debenture. Bono; debentura; certificado para reintegro.
Debit. Debitar; cargar; adeudar.
Debt. Deuda; obligación.
Debtor. Deudor.
Decedent. Difunto.
Deceit. Dolo; fraude.
Decentralization. Decentralización.
Decision. Decisión; fallo; auto; dictamen.
Declarant. Declarante.
Declaration. Declaración; proclama pública.
Declaration of acquisition of separate property. Declaración de adquisición de bienes privativos.
Declaration of dividends. Declaración de dividendos.
Declaration of independence. Declaración de independencia.
Declaration of intention. Declaración por parte de un extranjero de su intención de hacerse ciudadano de los E E.U U.
Declaration of rights. Declaración de derechos.
Declaration of trust. Declaración de fideicomiso; reconocimiento de alguien que ostenta el título legal de ciertos bienes que tiene los mismos como fiduciario para beneficio de otra persona.
Declaration of war. Declaración de guerra.
Declaration of will. Declaración de voluntad.
Declaratory decree. *Véase* declaratory judgment.
Declaratory judgment. Sentencia declaratoria de derechos; llámase así a la sentencia que sin otorgar un remedio en particular (tal como otorgar el resarcimiento del daño, ordenar la entrega de bienes, etc.) meramente declara los derechos de las partes.
Declaratory judgments act. Ley autorizando a los tribunales a dictar sentencias declaratorias
Declaratory relief. Reparación mediante sentencia declaratoria (declaratory judgment).
Declare (to). Declarar; testificar.

Declared capital. Capital declarado.
Declinatory exception. Excepción declinatoria.
Decree. Sentencia; decreto; orden; auto.
Decree law. Decreto ley.
Decree nisi. Fallo provisional; sentencia interlocutoria, generalmente en juicios de divorcio.
Decretal order. Fallo o resolución de un tribunal de equidad (equity).
De cujus. Causante; de cuyus; aquel de cuya sucesión se trata.
Dedicate to the public use. Donar bienes para el uso público.
Dedication. Dedicación; cesión para cierto propósito o uso en particular.
Deed. Escritura.
Deed of conveyance. Escritura de transmisión.
De facto. De hecho; de facto.
Defamation. Difamación.
Default. Incumplimiento; rebeldía; mora.
Default judgment. Sentencia por rebeldía.
Defeasance. Condición resolutoria; terminación de un derecho por motivo de la condición resolutoria.
Defeasible. Derecho sujeto a condición resolutoria.
Defect. Defecto.
Defect, latent. *Véase* latent defect.
Defect of design. Defecto en el diseño.
Defects, apparent. *Véase* apparent defects.
Defendant. Reo; demandado.
Defendant in error. Apelado; parte victoriosa en un juicio cuya sentencia ha sido recurrida en casación.
Defense. Defensa.
Defense of others. Defensa de otros; defensa de tercero.
Defense of property. Defensa de propiedad.
Deficiency judgment. Sentencia por el saldo; sentencia contra el deudor de una propiedad gravada y vendida para satisfacer la deuda, por la deficiencia entre el precio de la venta y el monto de la deuda.
Definitive judgment. Sentencia firme.
Definitive partition. Partición permanente o definitiva.
Deforce. Poseer sin derecho; poseer de mala fe.
Deforcement. Posesión sin derecho; posesión de mala fe.
Deforceor. Poseedor sin derecho; poseedor de mala fe.
Degree. Grado; graduación.
Deimmobilization. Separación de las partes integrantes de un inmueble y su consecuente conversión a muebles.
De jure. De derecho; de jure.
Delay rentals. Precio pagadero por el arrendatario de minas al comenzar el arrendamiento a cambio del derecho de demorar las excavaciones y otras operaciones mineras.
Delegate. Delegar; delegado.

Delegation. Delegación.
Delinquent taxes. Impuestos sobrevencidos.
Delivered weights. Pesos entregados.
Delivery. Tradición; entrega.
Delivery of immovables. Tradición (o entrega) de inmuebles.
Delivery of movables. Tradición o entrega de bienes muebles.
Delivery order. Orden de entrega.
Delivery term. Término de entrega o tradición.
Demand. Demanda; reclamo.
Demand instrument. Instrumento pagadero a la vista; instrumento pagadero a presentación.
Demand items. Valores pagaderos a la vista; instrumentos pagaderos a la vista.
Demand note. Pagaré a la vista o presentación.
Demise. Cesión; transferencia.
Demise charter. Carta de fletamento sin tripulación ni combustible.
Demonstrative legacy. Legado que debe ser pagado de un fondo o de ciertos bienes determinados.
Demurrage. Demora o sobreestadía de una nave; deuda dineraria debida al dueño de la nave por demora o sobreestadía.
Demurrer. Excepción.
Denial. Refutación; negación.
De novo. De nuevo; por segunda vez; de novo.
Departure. Desviación.
Deponent. Declarante (en una deposición); *véase* deposition.
Deport. Deportar.
Deportation. Deportación.
Depose. Tomar la declaración de un testigo; declarar bajo juramento.
Deposit. Depositar; depósito.
Depositary. Depositario.
Depositary bank. Banco depositario.
Deposit by the obligor. Consignación (por el deudor de la cosa debida).
Deposition. Declaración de un testigo hecha fuera del tribunal; deposición.
Deposition upon oral examination. Declaración bajo interrogatorio (o examen) oral.
Deposition upon written interrogatories. Declaración de testigo a base de interrogatorios por escrito.
Deposit, judicial. *Véase* judicial deposit.
Depositor. Depositante.
Depreciation. Depreciación.
Derelict. Abandonado; nave abandonada.
Derivative action. Acción basada en un derecho de la sociedad ejercitada por los accionistas.
Derivative action by shareholders. *Véase* derivative action.
Derogation. Derogación.
Descendant. Descendiente.
Descent. Transferencia de bienes raíces por ministerio de

ley cuando el causante muere intestado.

Desertion. Deserción; abandono de hogar.

De son tort. De su propia culpa. Generalmente se aplica a alguien que, sin haber sido nombrado como tal, actúa como albacea.

Destination bill. Conocimiento de embarque en el lugar de la entrega.

Detainer. Detención; retención sin derecho de propiedad inmueble,aunque al principio la posesión del predio pudo ser legítima.

Determinable. Derecho sujeto a terminación por condición resolutoria.

Detinue. Acción reivindicatoria.

Detinue, writ of. *Véase* writ of detinue.

Deviation. Desvío; desviación; desviarse de la ruta del viaje.

Devise. Legar inmuebles.

Devisee. Legatario de propiedad inmueble.

Devisor. Testador (de propiedad inmueble).

Devolutive appeal. Apelación devolutiva; apelación que no suspende la ejecución de la sentencia; apelación con efecto devolutivo.

Dicta. Plural de dictum (*véase* dictum).

Dictum. Declaración hecha en una sentencia que no forma parte de la decisión.

Digest. Repertorio; digesto; resumen.

Dilatory exception. Excepción dilatoria.

Dilatory plea. Alegato o defensa dilatoria.

Diligence. Diligencia.

Direct action statute. Ley que autoriza acción directa contra el asegurador, sin necesidad de acumular la acción contra el asegurado.

Directed verdict. Veredicto dirigido u ordenado; llámase así a la situación en un juicio ante jurado en la que el juez determina que, en realidad, no existe duda razonable respecto a la prueba y, por tanto, dicta él mismo la sentencia, dirigiendo u ordenando el fallo.

Direct evidence. Prueba directa; llámase así a la prueba que tiende a demostrar de un modo directo la existencia de un hecho.

Direct examination. Interrogatorio inicial a un testigo durante el juicio por la parte que lo llama a atestiguar.

Directions to the jury. *Véase* instructions to the jury.

Director. Director.

Direct taxes. Impuestos directos.

Disavowal. Impugnación; negación.

Disavowal, action in. *Véase* action in disavowal.

Disbar. Desaforar; separar a un abogado del ejercicio de la abogacía.

Discharge. Liberación; cumplimiento; finiquito; descargo.
Discharged bankrupt. Fallido rehabilitado o descargado.
Discharge in bankruptcy. Orden de descargo del deudor en un juicio de quiebra, eximiéndolo de responsabilidad por sus deudas.
Disclaim. Renuncia; renegación; abandono.
Discontinuance. *Véase* voluntary dismissal.
Discontinue. Descontinuar; suspender.
Discount. Descuento; descontar.
Discovery. Averiguaciones sobre las pruebas relevantes en un litigio.
Discovery devices. Medios o procedimientos de descubrir pruebas relevantes en un litigio.
Discredit. Desacreditar un testigo.
Discretion. Discreción.
Discretionary authority. Autoridad discrecional.
Discretionary relief. Reparación discrecional.
Discretionary trust. Fideicomiso discrecional; llámase así al fideicomiso en el cual el fiduciario tiene amplia discreción en el uso de los fondos del fideicomiso.
Discrimination. Discriminación.
Discussion. Excusión.
Disenfranchise. Privar a una persona del derecho al voto.
Disherison. Desheredación.
Disherit. Desheredar.
Dishonor. Deshonor; denegación de pago o aceptación de un valor.
Disinherison. Véase disherison.
Disinherit. *Véase* disherit.
Disinheritance. Desheredación.
Dismiss. Anular la instancia; declarar sin lugar; sobreseimiento.
Dismissal. Anulación de la instancia; declararar sin lugar; sobreseimiento.
Disorderly conduct. Conducta desordenada o inmoral.
Disposable portion. Porción disponible (de una sucesión).
Dispose. Disponer; enajenar; ceder.
Disqualification. Descalificación.
Disqualify. Descalificar.
Disseise. Desposeer.
Dissent. Disentir.
Dissenting opinion. Voto particular.
Dissolution. Disolución; rescisión.
Distrain. Embargo; ejecución.
Distraint, writ of . *Véase* writ of distraint.
Distress. Acción de distrain (*véase* distrain).
District attorney. Fiscal.
District court. Tribunal de distrito.
Distringas, writ of . Orden de embargo; auto de secuestro.

Disturbance. Perturbación; interferencia con el ejercicio de un derecho.
Disturbance of possession. Perturbación de la posesión.
Diversity of citizenship. Diversidad de ciudadanía.
Divest. Desposeer; despojar.
Dividend. Dividendo.
Divisible obligation. Obligación divisible.
Divisor. División.
Divorce. Divorcio.
Docket. Lista de casos en proceso ante un tribunal.
Doctrine. Doctrina.
Document. Documento.
Documentary credit. Crédito documentario.
Documentary draft. Giro documentario.
Documentary sale. Venta documentaria; venta por documentos.
Document in transit. Documento en tránsito.
Document of title. Documento de título; instrumento de título; documento de resguardo.
Domestic corporation. Corporación funcionando en el Estado donde fue organizada.
Domicile. Domicilio; residencia.
Dominant tenement. Predio dominante.
Dominion. Dominio.
Donation. Donación.
Donation, inter vivos. Donación inter vivos.
Donation, mortis causa. Testamento; donación por causa de muerte.
Donation, onerous. *Véase* onerous donation.
Donative intent. Intención de donar.
Donee. Donatario.
Donee, particular. *Véase* particular donee.
Donee, universal. *Véase* universal donee.
Donor. Donante.
Dormant judgment. Sentencia durmiente; llámase así a la sentencia que ha caducado por no haber sido ejecutada.
Dormant partner. Socio comanditario.
Dotal. Dotal; concerniente a la dote.
Double citizenship. Doble ciudadanía.
Double jeopardy. Procesar por segunda vez por el mismo delito.
Double liability. Responsabilidad doble.
Double pleading. Alegato doble.
Double waste. Devastación doble (*véase* waste).
Dower. Derecho de herencia de la esposa en la sucesión de su esposo bajo el common law.
Dowry. Dote.
Draft. Letra de cambio; giro.
Drainage. Extracción de hidrocarburos sitos en el subsuelo de un predio determinado mediante operaciones ubicadas en otro predio.

Dram shop acts. Leyes que imponen responsabilidad civil a vendedores de bebidas alcohólicas a personas ya embriagadas por el daño que éstas causen a tercero o a sí mismas.
Draw. Librar.
Drawee. Girado; librado.
Drawer. Girador; librador.
Dual citizenship. *Véase* double citizenship.
Dual nationality. *Véase* double citizenship.
Duces tecum. *Véase* subpoena duces tecum.
Due process clause. Cláusula de procedimiento debido.
Due process of law. Procedimiento debido.
Duly negotiated. Negociado debidamente.
Duplicity. Duplicidad.
Duress. Coacción; violencia.
Duty. Deber; obligación.
Duty of care. Deber de actuar con prudencia; diligencia de un buen padre de familia.
Duty of reasonable care. Diligencia de un buen padre de familia.
Duty-risk doctrine. Doctrina de deber y riesgo.
Dying declaration. Declaración de una persona en peligro inminente de muerte.

E

Earned income. Entradas ganadas; entradas resultantes del trabajo o de las ganancias de negocios.
Earned premium. Parte del pago de la póliza que el asegurador puede conservar aunque se cancele la póliza.
Earnest. Señal; seña.
Earnest money. *Véase* earnest.
Earnings. Salario; jornal.
Easement. Servidumbre.
Effect. Efecto.
Effective. Eficaz; efectivo.
Ejectment. Acción petitoria; acción posesoria.
Ejectment, writ of. *Véase* writ of ejectment.
Ejusdem generis. Del mismo género o naturaleza; ejusdem generis.
Election. Elecciones.
Election of remedies. Elección de remedios; elección entre dos o más cursos de acción.
Election of rights. Elección de derechos.
Elector. Persona con derecho a votar; cada uno de los miembros del colegio electoral que elige al presidente de los E E.U U.
Electoral college. Cuerpo de electores de los estados de los Estados Unidos que selecciona al presidente de los E E.U U.
Emancipate. Emancipar.
Emancipation. Emancipación.

Emancipation by marriage. Emancipación por causa de matrimonio.
Emancipation by notarial act. Emancipación por escritura pública.
Emancipation, judicial. *Véase* judicial emancipation.
Embargo. Embargo; detención de buques.
Embezzle. Estafar.
Embezzlement. Estafa.
Emblements. Frutos de la tierra y de los árboles antes de la cosecha.
Embracery. Intento doloso de influenciar la decisión del jurado.
Emergency powers. Poderes de emergencia del ejecutivo.
Emergent damages. Daños emergentes; daños no contemplados al momento de la perfección del contrato.
Emigrant. Emigrante.
Emigrate. Emigrar.
Eminent domain. Dominio eminente del Estado.
Empanel. *Véase* impanel.
Emphytheusis. Enfiteusis.
Emption. Compra; compraventa.
Emptor. Comprador.
Enabling act. Ley que elimina una restricción impuesta por una ley anterior.
Enact. Promulgar.
Enactment. El proceso de promulgación de una ley; ley promulgada.
Encroachment. Proyección indebida del derecho de propiedad de una persona sobre el derecho de propiedad de otra.
Encumbrance. Carga; pignoración; gravamen.
En demeure. En mora.
Endorse. Endosar.
Endorsed "for collection". Endosado para cobro.
Endorsed for surrender. Endosado para entrega.
Endorsee. Endosatario; tenedor por endoso.
Endorsement. Endoso.
Endorser. Endosante.
Enforce. Ejecutar; hacer cumplir.
Enjoin. Orden; prohibición; mandamiento.
Entail. Ostentar el derecho de fee tail; posesión de una heredad a título de fee tail.
Enter. Tomar posesión de un predio.
Enterprise. Empresa.
Enterprise liability. Responsabilidad empresarial.
Entrapment. Defensa consistente en que la comisión de un delito ha sido inducida por un agente de la autoridad cuándo el autor del delito no estaba predispuesto a cometerlo.
En ventre sa mere. En el vientre de su madre. Este término describe la situación en que la criatura ha sido concebida pero no ha nacido aún.
Equal dignity rule. Regla de "igualdad de dignidad"; según este principio, si la validez de un contrato depende de que sea por escrito, un poder para realizar

dicho contrato debe también ser hecho por escrito.

Equal protection of the laws. Igualdad de amparo o protección de las leyes.

Equipment leasing. Arrendamiento de equipo; arrendamiento de maquinaria.

Equipment trust. Fideicomiso sobre equipo.

Equitable. Equitativo; relativo al sistema jurídico de la "equity".

Equitable conversion. Transformación equitativa (transformación ficticia por el tribunal de equidad de la clasificación de los bienes para lograr un resultado justo en un caso en particular).

Equitable defense. Defensa equitativa (defensas admisibles en un tribunal de equidad).

Equitable estoppel. *Véase* estoppel.

Equitable mortgage. Hipoteca equitativa (escritura en la cual las partes demuestran su intención de que un inmueble sirva de seguridad o afianzamiento de una deuda).

Equity. Equidad; sistema jurídico basado en la equidad.

Equity acts in personam. *Véase* aequitas agit in personam.

Equity of redemption. Derecho equitativo de redención; derecho del deudor de un crédito hipotecario de conservar el dominio de la cosa mediante el pago de la deuda, cuyo derecho expira al firmarse la escritura que confirma el remate.

Equity pleading. Proceso de los tribunales de equidad.

Erasure of mortgages. Borradura de hipotecas.

Error induced by fraud. Error inducido por dolo o fraude.

Error of fact. Error en la apreciación de los hechos; error sobre los hechos.

Error of law. Error de derecho; error sobre el derecho.

Error that concerns cause. Error sobre la causa.

Error, writ of. *Véase* writ of error.

Escape. Fuga de un preso.

Escheat. Sucesión del estado (por falta de herederos).

Escrow. Plica.

Establishment clause. Cláusula sobre el establecimiento. Esta cláusula de la primera enmienda de la constitución de los E E. U U. prohibe al congreso aprobar leyes decretando el establecimiento (oficial) de una religión.

Establishment of credit. Establecimiento de un crédito.

Estate. Heredad; sucesión; patrimonio; bienes; cosas.

Estate and gift tax. Impuesto sobre la herencia y donaciones.

Estate at will. Arrendamiento de bienes raíces que el arrendador puede terminar a discreción.

Estate by sufferance. Situación legal que ocurre

cuando alguien con derecho a ocupar un predio, v. gr., un arrendatario, permanece en posesión después de extinguido su derecho, quedando en situación equivalente a la de un precarista.

Estate by the entirety. Copropiedad de un predio entre marido y mujer, con la peculiaridad de que el cónyuge supérstite hereda la porción del otro cónyuge.

Estate for years. Arrendamiento de bienes raíces por un término determinado.

Estate from year to year. Arrendamiento de bienes raíces por un plazo no determinado.

Estate in common. Copropiedad en indivisión.

Estate in expectancy. Derecho real futuro. El titular no tiene derecho a ejercitarlo sino hasta la terminación del derecho real de otro.

Estate in remainder. Derecho real que comienza al finalizar otro.

Estate in reversion. Derecho real remanente en la persona del cedente de un predio.

Estate in the land. Derecho real inmobiliario.

Estate tax. Impuesto sobre la herencia.

Estoppel. Doctrina de los actos propios.

Estovers. Servidumbre de madera; derecho a usar madera de la heredad.

Estrepe. Malgastar un inmueble con consecuente daño para su propietario.

Evict. Desahuciar; desalojar.

Eviction. Evicción; desahucio.

Eviction order. Orden de desahucio.

Evidence. Evidencia; prueba.

Evidence, weight of. *Véase* weight of the evidence.

Exaction. Extorsión.

Examination of the judgment debtor. Proceso para interrogar al deudor condenado.

Exception. Excepción.

Exception, declinatory. *Véase* declinatory exception.

Exception, dilatory. *Véase* dilatory exception.

Exception, peremptory. Véase peremptory exception.

Excessive damages. Daños excesivos; sentencia que condena al pago de una cantidad excesiva por concepto de daños.

Excessive force. Fuerza excesiva.

Excessive verdict. Fallo o veredicto excesivo (por la cantidad del resarcimiento).

Exchange. Permuta; cambio.

Excise tax. Impuesto o tributo indirecto sobre un producto u objeto en particular; e.g., impuesto sobre el licor o el tabaco.

Exclusion of warranty. Omisión o renuncia de garantía.

Excusable. Perdonable; excusable.

Excuse. Perdonar; eximir.

Excuses for nonperformance. Factores que excusan el incumplimiento.
Execute. Ejecutar.
Executed. Completo; cumplido; hecho; ejecutado.
Executed consideration. Consideración o causa cumplida.
Execution. Ejecución.
Execution of liens. Ejecución de privilegios.
Execution, stay of. *Véase* stay of execution.
Execution, writ of. *Véase* writ of execution.
Executive interest. *Véase* executive rights.
Executive order. Decreto; orden ejecutiva.
Executive rights. Derecho ejecutivo de minas. Llámase así al derecho de conceder arriendos de minas sobre un predio determinado o una servidumbre minera.
Executor. Albacea.
Executory. Por efectuar; imperfecto; por terminar; sin cumplir.
Executory contract. Contrato con prestaciones por efectuar.
Executory trust. Fideicomiso indeterminado.
Executrix. Mujer albacea.
Exemplary damages. Daños punitivos; daños punitorios.
Exemplification. Copia certificada de una sentencia o documento registrado.
Exemption. Exención.
Exhaustion of credit. Agotamiento del crédito.
Exhibit. Documento fehaciente presentado como prueba.
Exonerate. Exonerar; descargar.
Exoneration. Condonación; liberación; exoneración.
Expatriate. Expatriar.
Expatriation. Expatriación.
Expectancy. Derecho en expectativa.
Expense. Gasto.
Expenses of the marriage. Gastos del matrimonio.
Expert. Perito.
Expert opinion. Opinión pericial; opinión experta.
Explicit. Explícito.
Express. Explícito.
Express dissolution clause. Cláusula resolutoria.
Express mandate. Mandato expreso; mandato especial.
Express warranty. Garantía explícita; garantía escrita.
Ex proprio motu. De su propia moción.
Extenuating circumstances. Atenuantes.
Extinction of obligations. Extinción de las obligaciones.
Extinguish. Extinguir; liquidar.
Extinguishment. Extinción.
Extinguishment of easement. Extinción de servidumbre.
Extorsion. Extorsión.
Extradite. Extraditar.
Extradition. Extradición.

Extrajudicial. Extrajudicial; fuera del proceso judicial.
Extra legal. Fuera del Derecho.
Extraordinary care. Cuidado extraordinario; prudencia extraordinaria.
Extraordinary relief. Reparación extraordinaria; remedio extraordinario.
Extraordinary remedy. Remedio extraordinario.
Extraterritorial. Extraterritorial.
Extraterritoriality. Extraterritorialidad.
Extrinsic evidence. Evidencia fuera del documento.
Eye witness. Testigo ocular.

F

Fabricate. Presentar prueba falsa; dar falso testimonio.
Fabrication. Prueba falsa; falso testimonio.
Facsimile. Copia exacta; facsímil.
Fact. Hecho.
Fact finder. Juzgador de los hechos; persona o grupo de personas que tiene a su cargo el determinar los hechos en un pleito.
Factor. Factor.
Factor's lien. Privilegio de factor; derecho de rentención de factor.
Factual. De hecho; fáctico.
Facultative obligations. Obligaciones facultativas.
Failure of cause. Falla de la causa; falta de la causa.
Failure of consideration. Incumplimiento de una de las partes que deja sin consideración (consideration) la obligación de la otra parte.
Failure of issue. Muerte sin descendencia.
Failure of proof. Insuficiencia de la prueba.
Failure of record. Falta de introducción de un expediente en el proceso.
Failure to state a claim upon which relief can be granted. Demanda sin lugar.
Fair. Justo.
Fair comment. comentario justificado.
Fair hearing. Vista justa y apropiada que se ajusta a las garantías procesales de la constitución.
Fair market value. Valor de un objeto en el mercado bajo condicioines normales.
Fair use. Uso justificado; término utilizado en el derecho autoral para denominar el uso limitado que se puede hacer de una obra sin infringir el Derecho de autor.
False. Falso.
False arrest. Detención ilegal; arresto ilegal.
False impersonation. Usurpación de la identidad de otro.
False imprisonment. Detención injustificada; restricción ilegal de la libertad de movimiento de un sujeto.
False pretenses. Declaración falsa sobre un hecho.

False representation. *Véase* misrepresentation.

False return. Certificación falsa; declaración falsa.

False swearing. Falso testimonio.

Falsify. Falsificar.

Family. Familia.

Family arrangement. Convenio familiar.

Family law. Derecho de familia.

Family meeting. Consejo de familia.

Farm out. Cesión o arrendamiento de derechos.

Fatricide. Fatricidio; homicidio del hermano.

Fault. Culpa; negligencia; falta.

Federal. Federal.

Federal common law. Derecho común elaborado por los tribunales federales.

Federal court. Tribunal federal.

Federal government. Gobierno federal.

Federal jurisdiction. Jurisdicción federal.

Federal maritime board. Junta administrativa marítima federal.

Federal maritime commission. Comisión marítima federal.

Federal maritime lien act. Ley federal sobre privilegios marítimos.

Federal question. Problema o cuestión federal. Dícese de un problema que debe decidirse conforme al Derecho federal de los Estados Unidos.

Federal Rules of Civil Procedure. Reglas de procedimiento civil federal. Estas normas integran un verdadero código de procedimiento civil que ha servido de modelo a los códigos modernos de procedimiento civil en los Estados de la unión norteamericana.

Federal Rules of Criminal Procedure. Reglas de procedimiento penal federal.

Federal Rules of Evidence. Reglas federales sobre la prueba.

Fee. *Véase* fee simple.

Fee simple. Dominio. Derecho real del common law equivalente al dominio.

Fee simple absolute. *Véase* fee simple.

Fee tail. Derecho real limitado al titular y sus herederos o a algunos de ellos.

Fellow servant rule. Doctrina del coempleado. Según esta doctrina el empleado no tiene acción contra sus compañeros de trabajo por culpa o negligencia de éstos en el empleo ni contra el empleador común por dicha culpa o negligencia.

Felon. Delincuente; dícese del convicto de un crimen clasificado como *felony* (delito).

Felony. Delito.

Felony murder. Homicidio que ocurre durante la comisión de un acto delictuoso.

Femme sole. Mujer soltera.

Fiat. Orden; fiat.
Fictitious. Ficticio; imaginario.
Fictitious payee. Tomador o beneficiario ficticio.
Fiduciary. Fiduciario.
Fiduciary duty. Obligación fiduciaria.
Fiduciary relation. Relación fiduciaria o de confianza.
Fieri facias, writ of. Véase writ of fieri facias.
File. Archivar; *véase* filing.
Filiate. Filiar; determinar la paternidad.
Filiation. Filiación; proceso para determinar la paternidad.
Filing. Presentación de una escritura en el registro, o de una demanda u otro documento en el tribunal.
Filing a complaint. Presentación de una demanda.
Final decree. Orden final; orden o sentencia que concluye el proceso.
Final judgment. Sentencia definitiva.
Final order. Orden final; orden que finaliza el proceso.
Final payment. Pago final.
Financing agency. Entidad financiera; agencia de finanzas.
Financing statement. Estado financiero.
Finding. Fallo; resolución judicial; resolución judicial de un problema de hecho o de derecho.
Fine. Multa.
Fingerprint. Huellas digitales.
Firm. Firma; sociedad.
Firm offer. Oferta en la cuál el ofertante asegura que la oferta permanecerá abierta; oferta firme.
First impression, case of. *Véase* case of first impression.
First instance, court of. Tribunal de primera instancia.
Fiscal. Referente al fisco; fiscal.
Fitness, warranty of. *Véase* warranty of fitness.
Fixtures. Bienes muebles adheridos a un inmueble.
Flag. Bandera; pabellón.
Floating mortgage. Hipoteca flotante; hipoteca genérica que se aplica a un patrimonio o grupo de bienes en conjunto, como, por e.j., a las mercancías situadas en un almacén, cuyo monto varía de día a día.
Flotsam. Parte de un barco averiado, o de su cargamento, que se haya flotando.
Foeticide. Feticidio.
Forbearance. Privación voluntaria de un derecho.
Forbidden degrees. Prohibición de matrimonio por grado de parentesco existente entre el hombre y la mujer.
Force and arms, with. A la fuerza y armado.
Forced heirs. Herederos forzosos.
Forced respite. Espera forzosa.
Force majeure. Fuerza mayor.

Forcible detention. Retención ilegal de bienes muebles ajenos.
Forcible entry. Penetración a la fuerza; entrada ilegal y violenta en heredad poseída por otro.
Forcible rape. Violación.
For collection. Para cobro.
Foreclosure. Ejecución de hipoteca.
Foreign. Extranjero.
Foreign plea. Defensa procesal basada en la falta de jurisdicción o competencia del tribunal.
Foreign contracts. Contratos hechos en el extranjero.
Foreign corporation. Corporación incorporada en un Estado (de los E E.U U.) distinto de aquel en que tiene lugar el acto o proceso de que se trata; corporación extranjera; sociedad anónima extranjera.
Foreign judgment. Sentencia extranjera; fallo de un tribunal extranjero.
Foreign law. Derecho extranjero.
Foreign office. Ministerio del exterior o cancillería (Gran Bretaña).
Forensic medicine. Medicina forense o medicina legal.
Foreseeability. Predictabilidad.
Forfeit. Decomisar; confiscar; perder.
Forfeiture. Pérdida de derechos; confiscación; comiso.
Forfeiture of bond. Decomiso o confiscación de la fianza por no cumplirse la prestación para la cuál fue prestada.
Forge (to). Falsificar.
Forgery. Falsificación; falsedad.
Form. Forma.
Formal. Formal.
Formal contract. Contrato formal.
Formalism. Formalismo.
Formal party. *Véase* nominal party.
Formal requirements. Requisitos formales.
Forms of action. Catálogo de acciones del common law.
Formulary. Formulario.
For surrender. Para entrega.
Forswear. Renuncia bajo juramento; falso testimonio.
Forthcoming bond. Fianza de entrega de bienes embargados.
Fortuitous. Fortuito.
Fortuitous event. Caso fortuito.
Forum. Foro.
Forum contractus. El tribunal del lugar de la confección del contrato.
Forum domicilii. El tribunal del lugar del domicilio de una persona.
Forum non conviniens. Tribunal inconveniente. Doctrina que permite a un juez competente rehusar el conocimiento de una causa cuando el lugar del foro es inconveniente a las partes o los testigos.

Forum rei gestae. El tribunal del lugar donde fue realizado un hecho.

Forum rei sitae. El tribunal del lugar donde está ubicada la cosa.

For value. A título oneroso; por valor.

Foster parent. Adoptante; padre sustituto, generalmente pagado por el Estado.

Four corners. Cuatro esquinas (o costados) de un acto o ley.

Franchise. Franquicia; concesión; derecho a votar.

Fraud. Fraude; dolo; mala fe.

Fraud on creditors. Fraude a los acreedores; quiebra fraudulenta.

Frauds, statute of. Ley que establece el requisito de realizar por escrito ciertos actos jurídicos.

Fraudulent. Fraudulento.

Fraudulent conveyance. Enajenación o cesión fraudulenta.

Fraudulent misrepresentation. Representación falsa hecha de mala fe; engaño fraudulento.

Free alongside vessel (F.A.S.). Libre al costado de la nave.

Freedom. Libertad.

Freedom of contract. Libertad de contratación.

Freedom of disposition. Libertad de disposición.

Freedom of information act. Ley de libertad de información; ley que garantiza el acceso a información en poder del Estado.

Freedom of religion. Libertad de religión.

Freedom of speech. Libertad de palabra; libertad de expresión y difusión del pensamiento.

Freedom of the press. Libertad de prensa.

Free entry. (Derecho de) libre acceso. Derecho incidental al derecho de servidumbre.

Free egress and regress. (Derecho de) libre ingreso y regreso. Derecho incidental al derecho de servidumbre.

Free exercise clause. Cláusula de libre ejercicio; cláusula de la primera enmienda de la constitución de los E E. U U. que establece la libertad de religión.

Freehold. Clasificación de ciertos derechos reales equivalentes al dominio y al usufructo.

Freeholder. El titular de un freehold. *Véase* freehold.

Free on board (FOB). Libre a bordo, franco a bordo.

Free ships. Naves libres. Dícese de los barcos neutrales en tiempo de guerra.

Freight. Flete; porte; cargamento; carga.

Freightage. Fletamento; cargamento; flete; transportación.

Freight brokerage. Corretaje de fletamento.

Freight forwarder. Remitente de flete.

Friendly suit. Demanda amistosa. Demanda presentada con el propósito de obtener una opinión consultiva sobre un problema.

Fruits. Frutos.

Fruits, civil. *Véase* civil fruits.

Fruits, natural. *Véase* natural fruits.

Frustration of contract. Frustración del fin del contrato.

Frustration of purpose. Imprevisión; frustración del fin del contrato.

Frustration, supervening. *Véase* supervening frustration.

Fugitive. Fugitivo.

Full covenant and warranty deed. Escritura de compraventa con garantía.

Full faith and credit clause. Cláusula de la constitución de los E E.U U. exigiendo el reconocimiento de los actos públicos y decisiones judiciales de cada Estado por los demás estados de la Unión.

Fungible. Fungible.

Future estate. Derecho real futuro.

Future goods. Cosas futuras; bienes no existentes e identificados.

Future interest. Derecho real futuro.

Futures. Bienes cuya tradición se posterga hasta un momento dado en el futuro; futuros.

Future thing. Cosa futura.

G

Gage. Prenda.

Gambling. Juego de azar.

Game laws. Legislación sobre cacería de animales.

Gaming. Juegos de azar.

Gaming debt. Deuda de juego de azar.

Ganancial property. Bienes gananciales.

Garnish (to). *Véase* garnishment.

Garnishee. Persona adeudada al deudor embargado, o que posee algo de su pertenencia, cuyos bienes el acreedor intenta embargar. *Véase* garnishment.

Garnisher. Acreedor que embarga en un proceso de garnishment. *Véase* garnishment.

Garnishment. Embargo de bienes del deudor en posesión de tercero.

Garnishor. *Véase* garnisher.

General agent. Mandatario con poder general.

General appearance. Comparecencia sin reservas.

General assembly. Asamblea general; cuerpo legislador.

General assignment. Cesión de los bienes del deudor a sus acreedores.

General average. Avería gruesa; avería común.

General creditor. Acreedor quirografario.

General damages. Daño moral; daño que no necesita ser probado con particularidad.

General demurrer. Excepción general a la demanda.

General denial. Negación general de todos los alegatos de hecho presentados en la demanda.

General indorsement. Endoso en blanco.

General intent. Intención general.

General issue. Negación genérica de la demanda por parte del demandado.

General legacy. Legado general. Dícese del legado que ha de pagarse del total de los bienes de la herencia;por e.j., un legado de dinero.

General lien. Derecho pignorativo sobre uno o más de los bienes muebles del deudor que no afianzan una obligación en particular.

General mandate. Mandato general.

General mortgage. Hipoteca de bienes muebles que cubre todos los bienes muebles del deudor.

General partner. Socio de una sociedad civil o comercial.

General principles of law. Principios generales del derecho.

General property tax. Impuesto sobre la propiedad.

General ship. Barco que no ha sido fletado o arrendado. Dicho barco debe hacer uso del conocimiento de embarque al recibir cargamento.

General verdict. Fallo o veredicto del jurado en forma general.

Gentlemen's agreement. Acuerdo entre caballeros. Generalmente no crea vinculación jurídica alguna.

Gerrymander. Subdivisión de un área geográfica con fines políticos.

Gift. Donación.

Gift causa mortis. *Véase* donation mortis causa.

Gift inter vivos. *Véase* donation inter vivos.

Gift tax. Impuesto sobre donaciones.

Give on account. Rendir cuentas.

Giving in payment. Dación en pago.

Good behavior. Buen comportamiento.

Good cause. Just causa.

Good faith. Buena fe.

Good faith purchaser. Adquirente de buena fe; comprador de buena fe.

Goods. Bienes muebles; mercancías.

Good title. Título válido.

Good will. Plusvalía.

Graft. Peculado.

Grand jury. Gran jurado.

Grand larceny. Hurto mayor.

Grand theft. Hurto mayor.

Grant. Cesión; concesión; ceder otorgar; dar.

Grantee. Cesionario.

Grantor. Cedente; dador; otorgante.

Gratuitous. Gratuito.

Gratuitous bailee. Depositario a título gratuito.
Gratuitous bailment. Depósito a título gratuito.
Gratuitous cause. Causa donativa o gratuita.
Gratuitous contract. Contrato gratuito; contrato a título lucrativo.
Gratuitous title. Título lucrativo.
Gravamen. La esencia de una demanda o acusación.
Grievance committee. Comité de querellas.
Gross average. *Véase* general average.
Gross negligence. Culpa lata; negligencia enorme.
Grounds. Causa; causal.
Guarantee. Afianzamiento.
Guarantor. Garante.
Guaranty. *Véase* guarantee.
Guaranty, continuing. *Véase* continuing guaranty.
Guardian. Tutor; guardián.
Guardian, ad litem. Guardián o curador para el proceso.
Guardianship. Tutela; curatela.
Guilt. Culpabilidad penal.
Guilty. Culpable.
Guilty plea. Declaración de culpabilidad.

H

Habeas corpus. Hábeas corpus.
Habendum clause. Parte de la escritura de traslación de propiedad inmueble. El "habendum clause" comienza con la frase "to have and to hold." Dicha cláusula originalmente determinaba el carácter del derecho cedido y las condiciones a que estaba sujeto.
Habitation. Habitación.
Habitual offender. Criminal reincidente; criminal de carrera.
Habitual offender law. Ley que impone penas más severas al criminal reincidente.
Habitual offender statute. Véase habitual offender law.
Half brother. Medio hermano.
Hard labor. Trabajos forzados.
Harmless error. Error en el proceso que no causa perjuicio a ninguna de las partes.
Hazard. Riesgo.
Hazardous. Riesgoso.
Hearing. Vista.
Hearsay. Testimonio de oídas.
Hearsay evidence. Prueba de oídas.
Hearsay testimony. *Véase* hearsay.
Heir. Heredero.
Heir apparent. Heredero aparente.
Hereditary. Hereditario.
Heritable. Hereditable.

Heritable obligations. Obligaciones hereditables.
Heritable right. Derecho hereditario.
Hierarchy. Jerarquía.
High crimes and misdemeanors. Serios delitos y faltas.
High seas. Alta mar.
High treason. Alta traición; traición.
Hire. Arrendamiento de bienes muebles o servicios.
Hold. Tenencia; tener un valor; vincular contractualmente; decidir un caso.
Holder. Tenedor.
Holder for value. Tenedor a título oneroso.
Holder in due course. Tenedor legítimo; tenedor en debido curso; tenedor de buena fe.
Hold harmless. Indemnizar por perjuicios; amparar.
Holding. Tenencia; decisión judicial.
Holding company. Sociedad anónima cuyos únicos bienes son acciones de otras sociedades.
Hold over. Situación en la cuál el arrendatario permanece en el predio arrendado tras terminarse el arrendamiento.
Holiday. Día feriado.
Holograph. Ológrafo; testamento ológrafo.
Holographic will. Ológrafo; testamento ológrafo.
Homeowners' insurance. *Véase* homeowners' liability policy.
Homeowners' liability policy. Póliza contra responsabilidad del propietario de una casa.
Home rule charter. Carta municipal donde se establece el régimen político y administrativo de un municipio.
Homestead. Propiedad inmueble exenta de embargo, por constituir un hogar; homestead.
Homicide. Homicidio.
Homologate. Homologar.
Homologation. Homologación.
Honor. Honor; honrar, pagar, o aceptar un valor o instrumento negociable.
Hornbook. Manual o tratado jurídico en un solo volumen.
Housebreaking. Escalamiento.
House of detention. Cárcel de menores.
House of representatives. Cámara de representantes; cámara de diputados.
Hull average clause. Cláusula de avería del barco.
Hull insurance. Seguro del casco del barco.
Hull liability policy. Seguro contra responsibilidad del barco.
Husband. Esposo.
Hypothecary action. Acción hipotecaria.
Hypothecate. Hipotecar; pignorar.
Hypothecation. Hipotecar.

Hypothetical question. Cuestión o pregunta hipotética.

I

Identification. Identificación.

Identification of goods to the contract. Segregación de mercancías en cumplimiento de un contrato; separación de mercancías para un comprador en particular.

Identify. Identificar.

Ignorance of the law. Ignorancia del derecho.

Illegal Ilegal; antijurídico.

Illegal conditions. Condiciones ilícitas o contrarias a la ley.

Illegitimacy. Ilegitimidad.

Illegitimate. Ilegítimo.

Illegitimate child. Hijo ilegítimo.

Illicit. Ilícito; ilegal; antijurídico.

Illusory promise. Condición potestativa; promesa ilusoria; promesa aparente.

Immaterial. Impertinente o irrelevante.

Immaterial evidence. Prueba o evidencia impertinente o irrelevante.

Immigrant. Inmigrante.

Immigrate. Inmigrar.

Immigration. Inmigración.

Immoral. Inmoral.

Immoral contract. Contrato inmoral; contrato contra las buenas costumbres.

Immovable. Inmueble.

Immovables by declaration. Inmuebles por declaración; bienes muebles puestos en un inmueble para el uso del mismo y declarados parte componente del inmueble por el dueño.

Immovables by destination. Inmuebles por destinación.

Immovables by nature. Inmuebles por naturaleza.

Immunity. Inmunidad; exención.

Immunity, transactional. *Véase* transactional immunity.

Immunity, use. *Véase* use immunity.

Impairing the obligation of contracts. Afectar las obligaciones de los contratos (mediante leyes ex post facto).

Impairment of security. Menoscabo o deterioro de garantía.

Impanel. Seleccionar el jurado que ha de actuar en un juicio determinado.

Impart. Conferenciar con la parte opuesta en un litigio para tratar de llegar a un arreglo.

Impeach. Residenciar; acusar; impugnar.

Impeachment. Procedimiento de residencia; acusación; impugnación.

Impeachment of witness. Impugnar la veracidad del testigo.

Impediment. Impedimento.

Impediment of relationship. Impedimento de matrimonio por razón de parentesco.

Imperative. Obligatorio.

Imperative law. Derecho obligatorio o de orden público.

Imperfect obligation. Obligación imperfecta; obligación natural.

Imperfect trust. Fideicomiso imperfecto o incompleto.

Implead. Acción del demandado contra terecero responsable, cuya acción es acumulada con la acción original.

Impleader. Procedimiento mediante el cuál el demandado actúa contra un terecero responsable, acumulando dicha acción con la acción por él defendida.

Implication. Implícito.

Implied. Implícito.

Implied authority. Autorización implícita.

Implied in fact. Implícito de los hechos; se desprende de los hechos.

Implied in law. Implícito de derecho.

Implied powers. Poderes implícitos; autoridad implícita.

Implied warranty. Garantía implícita o legal.

Impossibility of performance. Imposibilidad de la prestación.

Impost. Impuesto o tributo de importación o exportación.

Impound. Incautar; depositar bajo la custodia del tribunal.

Impracticability of performance. Excesiva onerosidad de la prestación; imposibilidad económica.

Imprescriptible. Imprescriptible.

Imprison. Encarcelar.

Imprisonment for debt. Encarcelación por deudas no pagadas.

Improper delivery. Entrega impropia; entrega deficiente.

Improper venue. Incompetencia territorial de un tribunal.

Improvement. Mejoras.

Improvements of embellishments of luxury. Mejoras de recreo.

Imputation by obligees. Imputación de pagos por el acreedor.

Imputation by obligor. Imputación de pagos por el deudor.

Imputation of payments. Imputación de pagos.

Imputed contributory negligence. Negligencia contribuyente imputada.

Imputed negligence. Negligencia imputada; culpa imputada.

Inadequate remedy. Remedio (o derecho) inadecuado.

Inadmissible. No admisible; dícese de lo que no hace prueba en juicio.

Inadmissible evidence. Prueba inadmisible; prueba improcedente.

Inalienable. Inenajenable; inalienable.

In blank. En blanco.

In blank endorsement. Endoso en blanco.

Incapacity. Incapacidad.

Incapacity, absolute. *Véase* absolute incapacity.

Incapacity, relative. *Véase* relative incapacity.

Incest. Incesto.

In chief. Presentación original de la prueba en el juicio.

Inchoate. Imperfecto o incompleto.

Incidental. Incidental.

Incidental damages. Daño incidental.

Incite. Inducir o incitar a otro a cometer un delito.

Income. Entradas; rentas.

Income tax. Impuesto sobre las rentas; impuesto sobre las entradas.

Incompatible. Incompatible; irreconciliable.

Incompetence. Incapacidad; inhabilidad; incompetencia.

Incompetent. Incapaz; inhábil; incompetente.

Incorporate. Incorporar; certificación de una sociedad anónima.

Incorporated. Corporación o sociedad anónima debidamente autorizada y certificada por la autoridad.

Incorporation. Incorporación; certificación de una sociedad anónima.

Incorporator. Fundador de una corporación o sociedad anónima.

Incorporeal immovables. Inmuebles incorpóreos.

Incorporeal movables. Muebles incorpóreos.

Incorporeals. Bienes incorpóreos.

Incriminate. Incriminar; acusar.

Incumbent. Persona que ocupa un cargo oficial.

Incumbrance. *Véase* encumbrance.

Indecency. Indecencia.

Indecent. Indecente.

Indecent exposure. Excibición indecente.

Indemnification. Resarcimiento; indemnización.

Indemnify. Resarcir; indemnizar.

Indemnitee. Acreedor de una indemnización o resarcimiento.

Indemnitor. Persona que se obliga a indemnizar o a resarcir.

Indemnity. Resarcimiento; indemnización.

Indemnity agreement. Contrato por el cuál un tercero se obliga a reembolsar al deudor lo que éste se vea obligado a pagar al acreedor.

Indenture. Escritura.

Independent contractor. Contratista independiente.

Indictment. Acusación por el gran jurado; sumario.

Indifferent. Imparcial.
Indigent person. Pobre; indigente.
Indirect evidence. Prueba indirecta
Indispensable party. Parte indispensable.
Indivisible. Indivisible.
Indivisible obligation. Obligación indivisible.
Indorse. *Véase* endorse.
Indorsed for collection. *Véase* endorsed for collection.
Indorsement. *Véase* endorsement.
Indorser. *Véase* endorser.
Inducement. Motivo.
Ineffective. Ineficaz; inefectivo.
In extenso. En toda su extensión.
Infamy. Infamia; deshonra.
Infanticide. Infanticidio.
Infer. Inferir; deducir.
Inference. Deducción.
Inferior court. Tribunales inferiores o de menor jerarquía.
Infirmity. Defecto que usualmente conlleva la invalidez de un acto o documento.
In forma pauperis. Estado de pobre el cuál, debidamente acreditado, da derecho al acreditado como tal de litigar sin pagar costas inpuestas por la ley.
Information, bill of. Acusación formal del fiscal.
Informer. Informante o delator que proveee información a la autoridad pública sobre la comisión de delitos.
In fraudem legis. En fraude de ley.
Infringement. Infracción; contravención; transgresión.
Inhabitant. Habitante; domiciliado.
Inherent powers. Facultades implícitas o inherentes.
Inheritance. Herencia.
Inheritance tax. Impuesto estatal sobre la herencia. El impuesto federal sobre la herencia se denomina "estate and gift tax".
In judicio. En un proceso judicial; en un juicio.
Injunction. Mandamiento; orden; prohibición. Mandamiento o prohibición judicial.
Injunction, preliminary. *Véase* preliminary injunction.
Injunction, temporary. *Véase* temporary injunction.
Injury. Lesión.
Injustice. Injusticia.
Inmate. Preso; recluso.
Innocense. Inocencia.
Innocent. Inocente.
Innocent purchaser. Comprador de buena fe.
Innoficious. Inoficioso.
Innominate contract. Contrato innominado.
In pais. *Véase* act in pais.
In pari delicto. En igualdad de culpa.
In personam, judgment in. Sentencia que obliga a un deudor personalmente.
Inquest. Investigación.
Inquisition. Inquisición; investigación.

In rem, judgment in. Sentencia que afecta determinados bienes.

In rem proceeding. Acción real; proceso en contra de la nave en derecho marítimo.

Insane. Loco; demente; insano.

Insanity. Locura; demencia; insania.

Inscription of mortgages. Inscripción de hipotecas en el registro.

Insolvency. Insolvencia; quiebra.

Insolvent. Insolvente; quebrado.

Inspection. Inspección.

Installment contract. Contrato a plazos.

Installments. Plazos.

Installment sale. Venta a plazos.

Institution. Institución.

Instructions to the jury. Instrucciones del juez al jurado.

Instrument. Instrumento; documento; acto jurídico escrito.

Insurable. Asegurable.

Insurable interest. Interés asegurable; derecho asegurable.

Insurance. Seguro; contrato de seguro.

Insurance binder. Contrato de seguro provisional.

Insurance carrier. Asegurador; compañía de seguros.

Insurance certificate. Certificado de seguro.

Insurance policy. Póliza de seguro.

Insurance premium. Prima de seguro.

Insured. Asegurado.

Insurer. Asegurador.

Intangibles. Bienes incorpóreos.

Integrated agreement. Acuerdo integrado. Llámase así a la escritura o escrituras que constituyen la expresión final de una o más cláusulas de un acuerdo.

Intellectual property. Propiedad intelectual; derecho de autor.

Intendment. Significado; intención.

Intent. Intención.

Intent, general. *Véase* general intent.

Intention. Intención.

Intentional infliction of mental distress. *Véase* mental distress, intentional infliction of.

Intentional tort. Aspecto civil de un acto antijurídico premeditado.

Intent, specific. *Véase* specific intent.

Inter alia. Entre otras cosas.

Inter alios. Entre otras personas.

Interdiction. Incapacitación.

Interdiction, petition for. *Véase* petition for interdiction.

Interdiction proceedings. Proceso de incapacitación.

Interest. Interés; derecho; intereses.

Interests in land. Derechos reales inmobiliarios.

Interfere. Interferir; reclamación de identidad de patente.

Interference. *Véase* interfere.

Interlineation. Interlineación; entrerrenglonadura.

Interlocking directorates. Consejos de dirección que se cruzan; dícese de la situación existente cuándo dos o más sociedades tienen idéntico o casi idéntico consejo de dirección.

Interlocutory. Interlocutoria.

Interlocutory decree. *Véase* interlocutory judgment.

Interlocutory judgment. Sentencia interlocutoria.

Intermediary. Intermediario; corredor.

Intermediary bank. Banco intermediario.

Internal revenue. Rentas internas.

International agreement. Acuerdo internacional.

International arbitration. Arbitraje internacional.

International Court of Justice. Corte Internacional de Justicia.

International law. Derecho internacional.

International sight draft. Giro internacional a la vista.

Interpleader. Acción por la cuál el deudor o el tenedor de una suma de dinero u otros bienes deposita dicho dinero o bienes bajo la custodia del tribunal para compeler a los presuntos acreedores a que prueben su derecho a recibirlo.

Interpret. Interpretar.

Interpretation. Interpretación.

Interrogatories. Interrogatorios escritos.

Interrogatiories, written. *Véase* written interrogatories.

Interruption. Interrupción.

Interruption by acknowledgment. Interrupción de la prescripción por reconocimiento.

Interruption of prescription. Interrupción de la prescripción.

Interruption of the statute of limitations. Interrupción de la prescripción.

Interstate. Referente a transacciones entre dos o más Estados (de los E E.U U.).

Interstate commerce. Transacciones comerciales entre dos o más Estados (de los E E.U U.).

Intervener. *Véase* intervenor.

Intervening cause. Factor interviniente que influye en la causa.

Intervenor. Tercero que interviene como parte en una acción; interventor; tercerista.

Intervention. Intervención en una acción; intervención; tercería.

Intervention of right. Intervención de derecho.

Intervention, permissive. Intervención permisible.

Intestacy. Abintestato; intestado; muerte sin testamento.

Intestate. Persona que muere sin dejar testamento; intestado.
Intestate succession. Sucesión intestada; sucesión legítima.
Intestate successor. Heredero.
Intrastate commerce. Referente al comercio que tiene lugar dentro de un sólo Estado (de los E E.U U.).
Intrusion. Intrusión.
Invalid. Inválido; nulo.
Inventory. Inventario.
In ventre sa mere. *Véase* en ventre sa mere.
Invest (to). Invertir.
Investment. Inversión.
Investment securities. Valores o acciones propios para inversión.
Invitee. Invitado; alguien que entra en propiedad ajena en calidad de invitado.
Involuntary bankruptcy. Quiebra involuntaria o forzada.
Involuntary dismissal. *Véase* dismissal.
Ipso jure. De derecho; por ministerio de ley.
Irrebuttable presumption. Presunción juris et de jure; presunción absoluta.
Irrelevant. Impertinente; irrelevante.
Irreparable injury. Pérdida irreparable; perjuicio irreparable.
Irrevocability. Irrevocabilidad.
Irrevocable. Irrevocable.
Irrevocable agency. Poder irrevocable; mandato irrevocable.
Irrevocable letter of credit. Carta de crédito irrevocable.
Irrevocable offer. Oferta irrevocable.
Issue. Problema; cuestión; prole; expedir.
Issuer. Dador; emisor.
Issuer's lien. Privilegio o gravamen del emisor.

J

Jactitation. Jactancia.
Jail. Cárcel; prisión.
Jeopardy. Peligro.
Jetsam. Objeto lanzado al mar desde una nave para aliviarla.
Jettison. Aligeramiento; echazón; alijamiento.
Jobber. Intermediario.
Join. Acumular (acciones o partes).
Joinder. Unificación de acciones o partes en una misma causa.
Joinder of actions. Unificación de acciones en un mismo juicio.
Joinder of parties. Unificación de partes en un mismo juicio.
Joint adventure. *Véase* joint venture.
Joint and several. Solidario(a).
Joint and several liability. Responsabilidad solidaria.

Joint and several obligations. Obligaciones solidarias.
Joint and several obligees. Acreedores solidarios.
Joint and several obligors. Deudores solidarios.
Joint enterprise. Actividad conjunta; empresa conjunta.
Joint liability. Responsabilidad mancomunada.
Joint obligations. Obligaciones mancomunadas.
Joint obligees. Acreedores mancomunados; acreedores de una obligación mancomunada.
Joint obligors. Deudores mancomunados; deudores de una obligación mancomunada.
Joint stock company. Sociedad por acciones; sociedad en comandita por acciones.
Joint tenancy. Condominio o copropiedad con derecho de sucesión entre los condóminos.
Joint tort. Cuasidelito cometido por dos o más personas.
Joint tortfeasors. Copartícipes en un cuasidelito.
Joint venture. Sociedad creada con un fin específico.
Jones Act seaman. Marinero para los efectos de la ley Jones.
Journal. Libro de actas de un cuerpo legislativo.
Judge. Juez; magistrado.
Judge-advocate. Fiscal en la corte marcial (E E.U U.).
Judge made law. Jurisprudencia; derecho de las decisiones de los tribunales.
Judgment. Juicio; sentencia.
Judgment creditor. El vencedor en un juicio en el cuál se le reconoce un derecho de crédito.
Judgment debtor. La parte condenada en una sentencia a efectuar un pago o entregar bienes.
Judgment debtor, examination of. *Véase* examination of the judgment debtor.
Judgment, declaratory. *Véase* declaratory judgment.
Judgment, final. *Véase* final judgment.
Judgment, interlocutory. *Véase* interlocutory judgment.
Judgment lien. Derecho de embargo o retención por virtud de sentencia favorable.
Judgment non obstante veredicto. *Véase* judgment notwithstanding the verdict.
Judgment notwithstanding the verdict. Sentencia no obstante el veredicto del jurado.
Judgment of separation of property. Sentencia decretando la separación de bienes entre los cónyugues.
Judgment on the merits. Sentencia; sentencia sobre el problema o controversia en el juicio.
Judgment on the pleadings. Sentencia basada en los alegatos de las partes, sin examen de pruebas.
Judgment, summary. *Véase* summary judgment.
Judicature. Judicatura; la función de impartir justicia.

Judicial. Judicial.
Judicial action. Demanda; acción ejercitada por demanda.
Judicial admission. Admisión judicial; admisión de parte hecha durante el juicio.
Judicial authorization. Autorización judicial.
Judicial confession. confesión judicial.
Judicial deposit. Depósito judicial.
Judicial emancipation. Emancipación judicial.
Judicial mortgage. Hipoteca judicial. Hipoteca que afecta los bienes raíces del condenado en juicio, proveniente de la sentencia dictada en su contra.
Judicial notice. Reconocimiento judicial de la veracidad de ciertos hechos que no necesitan ser probados.
Judicial partition. Partición judicial.
Judicial personality. Personalidad jurídica.
Judicial power. El poder judicial; la autoridad de los tribunales de oir causas e impartir justicia.
Judicial process. Proceso; proceso judicial.
Judicial review. Revisión judicial.
Judicial sale. Compraventa judicial.
Judicial sequestration. Depósito judicial; secuestro judicial.
Judicial sequestrator. Depositario judicial.
Judiciary. El poder judicial.
Jumping bail. Falta de comparecencia a una vista del acusado en libertad bajo fianza. Dicha falta de comparecer conlleva el decomiso o confiscación de la finza judicial.
Juridical person. Persona jurídica.
Juridical personality. Personalidad jurídica.
Jurisconsult. Jurisconsulto.
Jurisdiction. Jurisdicción; competencia.
Jurisdiction, admiralty. *Véase* admiralty jurisdiction.
Jurisdiction, long-arm. Jurisdicción de "brazo largo". Llámase así a la jurisdicción que ejerce un Estado sobre un demandado no domiciliado en el foro por virtud de alguna actividad que afecta el interés de una persona domiciliada en el foro, o que tiene contactos significativos con el foro.
Jurisdiction, maritime. *Véase* maritime jurisdiction.
Jurisdiction, subject matter. *Véase* subject matter jurisdiction.
Jurisprudence. Filosofía del derecho; jurisprudencia.
Jurisprudent. *Véase* jurisconsult.
Jurist. Jurista; juez.
Juristic person. Persona jurídica.
Juror. Cada uno de los miembros del jurado.
Jury. Jurado.

Jury box. Lugar de ubicación del jurado dentro de la sala.
Just cause. Justa causa.
Just compensation. Compensación justa. Dícese de la compensación que debe dársele al dueño de bienes expropiados por causa de utilidad pública.
Justice. Justicia; juez de la corte suprema; juez.
Justice of the peace. Juez de paz.
Justice of the supreme court. Magistrado de la corte suprema.
Justiciable. Procesable. Aptitud de una disputa de ser procesada por los tribunales.
Justifiable. Justificable.
Justification. Justificación.
Justified. Justificado.
Justify. Justificar.
Just title. Justo título.
Juvenile court. Tribunal de menores; corte juvenil.
Juvenile delinquency. Delincuencia juvenil.

K

Kidnap. Secuestrar; raptar.
Kin. *Véase* kindred.
Kindred. Parentesco.
Kinship. *Véase* kindred.
Know all men. "Sepan todos los hombres"--preámbulo uitilizado en muchos contratos y otros actos jurídicos.

L

Labor arbitration. Arbitraje laboral.
Laborer. Obrero; trabajador.
Labor law. Derecho del trabajo.
Labor union. Sindicato obrero.
Laches. Tardanza irrazonable en el ejercicio de un derecho que produce la caducidad del mismo.
Land grant. Cesión de terrenos públicos.
Land lien. Privilegio (o derecho de rentención) terrestre.
Landlord. Arrendador de bienes inmuebles.
Landlord and tenant. Arrendador y arrendatario; relación arrendaticia.
Landlord and tenant law. Derecho de arrendamiento de inmuebles.
Landlord's lien. Privilegio del arrendador.
Land patent. Patente o título dado por el gobierno al beneficiario de una cesión de terrenos públicos.
Lapse. Caducidad; extinción; lapso.
Larceny. Hurto; robo sin violencia; latrocinio.
Last clear chance. Doctrina de la última oportunidad evidente de evitar el accidente.

Last will and testament. Testamento; disposición de última voluntad.
Latent ambiguity. Ambigüedad oculta en escritura pública o privada.
Latent defect. Defecto o vicio oculto.
Lateral support. Apoyo lateral. Derecho real del propietario de bienes raíces a que no se hagan cambios en el predio vecino que afecten el natural apoyo lateral del terreno.
Law. Derecho; ley.
Lawful. Lícito; legal.
Lawful age. Mayoría de edad.
Lawful permit. Permiso, licencia, o autorización con arreglo a derecho.
Law merchant. Derecho mercantil.
Law of nations. Derecho internacional público; derecho de gentes.
Law of the land. Derecho positivo; derecho aplicable.
Lawyer. Abogado; jurista.
Leading case. Precedente importante.
Leading question. Pregunta que sugiere la respuesta; pregunta sugestiva.
League of nations. Liga de las Naciones.
Lease. Arrendamiento.
Leasehold. Arrendamiendo de bienes inmuebles; tenencia de inmuebles bajo arrendamiento.
Lease, oral. *Véase* oral lease.
Lease-purchase. Contrato de arrendamiento-compraventa; leasing.
Leasing. Arrendamiento; arrendamiento de bienes muebles; arrendamiento-compraventa; leasing.
Leave of court. Autorización del tribunal.
Ledger. Libro de contabilidad.
Legacy, universal. *Véase* universal legacy.
Legal. Legal; legítimo; lícito.
Legal aid. Abogado del indigente; abogado de oficio.
Legal capacity. Capacidad para obrar; capacidad para realizar actos jurídicos.
Legal duty. Deber legal.
Legal fiction. Ficción jurídica.
Legal impediment. Impedimento legal.
Legalize. Legalizar; hacer legal.
Legal malice. Mala fe deducida del acto o las circunstancias.
Legal malpractice. Negligencia profesional del abogado.
Legal mortgage. Hipoteca legal.
Legal personality. Personalidad jurídica.
Legal regime. Régimen económico matrimonial legal; sociedad legal de gananciales.
Legal scholar. Jurisconsulto; estudioso del derecho.
Legal separation. Separación legal.

Legal servitude. Servidumbre legal.
Legal succession. Sucesión legítima; sucesión legal.
Legal suretyship. Fianza legal.
Legal tender. Moneda de curso legal.
Legatee. Legatario.
Legatee by universal title. Legatario a título universal.
Legatee, particular. *Véase* particular legatee.
Legatee, universal. *Véase* universal legatee.
Legation. Legación; embajada.
Legislation. Legislación.
Legislative. Legislativo; referente a la legislatura.
Legislative immunity. Inmunidad parlamentaria.
Legislative will. Voluntad del legislador.
Legislature. Legislatura; órgano constitucional que ostenta el poder legislativo.
Legitimacy. Legitimidad.
Legitimate. Legítimo; lícito; legitimar.
Legitimate child. Hijo legítimo.
Legitimation. Legitimación.
Légitime. Legítima.
Lender. Prestamista.
Lesion. Lesión.
Lesion beyond moiety. Lesión superior a la mitad.
Lessee. Arrendatario.
Lessor. Arrendador.
Lessor's privilege. Privilegio del arrendador.
Let. Arrendar.
Letter of advice. Carta de aviso.
Letter of attorney. Poder de abogado; poder.
Letter of credit. Carta de crédito; orden de crédito.
Letter of licence. Extensión convencional del vencimiento de deudas.
Letters of administration. Autorización de administración al albacea o administrador de la sucesión.
Letters of marque and reprisal. Patente de corso.
Letters of safe conduct. Salvoconducto.
Letters rogatory. Carta rogatoria; suplicatorio.
Letters testamentary. Autorización de albaceazgo; carta de albaceazgo.
Letting out of labor or industry. Arrendamiento de servicios.
Letting out of things. Arrendamiento de bienes.
Levy. Embargar; ejecutar (una sentencia); fijar (impuestos); embargo; ejecución.
Lex contractus. La ley del contrato.
Lex domicilii. La ley del domicilio.
Lex fori. La ley del foro; ley del lugar donde se radica la acción.
Lex loci. Ley del lugar del contrato o del acto antijurídico.
Liability. Responsabilidad; responsabilidad civil o criminal.

Liability insurance. Póliza de seguros de responsabilidad civil.
Liability insurance law. Derecho sobre seguros de responsabilidad civil.
Liability insurance policy. Seguro contra responsabilidad civil por cuasidelitos (generalmente del conductor de vehículos de motor).
Liability, limitation of. Limitación de responsabilidad.
Liability of seller for personal acts. Responsabilidad del vendedor por actos propios.
Liability, strict. Responsabilidad objetiva; responsabilidad absoluta; responsabilidad sin culpa.
Liability, without fault. Responsabilidad objetiva; responsabilidad absoluta; responsablidad sin culpa.
Libel. Difamación por escrito; libelo; demanda.
Libellant. Demandante, (der. mar.).
Libellee. Difamado; víctima de un acto de difamación por escrito.
Liberality. Liberalidad.
Liberative prescription. Prescripción liberatoria.
Liberty. Libertad; derecho constitucional a la libertad.
Liberty of speech. *Véase* freedom of speech.
Liberty of the press. *Véase* freedom of the press.
License. Permiso; concesión; cesión de derecho; licencia.
Licensee. Concesionario; autorizado.
Licitation. Venta en subasta pública; licitación.
Licitation, partition by. *Véase* partition by licitation.
Lien. Derecho de retención; privilegio; gravamen.
Lien creditor. Acreedor con garantía; acreedor con derecho de retención.
Lienee. Dueño de propiedad gravada por un derecho de retención.
Lienor. Acreedor con privilegio o derecho de retención; embargador.
Life estate. Usufructo; usufructo vitalicio.
Life insurance. Seguro de vida.
Life tenant. Usufructuario; usufructuario vitalicio.
Light. Servidumbre de luz.
Lights, ancient. *Véase* light.
Limitation of actions. Prescripción extintiva.
Limitation of liability. Limitación de responsabilidad.
Limitation, statute of. *Véase* limitation of actions.
Limitation, words of . Palabras de límite. Indicación de la extensión de la cesión inserta en un documento en particular.
Limited. Limitado.
Limited liability company. Sociedad de responsabilidad limitada; sociedad anónima.

Limited partner. socio comanditario.
Limited partnership. Sociedad en comandita.
Lineal. Parentesco en línea directa.
Liquidate. Liquidar.
Liquidated damages. Daños liquidados.
Liquidation. Liquidación.
Liquidator. Liquidador; síndico.
Literal construction. Interpretación literal.
Literal interpretation. Interpretación literal.
Litigant. Litigante; una de las partes en un juicio o litigio.
Litigate. Litigado; procesado; litigar; procesar.
Litigator. Litigante; abogado litigante; abogado que se dedica a llevar pleitos ante los tribunales.
Litigious. Litigado; relativo al litigio.
Litigious rights. Derechos litigiosos; créditos litigiosos.
Livery. Entrega; tradición.
Livery of seisin. Tradición o entrega de bienes inmuebles (arcaico).
Loan. Préstamo; mutuo; comodato.
Loan for consumption. Mutuo.
Loan for use. Comodato.
Lobby. Cabildeo.
Lobbyist. Cabildero.
Local action. Acción que debe ser ejercitada en un lugar específico; acción local.
Lockout. Cierre; cierre de la planta o centro de trabajo por el empresario.
Locus contractus. Lugar del contrato.
Locus rei sitae. Lugar donde la cosa está situada.
Long arm jurisdiction. *Véase* jurisdiction, longarm.
Long arm service. Citación de brazo largo. Dícese de la citación por correo, o personal, efectuada por virtud de existir la jurisdicción de brazo largo (long arm jurisdiction). *Véase* jurisdiction, long arm.
Long arm statute. Ley de brazo largo. Llámase así a la ley que establece la jurisdicción de brazo largo. *Véase* jurisdiction, long arm.
Longshoremen's and harborworkers' compensation act. Ley de compensación a estibadores y trabajadores portuarios.
Loss. Pérdida; daño; avería.
Lost profits. Lucro cesante; pérdida de ganancias.
Lot. Lote de mercancías.
Lower court. Tribunal inferior.
Lowest responsible bidder. Ofertante de servicios en un contrato administrativo que, siendo un contratista responsable, ofrece el mejor (más bajo) precio para efectuar la prestación de que se trata.
Loyalty oath. Juramento de lealtad.

Lucid interval. Intervalo o momento lúcido.

Lump sale. Venta a precio alzado; venta a precio global.

Lump sum. Suma global; precio alzado.

M

Magistrate. Magistrado; juez.

Maiden name Apellido de soltera.

Maintenance. Mantenimiento.

Maintenance and cure. Manutención y cura.

Majority. Mayoría.

Majority, age of. Mayoría de edad.

Maker. Librador; girador; otorgante.

Mala fides. Mala fe.

Malfeasance. Acto antijurídico; fechoría.

Malice aforethought. Malicia premeditada; alevosía.

Malice in fact. Malicia de hecho; deseo real de causar daño a la víctima.

Malice in law. Malicia legal o de derecho; malicia donde no hay necesariamente deseo de causar daño a la víctima.

Malicious. Malicioso.

Malicious mischief. Daño malicioso; daño a la propiedad ajena causado intencionalmente o por culpa grave.

Malicious prosecution. Procesamiento malicioso.

Malpractice. Negligencia profesional.

Malum per se. Acto intrínsicamente malo.

Malum prohibitum. Acto prohibido por el derecho pero que no es, objetivamente, intrínsicamente malo.

Management of affairs of another. Gestión de negocios.

Management of the community of gains. Administración de la sociedad de gananciales.

Mandamus, writ of. *Véase* writ of mandamus.

Mandatary. Mandatario; agente.

Mandate, express. *Véase* express mandate.

Mandate, general. *Véase* general mandate.

Mandate in blank. Mandato en blanco; mandato al portador.

Mandate, special. *Véase* special mandate.

Manifest. Manifiesto.

Manslaughter. Homicidio involuntario; homicidio cometido "en el calor de la pasión."

Manual gift. Dación gratuita de bienes muebles y consecuente tradición.

Marine contract. *Véase* maritime contract.

Marine insurance. Seguro marítimo.

Marital. Marital; relativo al matrimonio; matrimonial.

Marital duties. Deberes matrimoniales.

Marital portion. Porción conyugal; derecho del cónyuge supérstite en la sucesión de su consorte.

Marital rights. Derechos matrimoniales.

Maritime but local. Asunto marítimo primordialmente local. En estos casos generalmente se aplica el derecho privado del Estado de mayor relación con el problema en vez del Derecho marítimo.

Maritime causes. Causas o casos marítimos.

Maritime collision. *Véase* collision at sea.

Maritime contract. Contrato marítimo.

Maritime jurisdiction. Jurisdicción marítima.

Maritime law. Derecho marítimo.

Maritime lien. Privilegio marítimo; derecho de embargo o retención marítimo.

Maritime personal injuries. Lesiones sufridas en accidente marítimo.

Market of rejection. Mercado o plaza donde el comprador ha rechazado la mercancía.

Market share liablity. Reponsabilidad del fabricante de un producto defectuoso basada en la parte del mercado del producto de que se trata que tiene el fabricante.

Marriage. Matrimonio.

Marriage articles. Contrato matrimonial sobre propiedad.

Marriage by procuration. Matrimonio por poder.

Marriage ceremony. Boda; ceremonia matrimonial.

Marriage portion. *Véase* dowry.

Marriage settlement. Capitulaciones matrimoniales; contrato entre los cónyuges concerniente a la propiedad de los mismos.

Married name. Apellido de casada.

Marshalling of assets. Distribución de bienes del deudor entre sus acreedores.

Martial law. Ley marcial.

Master. Empleador; árbitro especial nombrado por el tribunal.

Master of a vessel. Capitán de una nave.

Material alteration. Alteración; alteración material; alteración substancial.

Materialman's privilege. Privilegio sobre el edificio o la nave del abastecedor y del reparador de los mismos.

Matrimonial agreement. Contrato matrimonial.

Matrimonial regime. Régimen económico matrimonial.

Matter of fact. Problema o cuestión de hecho.

Matter of law. Problema o cuestión de derecho.

Maturity of an obligation. Vencimiento de la obligación.

Maxim. Máxima; principio general del derecho.
Maxims of equity. Máximas de equidad.
Maximum cure. Cura máxima.
Measure of damages. Monto de los daños; determinación del monto de los daños.
Mediator. Mediador; amigable componedor.
Medical malpractice. Negligencia profesional del médico.
Meeting of the minds. Compenetración de las mentes.
Memorandum. Memorial.
Mental cruelty. Crueldad mental.
Mental distress, infliction of . Causar angustia mental.
Mental distress, intentional infliction of. Causar angustia mental intencionalmente.
Mental distress, negligent infliction of. Causar angustia mental negligentemente.
Mercantile law. Derecho mercantil.
Merchant. Comerciante.
Merchantability. Comerciabilidad; negociabilidad.
Merchantable. Vendible.
Merchantable title. Título válido.
Merger. Fusión de sociedades; fusión.
Merits. El problema o controversia en el juicio.
Merits, judgment on the. Sentencia; sentencia sobre el fondo del asunto.
Merits (of the case). El problema central del pleito.
Mesne process. Proceso de un juicio entre el principio y el fin del mismo.
Metes and bounds. Límites de un predio.
Middleman. Intermediario.
Midnight deadline. Plazo fatal de medianoche; plazo improrrogable de medianoche (Der. banc.).
Military law. Derecho militar; Código militar.
Military testament. Testamento militar.
Mineral estate. Servidumbre minera; servidumbre de minas.
Mineral law. Derecho de minas; Derecho minero.
Mineral lease. Arredamiento minero; arrendamiento de minas.
Mineral right. Llámase así a cada uno de los derechos mineros, como, por e.j., el de exploración de minas.
Mineral rights. Derechos de exploración de minas y extracción de minerales; derechos mineros.
Mineral royalty. Derecho o canon de producción minera; regalía minera.
Mineral servitude. Servidumbre minera; servidumbre de minas.
Ministerial. Ministerial.
Ministerial act. Acto ministerial.

Minor. Menor; menor de edad.
Minority. Minoría; minoría de edad.
Minute clerk. Secretario de actas de un tribunal.
Minutes. Minutas; actas.
Mirror image rule. Principio de la imagen del espejo. Llámase así al principio según el cuál la aceptación de una oferta deber ser fiel a los términos de la oferta, o de lo contrario se la considerará una contraoferta.
Misappropriate. Malversar.
Misappropriation. Malversación.
Misbehavior. Mala conducta; mal comportamiento.
Miscegenation. Matrimonio mixto; matrimonio entre personas de diferentes razas.
Misfeasance. Acto legal realizado de forma ilegal.
Misjoinder of actions. Acumulación impropia de acciones.
Misjoinder of parties. Acumulación impropia de partes.
Misnomer. Designación errónea del nombre; nombre erróneo.
Mispleading. Alegación errónea.
Misprison of felony. Encubrimiento.
Misrepresentation. Tergiversación; falsedad.
Mistake. Error.
Mistrial. Anulación del juicio; anulación del juicio por error procesal.
Mitigate. Mitigar.
Mitigation. Mitigación.
Mitigation of damages. Mitagar el daño.
Mixed action. Acción mixta.
Mixed larceny. Hurto con agravantes.
Mixed personalty. Bienes muebles mezclados.
Mixed property. Bienes con características de muebles e inmuebles; propiedad mixta.
Mixed question of law and fact. Problema con cuestiones de hecho y de derecho entrelazadas.
Mobilia non habent situm. Los muebles no tienen sitio.
Modification. Modificación; alteración.
Moiety. Mitad; una de dos partes iguales.
Monarchy. Monarquía.
Monetary obligation. Obligación dineraria.
Money. Dinero; moneda de curso legal.
Money bill. Proyecto de ley de impuestos.
Moneyed corporation. Empresa monetaria (v.g. bancos, etc.).
Money judgment. Sentencia que ordena el pago de una suma de dinero.
Money order. Libranza o giro postal.
Monopoly. Monopolio.

Moot. Problema sin importancia práctica.

Moot court. Tribunal de aprendizaje para estudiantes de derecho.

Moral certainty. Certeza moral. Llámase así a la certeza que no deja lugar a duda razonable alguna.

Moral damages. Daño moral.

Moral duty. Deber moral.

Moral obligation. Deber moral.

Moral turpitude. Deshonestidad; depravación; contrario a la moral y las buenas costumbres.

Moratorium. Moratoria.

More definite statement, motion for. *Véase* motion for a more definite statement.

Mortgage. Hipoteca.

Mortgage, assumption of. *Véase* assumption of mortgage.

Mortgage, collateral. *Véase* collateral mortgage.

Mortgage, conventional. *Véase* conventional mortgage.

Mortgagee. Acreedor hipotecario.

Mortgage, general. *Véase* general mortgage.

Mortgage, inscription of. *Véase* inscription of mortgages.

Mortgage, judicial. *Véase* judicial mortgage.

Mortgage, legal. *Véase* legal mortgage.

Mortgages, erasure of. *Véase* erasure of mortgages.

Mortgage, special. *Véase* special mortgage.

Mortgage, tacit. *Véase* tacit mortgage.

Mortgage, unrecorded. *Véase* unrecorded mortgage.

Mortgagor. Hipotecante; deudor hipotecario.

Most favored nation clause. Cláusula de nación más favorecida.

Motion. Moción; pedimento; ponencia.

Motion for a more definite statement. Moción o pedimento de clarificación de alegatos.

Motion for a new trial. Moción o pedimento de juicio nuevo.

Motion for judgment notwithstanding the verdict (J.N.O.V.). Moción o pedimento solicitando que el juez dicte sentencia no obstante el veredicto del jurado (que ha resultado adverso al interés de la parte solicitando la decisión aludida.).

Motion to dismiss. Moción para anular la instancia; moción solicitando sobreseimiento.

Motion to strike. Moción de eliminación. Llámase así a la moción que procura una interlocutoria ordenando la eliminación de ciertos alegatos impropios hechos en el caso.

Motive. Motivo.

Movable property. Bienes muebles; propiedad mueble.

Movables. Muebles; bienes muebles.

Movables by anticipation. Muebles por anticipación; parte de un inmueble que se convierte en mueble, tal como los frutos de los árboles antes de ser cortados.

Movables transiently on premises. Bienes muebles sitos transitoriamente en el predio arrendado.

Movant. Parte que presenta una moción o pedimento.

Mover. *Véase* movant.

Moving party. *Véase* movant.

Multifariousness. Acumulación impropia de acciones.

Multiple taxation. Tributación múltiple; imposición de impuestos múltiple.

Multiplicity of actions. Multiplicidad de acciones.

Multiplicity of suits. Multiplicidad de acciones.

Municipal. Municipal.

Municipal corporation. Municipalidad; corporación municipal.

Municipal council. Ayuntamiento; cabildo; consejo municipal.

Municipal law. Derecho o ley municipal; derecho o ley nacional.

Muniment of title. *Véase* title deed.

Muniments. Documentos para probar título a bienes raíces; documentos para demostrar la existencia de un derecho.

Murder. Asesinato; homicidio con premeditación.

Murder in the first degree. Asesinato en primer grado; asesinato con agravantes.

Murder in the second degree. Asesinato en segundo grado.

Mutiny. Motín.

Mutual assent. Mutuo consentimiento.

Mutual fault. Culpa mútua; culpa de ambas partes.

Mutual insurance. Seguro mutuo.

Mutuality. Reciprocidad o bilateralidad (en las obligaciones).

Mutuality of obligations. Reciprocidad de las obligaciones; mutualidad de las obligaciones.

Mutual promises. Promesas recíprocas; promesas mutuas.

Mystic testament. Testamento cerrado.

Mystic will. Testamento cerrado.

N

Naked bailment. Nudo depósito. Dícese del depósito en que el depositario no tiene el deber de cuidar el objeto depositado.

Naked contract. Nudo contrato; Dícese del contrato hecho sin consideración o causa.

Naked owner. Nudo propietario.
Naked ownership. Nuda propiedad.
Naked title. Nudo título. Dícese del título que no da derecho alguno a su dueño a la propiedad en cuestión.
Naked trust. Nudo fideicomiso.
Named insured. Persona asegurada específicamente en la póliza.
Nation. Nación.
National. Nacional.
Nationality. Nacionalidad.
National supremacy. Supremacía nacional; supremacía de la nación sobre los Estados de la federación.
Native. Nativo.
Natural allegiance. Lealtad debida a la patria por virtud del nacimiento.
Natural born citizen. Ciudadano de nacimiento.
Natural child. Hijo natural.
Natural consequences. Consecuancias naturales.
Natural fruits. Frutos naturales.
Natural guardian. Tutor natural; curador natural.
Naturalization. Naturalización; adquisición de la cuidadanía estadounidense.
Naturalize. Naturalizar; adquirir la ciudadanía estadounidense.
Natural law. Derecho natural.
Natural monopoly. Monopolio natural.
Natural person. Persona física; persona natural.
Natural personality. Personalidad natural; personalidad del ser humano.
Natural servitude. Servidumbre natural; servidumbre de aguas.
Natural tutor. Tutor natural.
Navigation. Navegación.
Necessaries. Artículos de primera necesidad.
Necessary and proper clause. Cláusula de lo necesario y apropiado (de la constitución de los E E.U U.).
Necessary deposit. Depósito necesario; depósito miserable.
Necessary domicile. Domicilio fijado por la ley.
Necessary expenses. Gastos necesarios.
Necessary party. Parte necesaria.
Necessity. Necesidad; defensa en ciertos casos en que el autor de un acto actúa para prevenir un daño inminente.
Negative pregnant. Alegato ambiguo; negación ambigua.
Negative servitude. Servidumbre negativa.
Negligence. Negligencia; culpa.
Negligence per se. Culpa o negligencia de derecho ; v.gr., la violación de la ley.
Negligent infliction of mental distress. *Véase* mental distress, negligent infliction of.

Negotiability. Negociabilidad; transferabilidad.
Negotiable. Negociable; cesible; transferible.
Negotiable bill of lading. Conocimiento de embarque negociable; carta de porte negociable.
Negotiable instrument. Valor negociable; instrumento negociable.
Negotiate. Negociar; ceder (un valor).
Negotiation. Negociación.
Negotiation credit. Carta de crédito que autoriza la negociación o descuento de giros o letras de cambio a terceros.
Net income. Entradas netas; rentas netas.
Net landed weights. Peso líquido de descarga.
Neutral. Neutral.
Neutrality. Neutralidad.
New servitude. *Véase* additional servitude.
New trial. Nuevo juicio; nuevo proceso.
New trial, motion for. *Véase* motion for a new trial.
Next friend. Representante de un menor o incapaz ante un tribunal sin designación oficial.
Next of kin. Parentesco más cercano.
No cause of action. Sin lugar.
No-fault plan. Plan de indemnización sin considerar la culpa de las partes.
Nominal damages. Indemnización insignificante o nominal.
Nominal partner. Socio nominal; persona que permite que su nombre se use en una sociedad sin ser en realidad socio.
Nominal party. Persona que, sin ser parte interesada, figura como parte en un juicio por razones formales (v.gr., el tutor por el pupilo).
Nominal plaintiff. Demandante nominal; demandante cuyo nombre aparece en una causa sin tener interés en ella.
Nominate. Postular; nominado (contrato).
Nominate contract. Contrato nominado.
Nonacceptance. Rechazo; no aceptación.
Nonapparent servitude. Servidumbre no aparente.
Noncomformity. No se ajusta a.
Nonconforming goods. Mercancías que no están en conformidad con el contrato.
Nonconsumable things. Bienes no consumibles.
Nondelegable duty. Deber (o responsabilidad) no delegable.
Nonexecutive interest. Derecho o interés minero no ejecutivo. *Véase* executive rights.
Nonfeasance. Falta de hacer algo cuando se tiene el deber de hacerlo.

Nonjoinder. Falta de acumulación de parte necesaria en el litigio.

Nonnegotiable bill of lading. Conocimiento de embarque no negociable; carta de porte no negociable.

Nonnegotiable credits. Créditos no negociables.

Nonnegotiable instruments. Valores no negociables; instrumentos comerciales no negociables.

Non obstante. No obstante.

Non obstante veredicto. *Véase* notwithstanding the verdict.

Nonpecuniary damages. Daño moral.

Nonpossessory interest. Derecho no posesorio.

Nonquota immigrant. Inmigrante no sometido a cuotas de admisión.

Nonresident. Residente de otro Estado (de los E E.U U.).

Nonsuit. Juicio contra el demandante que no hace cosa juzgada.

Nonuser. No ejercitación de un derecho.

No right of action. Falta de derecho de actuar.

Notary. Notario; notario público.

Notary public. Notario público.

Notation of credit. Anotación de crédito.

Note. Pagaré; nota.

Note of hand. Reconocimiento de deuda; pagaré.

Not found. Rechazo de acusación por parte del gran jurado.

Not guilty. Inocente.

Not guilty, and not guilty by reason of insanity. Inocente por motivo de demencia.

Not guilty, plea of. Declaración de inocencia.

Notice. Notificación; aviso.

Notice of deposition. Notificación de que se va a tomar la declaración jurada o deposición a un testigo.

Notice of dishonor. Notificación de deshonor o rechazo (de aceptar o pagar un valor).

Notice of issue. Fijación de la causa para vista o juicio dispositivo.

Notice of protest. Protesto; notificación de protesto.

Notice of repudiation. Aviso de rechazo.

Notice of termination of lease. Notificación de terminación del arrendamiento.

Notice of trial. Notificación de vista o juicio definitivo.

Notice to perform. Aviso formal exigiendo cumplimiento; puesta en mora.

Notice to plead. Notificación avisando la necesidad de presentar alegatos dentro de un plazo determinado.

Notice to produce. Notificación de parte a la contraparte pidiendo producción de documentos o pruebas en posesión de la parte notificada.

Notice to quit. Notificación de deshabitar o deshaucio (dada al arrendatario por el arrendador).

Notification. Notificación; aviso; emplazamiento.

Notorious possession. Posesión notoria; dícese de la clase de posesión necesaria para la usucapión.

Not true bill. Determinación del gran jurado que no debe acusarse.

Notwithstanding the verdict (or nonobstante veredicto). (Dictar sentencia) no obstante el veredicto del jurado.

Novation. Novación.

Nuissance. Perjuicio; actividad que produce interferencia en el derecho ajeno.

Null. Nulo.

Null and void. Nulo.

Nullity. Nulidad; nulo.

Nullity, absolute. *Véase* absolute nullity.

Nullity of marriage. Nulidad del matrimonio.

Nullity, relative. *Véase* relative nullity.

Null marriage. Matrimonio nulo.

Nuncupative testament. *Véase* nuncupative will.

Nuncupative testament by public act. Testamento abierto por escritura pública.

Nuncupative will. Testamento nuncupativo; testamento abierto.

O

Oath. Juramento.

Oath of office. Juramento en la toma de posesión de un cargo público.

Objection. Objeción; oposición. Objeción u oposición de parte sobre alguna acción de la otra parte, usualmente de carácter procesal, durante el juicio.

Obligation. Obligación.

Obligation, alternative. *Véase* alternative obligations.

Obligation, assumption of. *Véase* assumption of obligations.

Obligation, civil. *Véase* civil obligation.

Obligation, divisible. *Véase* divisible obligation.

Obligation, extinction of. *Véase* extinction of obligations.

Obligation, facultative. *Véase* facultative obligations.

Obligation, heritable. *Véase* heritable obligation.

Obligation, indivisible. *Véase* indivisible obligation.

Obligation, joint. *Véase* joint obligation.

Obligation, joint and several. *Véase* joint and several obligation.

Obligation, moral. *Véase* moral obligation.

Obligation, principal. *Véase* principal obligation.
Obligation, real. *Véase* real obligation.
Obligation, secondary. *Véase* secondary obligation.
Obligation, several. *Véase* several obligations.
Obligations, mutuality of. *Véase* mutuality of obligations.
Obligation, solidary. *Véase* solidary obligation.
Obligations, reciprocal. *Véase* reciprocal obligations.
Obligations, transfer of. *Véase* transfer of obligations.
Obligation, strictly personal. *Véase* strictly personal obligation.
Obligee. Acreedor.
Obligor. Deudor.
Oblique action. Acción oblícua.
Obscene. Obsceno.
Obstruction of justice. Obstrucción de la administración de la justicia. Delito que consiste en intencionalmente obstruir el arresto o alguna parte del proceso penal.
Occupancy. Ocupación.
Occupant. Ocupante; poseedor.
Occupation. Ocupación.
Occupational tax. Impuesto o tributo sobre la ocupación o trabajo.
Of counsel. Abogado afiliado a un bufete como asesor sin ser miembro de la firma.
Offense. Ofensa; violación de la ley; crimen.
Offer. Oferta.
Offeree. Aceptante; persona a quien se le hace una oferta.
Offer of reward made to the public. Oferta de recompensa hecha al público.
Offeror. Oferente.
Office. Cargo; posición; oficina.
Office of recordation. Registro; lugar del registro.
Officer. Funcionario; oficial.
Official. Relativo a un cargo público; funcionario; oficial.
Oil and gas law. Derecho de hidrocarburos en forma líquida o gaseosa; Derecho del petróleo y del gas.
Olograph. Ológrafo.
Olographic testament. Testamento ológrafo.
Olographic will. Ológrafo; (testamento) ológrafo.
Omission. Omisión; falta de cumplir un deber legal.
On account. A cuenta.
Onerous. Oneroso.
Onerous cause. Causa onerosa.
Onerous contract. Contrato oneroso.
Onerous donation. Donación onerosa.
On or about. "En o sobre". Frase usada en documentos cuando no se conoce con certeza la fecha de un acontecimiento.
Onus probandi. Carga de la prueba.

Open court. Audiencia pública en sesión del tribunal.
Opening of succession. Apertura de la sucesión.
Open policy. Póliza abierta; póliza flotante.
Open price. Precio a determinar; precio abierto; contrato concluído con precio indeterminado.
Open shop. Centro de trabajo donde el empleador puede utilizar empleados sindicalizados o no sindicalizados a su arbitrio.
Open testament. Testamento abierto.
Operation of law. De derecho; por virtud de la ley.
Operative (words). Palabras claves; dícese de la clase de palabras que son necesarias para que un documento dado surta efecto.
Opinion. Opinión.
Oppression. Opresión.
Option. Opción.
Optionee. Persona que ostenta un derecho de opción.
Optioner. *Véase* optionor.
Optionor. Persona que ha concedido un derecho de opción.
Oral argument. Exposición oral en un juicio.
Oral complaint. Demanda oral.
Oral lease. Arrendamiento oral.
Oral pleading. Alegatos orales.
Order. Orden; mandamiento.
Ordinance. Ordenanza; decreto.
Ordinary care. Prudencia o cuidado ordinario. Llámase así a la prudencia o cuidado que toda persona debe observar, como mínimo, en sus actos.
Ordinary course of business. Curso ordinario del comercio.
Ordinary creditor. Acreedor ordinario.
Ordinary proceedings. Proceso ordinario.
Ordinary suretyship. Fianza; fianza ordinaria.
Organic law. Derecho constitucional.
Organization. Organización.
Organization of American States. Organización de Estados Americanos.
Original bill. Demanda en un tribunal de equidad.
Original complaint. Demanda original.
Original jurisdiction. Jurisdicción o competencia en primera instancia.
Original package. Envase o paquete original.
Orphans' court. Tribunal de testamentaría.
Ostensible authority. Autoridad aparente; autoridad pretendida.
Ostensible partner. Socio aparente. Dícese de alguien que, sin ser socio de una firma, permite que se use su nombre tal como si lo fuera.
Ouster. Evicción; desahucio.
Outlaw. Delincuente; bandido.

Output contract. Contrato de rendimiento. Llámase así al contrato de tracto sucesivo en que el objeto de la prestación depende del rendimiento o producción de una de las partes que la otra parte se compromente a comprar.
Overdraft. Sobregiro; sobregirar.
Overdraw. Sobregirar.
Overdue. Vencida (cuenta, paragé, etc.).
Overissue. Emisión excesiva.
Overreaching. Aprovecharse de otro a través de prácticas desleales o de mala fe.
Overriding royalty. Derecho de participación en un canon o derecho de producción minero (o de regalía minera).
Overrule. Negar una objeción; anular la vigencia de un precedente.
Owner. Propietario; dueño.
Ownership. Dominio; propiedad.
Oyer of a deed. Inspección de un documento en audiencia pública.
Oyez. Aviso oral del oficial del tribunal anunciando la apertura de la audiencia y pidiendo silencio.

P

Pact. Pacto; acuerdo.
Paid-in capital. Capital pagado.
Panel. Panel; lista de personas disponibles para formar un jurado.
Paper money. Papel moneda.
Paramount. Supremo; (título) superior; o de más valía.
Paramount title. *Véase* paramount.
Parapherna. Bienes parafernales.
Paraphernalia. Bienes parafernales.
Paraph for identification. Rubricación notarial de un pagaré para identificarlo como relacionado a una hipoteca.
Parcel. Parcela.
Pardon. indulto; perdón.
Parens patriae. Padre de la patria. Dícese del Estado en su capacidad de protector de menores e incapaces.
Parental authority. Patria potestad; autoridad paternal.
Parental usufruct. Usufructo que gozan los padres sobre los bienes de sus hijos menores.
Parenticide. Homicidio de padre o madre.
Pari delicto, in. Igual culpabilidad.
Pari materia, in. Sobre el mismo tema o materia.
Pari passu. Al mismo paso; sin preferencia.
Parish. Parroquia.
Parliament. Parlamento.

Parliamentary law. Derecho parlamentario; procedimiento parlamentario.
Parliamentary procedure. Derecho parlamentario; procedimiento parlamentario.
Parol contract. Contrato oral.
Parole. *Véase* probation and parole.
Parol evidence. Prueba testifical o de testigos.
Parol evidence rule. Regla de la prueba oral. Dícese de la regla que prohibe la prueba oral para variar o contradecir las cláusulas de un contrato escrito.
Parricide. Parricidio.
Partial assignment. Cesión parcial.
Partial breach. Incumplimiento parcial.
Partial eviction. Evicción parcial.
Particular average. Avería particular; avería simple.
Particular donee. Donatario a título particular o singular.
Particular estate. Heredad limitada. Derecho real de carácter temporal.
Particular legacy. Legado particular.
Particular legatee. Legatario de un legado en particular.
Particular lien. Derecho de retención particularizado; privilegio.
Particular tenant. Tenedor particular. Dícese del dueño de una heredad limitada. *Véase* particular estate.
Parties, substitution of. Substitución de partes.
Partition. Partición; división; repartimiento.
Partition by licitation. Partición por licitación.
Partition, definitive. *Véase* definitive partition.
Partition in kind. Partición en especie.
Partition, judicial. *Véase* judicial partition.
Partition, provisional. *Véase* provisional partition.
Partition, voluntary. *Véase* voluntary partition.
Partner. Socio.
Partner, dormant. *Véase* dormant partner.
Partner in commendam. Socio comanditario.
Partnership. Sociedad.
Partnership, civil. Sociedad civil.
Partnership, commercial. Sociedad mercantil; sociedad comercial.
Partnership in commendam. Sociedad en comandita; sociedad limitada.
Partnership, limited. Sociedad en comandita; sociedad limitada.
Partnership, universal. *Véase* universal partnership.
Part owner. Condueño; condómino; dueño pro indiviso; comunero.
Part payment. Pago parcial.
Part performance. Cumplimiento parcial.

Party. Parte; partido; partido político.
Party in interest. Parte interesada; parte con interés; persona interesada o con derecho.
Party-wall. Pared o muralla divisoria entre dos edificios.
Pass. Traspasar; transferir; decidir; determinar.
Passage. (servidumbre de) paso.
Passim. Regado. Término usado para expresar el hecho de que un vocablo o frase ocurre con frecuencia en una ley o estatuto.
Passive. Pasivo. Dícese de bonos o debentures que no devengan interés.
Passive trust. Fideicomiso pasivo (o inactivo). Dícese del fideicomiso donde al fideicomisario no le restan deberes activos que cumplir.
Passport. Pasaporte.
Past consideration. Beneficio recibido por el promitente en el pasado; contraprestación recibida en el pasado.
Past due. Sobrevencida (deuda).
Patent. Patente de invención.
Patentable. Patentizable.
Patentee. Poseedor de patente; beneficiario de patente.
Patentor. Dueño de patente.
Paternity. Paternidad.
Patrimony. Patrimonio.
Pauper. Pobre.
Pawn. Prenda de bienes muebles.
Pay. Pagar.
Payable at a definite time. Pagadero a una fecha determinada.
Payable on demand. Pagadero a la vista.
Payable to bearer. Pagadero al portador.
Payable to order. Pagadero a la orden.
Payee. Beneficiario; tenedor; portador.
Payment. Pago.
Payment against documents. Pago contra documentos.
Payment into registry of the court. Pago hecho por consignación al tribunal.
Payment of a thing not due. Pago de lo indebido.
Payment on account. Pago a cuenta.
Payments, application of. *Véase* application of payments.
Payment under protest. Pago bajo protesto.
Payor. Pagador.
Payor bank. Banco pagador.
Peaceful possession. Posesión pacífica.
Peace, justice of the . Juez de paz.
Peers. Pares.
Peers, jury of. Jurado de los pares; jurado compuesto de miembros de una comunidad.
Penal. Penal.
Penal clause. Cláusula penal.
Penal damages. Daños punitivos; daños punitorios.

Penal law. Derecho penal; Derecho criminal.
Penal statute. Ley penal; ley de Derecho criminal.
Penal sum. Cláusula penal.
Penalty. Condena; pena; castigo; penalidad.
Pendente lite. Mientras el litigio está en proceso; pendiente el litigio.
Pendent jurisdiction. Jurisdicción apoyada. Llámase así a la jurisdicción de los tribunales federales sobre causas que surgen bajo el derecho estatal, en ciertos casos, por la conexión que ostentan con una reclamación de derecho federal.
Penitentiary. Prisión; presidio.
Pension. Pensión.
Per autre vie. Por la vida de otro; derecho real temporal cuya duración se mide por la vida de alguien que no es el poseedor del derecho real de que se trata.
Per curiam. Por el tribunal; decisión colegiada sin ponente en particular.
Per diem. Por día; viático; diariamente.
Peremption. Caducidad.
Peremption of action. Caducidad de la acción.
Peremptory. Perentoria; perentorio.
Peremptory challenge. Impugnación facultativa de un miembro del jurado.
Peremptory exception. Excepción perentoria.
Perfected security interest. Derecho de garantía perfeccionado.
Performance. Cumplimiento; prestación.
Perils clause. Cláusula de peligros.
Perils of the sea. Peligros del mar.
Per, in the. Pretensión al título por sucesión, a título universal o singular, del dueño.
Perjury. Perjurio; falso testimonio.
Permanent alimony. Pensión definitiva o permanente.
Permanent injunction. Mandamiento permanente; interdicto permanente; prohibición permanente.
Permissive. Permitido.
Permissive counterclaim. Reconvención permisible.
Permissive intervention. Intervención permisible.
Permissive waste. Daño sufrido por una heredad debido a la imprudencia del poseedor o arrendatario.
Permit. Permiso; licencia; autorización.
Perpetual injunction. Mandamiento permanente; interdicto permanente; prohibición permanente.
Perpetual lease. Arrendamiento perpetuo. Arrendamiento en que el arrendatario tiene la opción de renovar el arrendamiento al vencimiento del término.

Perpetuate testimony. Perpetuar el testimonio; preservar el testimonio o declaración.
Perpetuties, rule against. *Véase* rule against perpetuities.
Perquisite. Compensación más allá de su sueldo legalmente recibida por alguien que ostenta un cargo oficial.
Person. Persona.
Personal. Personal.
Personal action. Acción personal.
Personal contract. Contrato cuyo objeto es una cosa mueble.
Personal injury claim. Demanda por daño ocasionado por lesiones físicas sufridas.
Personality. Personalidad.
Personality, juridical. *Véase* juridical personality.
Personal jurisdiction. Competencia sobre la persona del demandado.
Personal property. Bienes muebles.
Personal right. Derecho personal.
Personal servitude. Servidumbre personal.
Personalty. Bienes muebles.
Personate. Pretender ser otra persona.
Personification of ship. Personificación de la nave.
Person interposed. Interpósita persona.
Person, juridical. *Véase* juridical person.
Pertinent. Pertinente; relevante; relacionado.
Petition. Demanda; pedimento; petición; súplica.
Petition for interdiction. Demanda de incapacitación.
Petition of intervention. *Véase* intervention.
Petit jury. Pequeño jurado; jurado.
Petitory action. Acción petitoria.
Petty jury. *Véase* petit jury.
Petty larceny. Hurto de propiedad de pequeño valor.
Petty theft. *Véase* petty larceny.
Pilotage. Pilotaje; timonaje.
Piracy. Piratería.
Piracy, air. Piratería aérea.
Pirate. Pirata.
Place of destination. Lugar de destino.
Place of shipment. Lugar de embarque.
Plaintiff. Demandante.
Plea. Contestación; respuesta; alegato; contestación del reo a la acusación.
Plea bargain. Negociación sobre la contestación del reo a la acusación.
Plead. Contestar; argüir; alegar.
Pleader. Parte que presenta un alegato en un juicio.
Pleading. Alegatos; presentación de escritos; escritos; pieza de autos.
Pleading, responsive. *Véase* responsive pleading.
Pleadings, amendment of. Enmienda de alegatos.

Pleading, supplemental. Alegato suplementario.
Plebiscite. Plebiscito.
Pledge. Prenda.
Plenary suit. Juicio ordinario; procedimiento ordinario.
Plurality. Pluralidad.
Pocket veto. Veto técnico; veto de bolsillo. Dícese del veto producido cuando la sesión del congreso de los E E. U U. termina antes de expirar el período de diez días de que goza el presidente para firmar o vetar una ley.
Policy. Política (legislativa); póliza (de seguros).
Political party. Partido político.
Poll. Encuesta; encuesta del jurado para determinar si están de acuerdo con el veredicto.
Pollicitation. Policitación; oferta.
Polling place. Urnas; ubicación de las urnas.
Poll tax. Capitación.
Polygamy. Poligamia.
Poor law. Legislación de asistencia a los pobres.
Port commission. Autoridad portuaria; junta administrativa del puerto.
Positive law. Derecho positivo.
Possession. Posesión.
Possession as owner. Posesión en concepto de dueño.
Possession, clandestine. *Véase* clandestine possession.
Possession, precarious. *Véase* precarious possession.
Possession, violent. *Véase* violent possession.
Possession, writ of. Mandamiento de posesión.
Possessor. Poseedor.
Possessor in good faith. Poseedor de buena fe.
Possessory action. Acción posesoria.
Possessory interest. Derecho posesorio.
Possibility of reverter. Derecho real del cedente de recobrar el derecho real cedido.
Posting, process of. Proceso de anotación bancaria.
Potestative condition. Condición potestativa.
Poverty affidavit. Declaración jurada de pobreza.
Power. Autorización; autoridad.
Power coupled with an interest. Mandato irrevocable.
Power of acceptance. Derecho de aceptar.
Power of application. Derecho a imputar pagos.
Power of appointment. Autoridad para nombrar beneficiarios.
Power of attorney. Poder; poder de abogado.
Practice of law. Abogacía; ejercicio de la profesión de abogado.
Precarious. Precario.
Precarious possession. Posesión precaria; precaria.

Precarious possessor. Poseedor precario.
Precatory. Exhortante; suplicante.
Precatory words. Sugerencia, recomendación, o pedimento contenido en un acto jurídico.
Precedent. Precedente.
Precept. Precepto; orden; mandamiento.
Precinct. Distrito; precinto.
Precontract. Promesa de matrimonio; precontrato; contrato que cohibe la celebración posterior de otro contrato de la misma índole.
Predecessor. Predecesor.
Predial servitude. Servidumbre real.
Preemption. Preferencia; prioridad.
Preemptive rights. Derechos de preferencia; derechos de prioridad.
Pre-existing duty. Deber preexistente.
Preference. Preferencia; cesión de bienes por un deudor insolvente dando preferencia injusta a un acreedor.
Preferred stock. Acciones con preferencia; acciones preferentes.
Prejudice. Prejuicio; perjuicio; daño.
Preliminary examination. Vista preliminar del proceso penal.
Preliminary injunction. Mandamiento provisional; prohibición provisional.
Preliminary negotiation. Negociación preliminar; negociación con miras a la formación de un contrato.
Premeditation. Premeditación.
Premier. Primer ministro.
Premises. Lugar; local; derecho transferido.
Premium. Prima.
Prescribe. Prescribir.
Prescription. Prescripción; usucapión.
Prescription, acquisitive. *Véase* acquisitive prescription.
Prescription, interruption of. *Véase* interruption of prescription.
Prescription, liberative. *Véase* liberative prescription.
Prescription of nonuse. Prescripción de desuso (por) no usar un derecho real.
Prescription, suspension of. *Véase* suspension of prescription.
Presenter. Presentante.
Presenting bank. Banco presentante.
Presentment. Presentación (de un valor); acusación.
Presentment for payment. Presentación para el pago.
Present sale. Venta.
President. Presidente.
Presidential elector. Miembro del colegio electoral que elige al presidente (E E.U U.).
Press, freedom of. Libertad de prensa.
Presumption. Presunción.

Presumption of fact. Deducción de los hechos; presunción de hecho.
Presumption of law. Conclusión jurídica basada en la prueba; presunción de derecho.
Presumption of paternity. Presunción de paternidad.
Presumption of survivorship. Presunción de supervivencia.
Presumptive heir. Heredero aparente.
Presumptive title. Título aparente; título que puede deducirse de la posesión,o del uso, de un predio.
Presuppositions, contractual. Presuposición contractual.
Pretrial conference. conferencia con antelación a la vista definitiva.
Pretrial order. Orden sobre la conducción del proceso hasta la vista definitiva.
Prevarication. Prevaricación; prevaricato.
Price. Precio.
Price certain. Precio cierto.
Prima facie case. *Véase* prima facie evidence.
Prima facie evidence. Prueba suficiente para demostrar la existencia de un hecho.
Primary election. Elecciones preliminares; elecciones primarias.
Primary evidence. Prueba principal; la mejor prueba para probar un hecho; prueba primaria.
Primary legacy. Legado de dinero.
Primary obligation. Obligación primaria.
Primary right. Derecho primario.
Primary sources. Fuentes principales.
Prime minister. Primer ministro.
Principal. Mandante; autor de un delito.
Principal contract. Contrato principal.
Principal obligation. Obligación principal.
Principal place of business. *Véase* chief place of business.
Principal, undisclosed. *Véase* undisclosed principal.
Principle. Principio.
Priority. Preferencia; prioridad; prelación.
Priority of claims. Prelación de créditos.
Prior restraint. Censura previa.
Prison. Prisión.
Private international law. Derecho internacional privado.
Private law. Derecho privado.
Private property. Propiedad privada.
Private road. Camino o vía privada.
Private things. Bienes de dominio privado; bienes privados.

Private written instrument. Documento privado; documento sin notarizar.

Privilege. Privilegio; derecho; facultad.

Privilege against self-incrimination. Privilegio (constitucional) contra la autoincriminación.

Privileged communications. Comunicación de confianza; comunicación privilegiada.

Privileges and immunities clause. Cláusula sobre privilegios e inmunidades (de la constitución de los E E.U U.).

Privileges, ranking of. *Véase* ranking of privileges.

Privity of contract. Relación contractual.

Prize. Presas.

Prize court. Tribunal de presas.

Prize law. Derecho de presas.

Prize proceedings. Proceso sobre presas.

Probable cause. Causa probable. Dícese de la situación que hace razonable la estimación de que el reo haya cometido el delito de que se le acusa. La causa probable no basta para probar la culpabilidad del reo. *Véase* proof beyond a reasonable doubt.

Probate. Proceso de validar un testamento; testamentaría.

Probate court. Tribunal competente para oir juicio de testamentarías, herencias, donaciones y asuntos afines.

Probate of a will. Proceso de probar la validez de un testamento.

Probation. *Véase* probation and parole.

Probation and parole. Probatoria; libertad condicionada.

Probative. Tendiente a probar.

Pro bono publico. Por el bien de la comunidad. Esta frase generalmente es usada para describir la prestación gratuita de servicios legales, por ameritarlo el caso o por la calidad de pobre del cliente.

Procedural law. Derecho procesal.

Procedure. Procedimiento, proceso.

Procedure for recordation. Procedimiento de registración.

Proceedings. Vista; autos; proceso judicial.

Proceeds. Producto.

Process. Proceso; citación.

Proces verbal. Declaración autenticada.

Proctor. Abogado (esp. de almirantazgo o testamentaría).

Proctor in admiralty. Abogado especializado en Derecho marítimo.

Procuration. Procuración; poder.

Procurator. Mandatario; *véase* proctor.

Products liability. Responsabilidad objetiva del fabricante y el vendedor profesional por el

daño causado por productos defectuosos.
Profert. *Véase* proffer.
Proffer. Solicitación de introducción de prueba en el expediente de un juicio.
Profit. Ganancia; servidumbre de aprovechamiento.
Profits. Ganancias; utilidades.
Pro hac vice. Por esta ocasión.
Prohibition. Prohibición.
Prohibition, writ of. Auto de prohibición.
Promise. Promesa.
Promisee. Promisario.
Promise to sell. Promesa de venta.
Promissor. Promitente.
Promissory estoppel. Actos propios del promitente. Llámase así al principio que obliga al promitente a cumplir una promesa cuando el promitente sabe, o debería saber, que el promisario actuaría en consecuencia, y el promisario actúa consecuentemente. Este principio se aplica, aún sin acto consecuente del promisario, en casos de donaciones a sociedades benéficas y convenios matrimoniales.
Promissory note. Pagaré.
Promoter. Promotor; organizador de una sociedad anónima o corporación.
Promulgate. Promulgar.
Proof. Prueba.
Proof beyond a reasonable doubt. Prueba más allá de toda duda razonable. Dícese del tipo de prueba necesario para demostrar la culpabilidad del acusado.
Proof by reputation. Prueba (de filiación) por posesión de estado.
Proof of obligations. Prueba de las obligaciones.
Proper party. Parte interesada; parte que puede ser adherida a un juicio.
Property. Propiedad; dominio.
Propinquity. Parentesco cercano.
Proposal. Propuesta.
Prorogation. Prórroga.
Prosecute a claim. Procesar una acción; actuar.
Protection and indemnity policy. Póliza de protección e indemnidad; póliza de protección e indemnización.
Protective order. Orden protectora del tribunal.
Protest. Protesto.
Prothonotarial certificate. Certificación del secretario de administración (clerk of court) del tribunal.
Prothonotary. Secretario de administracion.
Protocol. Protocolo.
Protonotarial certificate. *Véase* Prothonotarial certificate.
Prove. Probar.
Provisional partition. Partición provisional.
Provisional possession. Posesión provisional; posesión temporal.
Provisional remedies. Medidas provisionales; remedios

provisionales; medidas cautelares.

Provisional settlement. Liquidación provisional.

Provisional tutor. Tutor provisional.

Proviso. Condición; excepción.

Proximate cause. Causa legal; causa legal de un accidente.

Proxy. Poder especial para votar; poder; proxy.

Prudent administrator. Buen padre de familia; administrador prudente.

Public administrator. Administrador público de sucesiones; albacea público.

Public auction. Subasta pública.

Public authorities. La autoridad pública; la autoridad.

Public defender. Abogado de oficio; defensor del indigente.

Public domain. Dominio público.

Public drunkenness. Embriaguez pública.

Public enemy. Enemigo público.

Public figure. Personaje público.

Public interest. El interés público.

Public international law. Derecho internacional público.

Public law. Derecho público.

Public policy. Orden público; política pública.

Public records. Registro; registro público.

Public road. Camino o vía pública; camino sujeto al uso público.

Public things. Bienes de dominio público destinados al uso público; bienes públicos.

Public use. El uso público; el uso del público.

Public utility. Utilidad pública.

Public vessel. Nave pública.

Public written instrument. Documento público; documento notarizado.

Punitive damages. Daños punitivos; daño punitorio.

Purchase. Compra; adquisición.

Purchase and sale. Compraventa.

Purchase at peril and risk. Compra a riesgo.

Purchase money security interest. Derecho de garantía que resguarda el precio de la venta.

Purchaser. Comprador; adquirente.

Purchaser for value. Comprador a título oneroso; adquirente a título oneroso.

Putative. Putativo.

Putative marriage. Matrimonio putativo.

Putative spouse. Cónyuge putativo.

Putting in default. Poner en mora.

Q

Qualified endorsement. Endoso condicional; endoso sin recurso; endoso limitado.

Qualified fee. Derecho real sometido a condición resolutoria.

Qualified property. Derecho real condicionado en la posesión contínua.

Qualified voter. Votante registrado.

Quality. Calidad.

Quantum meruit. Tanto como se ha ganado; tanto como se merece.

Quantum valebant. Cuanto valen.

Quarantine. Cuarentena.

Quash. Invalidar; anular.

Quasicontract. Cuasicontrato.

Quasi-corporation. Cuasicorporación; cuasisociedad anónima.

Quasi-delict. Cuasidelito.

Quasi-deposit. Depósito efectuado sin el consentimiento del depositario de asumir las obligaciones del contrato de depósito.

Quasi-easement. Cuasiservidumbre.

Quasi in rem. Cuasi in rem.

Quasi in rem jurisdiction. Jurisdicción cuasi in rem. Jurisdicción basada en el hecho de la posesión o dominio de bienes por el demandado en el foro donde radica la demanda.

Quasi-judicial. Cuasijudicial.

Quasi-legislative. Cuasilegislativo.

Quasi-offense. Cuasidelito; hecho culposo o negligente.

Quasi-personalty. Bienes muebles relacionados con inmuebles.

Quasi-realty. Bienes muebles tratados jurídicamente como inmuebles.

Quasi-trustee. Cuasifideicomisario.

Question of fact. Problema de hecho; cuestión sobre los hechos.

Question of law. Problema de derecho; cuestión sobre el derecho.

Quia timet. Porque teme.

Quick assets. Bienes líquidos; dinero y bienes muebles que pueden facilmente convertirse en dinero.

Quid pro quo. Algo por algo.

Quiet enjoyment. Posesión pacífica.

Quiet possession. Posesión quieta (o pacífica).

Quiet title. (Acción para) validar el título.

Quit-claim. Cesión sin garantía; cesión de un derecho real, usualmente dudoso, sin garantía.

Quittance. Recibo; finiquito; descargo.

Quorum. Quorum.

Quota. Cuota.

R

Railroad bill of lading. Carta de porte de ferrocarril.

Rank. rango.

Ranking of credits. Prelación de créditos.

Ranking of privileges. Prelación de créditos privilegiados o preferenciales.

Rape. Violación; rapto.

Rate of exchange. Tipo de cambio.

Ratification. Ratificación; confirmación.

Ratify. Ratificar; confirmar.

Ratio decidendi. Razón que motiva la decisión.

Ravish. Violación; rapto.

Real action. Acción real.

Real chattels. *Véase* chattels real.

Real contract. Contrato sobre propiedad inmueble.

Real covenant. Pacto relacionado con bienes inmuebles.

Real estate. Propiedad inmueble; inmueble; bienes raíces.

Real estate broker. Corredor de bienes raíces.

Real evidence. Prueba real; prueba material; evidencia real; evidencia material.

Real obligation. Obligación real.

Real party in interest. Parte interesada; parte con derecho.

Real property. Bienes raíces; propiedad inmueble.

Real right. Derecho real.

Real things. Bienes inmuebles; bienes raíces.

Realty. Propiedad inmueble; heredad; inmueble; bienes raíces.

Reasonable care. *Véase* ordinary care.

Reasonable doubt. Duda razonable; *véase* proof beyond a reasonable doubt.

Reasonable expectation. Esperanza razonable; esperanza fundamentada.

Reasonable fee. Honorario razonable.

Reasonable man. Buen padre de familia; hombre razonable.

Reasonableness. Razonabilidad.

Reasonable price. Precio razonable.

Reasonable time. Período de tiempo razonable.

Reassurance. Reaseguro.

Rebut. Refutar.

Rebuttable presumption. Presunción refutable; presunción juris tantum.

Rebuttal evidence. Prueba ofrecida para refutar la oposición de la parte contraria.

Recaption. Recuperación de bienes; rescate de bienes.

Recapture. Rescate; recapturar; recuperar.

Receipt. Recibo; descargo; finiquito.
Receiver. Síndico.
Receivership. Sindicatura.
Receive stolen property. Encubrir propiedad robada.
Recidivist. Reincidente.
Reciprocal contract. Contrato bilateral.
Reciprocal obligations. Obligaciones recíprocas.
Reciprocal will. Testamento recíproco.
Reciprocity. Reciprocidad.
Recital. Declaración hecha en un documento o ley; declaración.
Recite. Hacer una declaración específica en un documento o ley; rezar.
Recklessness. Imprudencia grande; culpa lata.
Reclamation. Reclamación; reivindicación (espec. quiebra).
Recognition. Reconocimiento.
Recognizance. Reconocimiento.
Recognizance, release on his own (R.O.R). Libertad provisional bajo la propia palabra del reo (pendiente el juicio).
Reconciliation. Reconciliación.
Reconduction. Reconducción.
Reconvention. Reconvención.
Reconventional demand. Demanda reconvencional.
Reconversion. Reintegro de bienes a su condición jurídica original; derecho del legatario del producto de la venta de un predio a recibir el predio en vez del producto de su venta.
Reconveyance. Retrocesión; retrocesión por el acreedor hipotecario al deudor hipotecario del predio hipotecado al liquidarse la deuda.
Record. Expediente; actas; registrar.
Recordation. Registro; presentación en el registro; registración.
Record, court of. Tribunal ordinario; tribunal legítimamente establecido.
Record, criminal. Antecedentes penales.
Recorder. Registrador.
Recoupment. Derecho a rebajar (o compensar) la reclamación del demandante por virtud de daños ocasionados al demandado por el demandante.
Recovery. Recuperación; obtención de sentencia favorable por el demandante, en la cuál se condena al demandado al resarcimiento de daños y perjuicios.
Recovery of damages. *Véase* recovery.
Recrimination. Recriminación.
Recross examination. Segundo careo; volver a carear.
Recusation. Recusación.
Recuse. Recusar.
Redeemable bonds. *Véase* callable bonds.

Redemption. Retroventa; redención.
Redhibition. Redhibición.
Redhibitory action. Acción redhibitoria.
Redirect examination. Segunda interrogación (después del careo); segunda interrogación directa.
Re-entry, right of. Derecho de volver a poseer. Derecho del cedente del derecho a poseer un inmueble a reocupar o reposeer el inmueble.
Referee. Componedor; árbitro; juez auxiliar.
Referendum. Referendum.
Reform. Reformar.
Reformation. Reforma; reforma de un documento.
Reformation of contract. Reforma de contrato (para hacerlo consecuente con la voluntad de las partes).
Reformatory. Reformatorio; cárcel de menores.
Reform school. *Véase* reformatory.
Refund. Reembolso.
Register. Registrar; presentar en el registro; asentar.
Registered owner. Persona que aparece como dueño en el registro.
Registration. Registrar (proceso de); registro.
Registration certificate. Certificación de registro.
Registry. Registro.
Regulate. Regular; reglamentar.
Regulation. Reglamento; ordenanza.
Rehabilitation. Rehabilitación.
Rehearing. Revisión de la causa; nueva audiencia.
Reimbursement. Reembolso.
Reinscription of mortgages. Reinscripción de hipotecas.
Reinsurance. Reaseguro.
Reject. Rechazar.
Rejection. Rechazo.
Relation. Relación; parentesco.
Relationship. Relación; vínculo.
Relative incapacity. Incapacidad relativa.
Relatively null. Nulidad relativa; nulidad subsanable.
Relative nullity. Nulidad relativa.
Relative simulation. Simulación relativa.
Release. Descargo; quita.
Relevancy. Pertinencia; relevancia.
Remainder. Derecho real futuro que comienza al finalizar un derecho real limitado.
Remainderman. Substituto fideicomisario; reservatario.
Remand. Reenviar a la cárcel; reenvío de un caso al tribunal de primera instancia por orden del tribunal de apelación.
Remarriage. Segundas nupcias; segundo matrimonio.
Remedial statute. Ley remediadora.

Remedy. Remedio; recurso.
Remission. Remisión.
Remission of debt. Remisión de la deuda.
Remittance check. Cheque de remesa.
Remittance instrument. Instrumento de remesa.
Remitting bank. Banco remitente.
Remittitur. Devolución; rebaja. Rebaja del monto de la indemnización de la sentencia o veredicto del jurado.
Removal. Mudanza o transmisión de un caso a otro tribunal (generalmente de un tribunal estatal a un tribunal federal.)
Removal of causes. *Véase* removal.
Remover. *Véase* removal.
Remunerative donation. Donación remuneratoria.
Render on account. Rendir cuentas.
Renouncing probate. Renuncia de albaceazgo.
Rent. Alquiler; renta.
Rentals. Renta; precio pagadero por el arrendatario de minas para mantener el arriendo vigente cuando no hay excavaciones, operaciones mineras o producción.
Rent of lands. Censo.
Renunciation of claim. Renuncia de pretensión; renuncia de derecho.
Renunciation of rights. Renuncia de derechos.
Renunciation of the succession. Repudiación de la herencia.
Renvoi. Reenvío.
Reorganization. Reorganización; reestructuración. Regorganización de una corporación o sociedad anónima.
Reorganization of a corporation. Reconstitución de una corporación o sociedad anónima.
Repatriate. Repatriar.
Repatriation. Repatriación.
Repeal. Abrogar; derogar.
Replevin. Reivindicación; acto para recobrar la posesión de bienes muebles.
Replevin, writ of. *Véase* writ of replevin.
Reply. Réplica.
Report. Informe.
Reports. Colección de sentencias.
Repossession. Reivindicación; reposesión; recuperar.
Representation. Representación.
Representative. Representante; diputado; mandatario.
Representative parties. Partes representantes (de una acción de clase; *véase* class action).
Re-presentment. Presentación por segunda vez.
Republic. República.
Republican form of government. Gobierno de tipo republicano.
Republication. Restauración de un testamento revocado.

Repudiation. Repudio; rechazo.
Reputation of status as child. Posesión de estado (de hijo).
Reputed owner. Presunto dueño; poseedor, con el consentimiento del dueño, a quién se le presume ser dueño.
Request for admissions. Solicitud de confesión de parte.
Request for documents. Solicitud de documentos en poder de la otra parte.
Requirements contract. Contrato de suministro. Contrato en el cual el objeto de la prestación depende de las órdenes, exigencias, o necesidades de una de las partes.
Requisition. Requisición; solicitud de extradición.
Res adjudicata. Cosa juzgada.
Resale. Reventa; venta de mercancías por segunda vez.
Rescind. Rescindir.
Rescission. Rescisión.
Reservation. Reserva.
Reservation for security. Reserva de dominio como garantía.
Reservation of rights. Reservación de derechos.
Reserve. Reservar.
Reserve rights. Reservar derechos.
Residence. Domicilio; residencia.
Resident. Residente; domiciliado.
Residuary estate. Parte remanente de la herencia (por no haberse legado).
Residuary legatee. Legatario remanente.
Res inter alios acta. Acto realizado entre otros. Según este principio, los contratos no deben afectar a terceros, ya que, respecto a ellos, son actos realizados "entre otros."
Res ipsa loquitur. Situación que sugiere imprudencia.
Res judicata. Cosa juzgada.
Resolution. Resolución; decisión formal.
Resolutory condition. Condición resolutoria.
Respite. Espera.
Respite, forced. *Véase* forced respite.
Respite, voluntary. *Véase* voluntary respite.
Respondeat superior. Responsabilidad vicaria del patrón por la culpa del empleado.
Responsive pleading. Alegato respondiente; réplica al alegato de la otra parte.
Restatement of the law. Nueva exposición del derecho; síntesis de una rama del derecho; nuevo planteamiento de una rama del derecho.
Restitution. Restitución.
Restraint of trade. Represión del comercio.
Restraint on alienation. Restricción convencional de enajenación de propiedad.

Restricted indorsement. Endoso limitado; endoso condicional; endoso restrictivo.

Resulting trust. Fideicomiso resultante; fideicomiso de hecho.

Retainer. Iguala (pagada a un abogado); honorarios.

Retribution. Compensación; retribución.

Retributive damages. *Véase* punitive damages.

Retroactivity. Retroactividad.

Retroactivity of laws. Retroactividad de la ley.

Return. Informe de emplazamiento rendido por el alguacil u otro emplazador.

Return day. Fecha de comparecencia.

Revenue. Ingresos del Estado; ingresos.

Revenue laws. Legislación tributaria; legislación fiscal; leyes tributarias; leyes fiscales.

Reversal. Anulación de sentencia; casación de sentencia.

Reverse. *Véase* reversal.

Reversion. Reversión; derecho de reversión. Llámase así al derecho del cedente de un derecho real temporario a recuperar la posesión al expirar el derecho real cedido.

Reversionary lease. Arrendamiento futuro que comienza cuando el actual arrendamiento expire.

Reversioner. Titular de un derecho de reversión. *Véase* reversion.

Revert. *Véase* reverter.

Reverter. Reversión; recuperación. *Véase* reversion.

Reverter, possibility of. Posibilidad de reversión. *Véase* reversion.

Review. Revisión; examen.

Revival. Restablecimiento.

Revival of actions. Restablecimiento de acciones.

Revival of judgment. Restauración de sentencia; restablecimiento de sentencia.

Revocability. Revocabilidad.

Revocable offer. Oferta revocable.

Revocation. Revocación.

Revocation of acceptance. Revocación de la aceptación.

Revocation for ingratitude. Revocación (de donación) por ingratitud.

Revocatory action. Acción revocatoria.

Revoke. Revocar.

Right. Derecho; pretensión legítima.

Rightful. Legítimo; verdadero; de derecho.

Rightful claim. Pretensión legítima; pretensión justificada.

Rightful rejection of goods. Rechazo justificado de mercancías.

Rightful transfer. Traspaso legítimo; traspaso válido.

Right of action. Derecho de actuar; titularidad de la acción.

Right of exploration for minerals. Derecho de exploración de yacimientos de minerales.

Right of passage. Servidumbre de paso; derecho de paso.
Right of retention. Derecho de retención.
Right of use. Derecho de uso.
Rights, bill of. Declaración de derechos; carta de derechos.
Rights, civil. Derechos fundamentales; libertades públicas; derechos civiles.
Rights in things. Derechos en, o sobre, las cosas.
Right to inspection of goods. Derecho de inspección de mercancías.
Riparian rights. Derechos ribereños.
Risk. Riesgo.
Risk of loss Riesgo de pérdida.
Robber. Ladrón; asaltante; salteador.
Robbery. Robo; asalto.
Robbery, armed. Robo a mano armada; asalto a mano armada.
Rogatory, letters. Carta rogatoria; carta suplicatoria.
Royalty. Derechos; gabela; regalía; cánones.
Royalty, mineral. *Véase* mineral royalty.
Royalty, overriding. *Véase* overriding royalty.
Rule. Regla; reglamento.
Rule against perpetuities. Regla contra disposiciones que aten la propiedad de forma perpetua.
Rule of law. Precepto normativo; principio de derecho; el imperio de la ley.
Ruling. Decisión del tribunal.

S

Safe port. Puerto seguro.
Sale. Compraventa.
Sale by auction. Subasta; venta a subasta.
Sale by installments. Compraventa a plazos.
Sale by lump. *Véase* lump sale.
Sale by sample. Venta por muestra.
Sale by weight, count, or measure. Venta por peso, número, o medida.
Sale, conditional. Compraventa con reserva de dominio.
Sale, credit. Venta a plazos.
Sale, documentary. *Véase* documentary sale.
Sale, executory. Venta ejecutiva.
Sale, forced. Venta forzosa.
Sale note. Nota de venta.
Sale of a future thing. Venta de cosa futura.
Sale of a hope. Venta de esperanza.
Sale of a thing belonging to another. Venta de propiedad ajena.
Sale of immovables. Venta de inmuebles.

Sale of immovables by measure. Venta de inmuebles por medida.
Sale of immovable for lump sum. Venta de inmueble a precio alzado o global.
Sale of litigious rights. Venta de bienes litigiosos.
Sale of movables. Venta de bienes muebles.
Sale of succession of a living person. Venta de sucesión de persona viva.
Sale on approval. Venta a prueba; venta sujeta a ensayo.
Sale or return. Venta con pacto de retro.
Sale per aversionem. Venta de inmueble a precio alzado de lindero a lindero.
Sale, unrecorded. *Véase* unrecorded sale.
Sale with reservation of view and trial. Venta por ensayo.
Sale with the right of redemption. Venta con pacto de retroventa; retracto convencional.
Salvage. Salvamento.
Salvage lien. Privilegio de salvamento.
Sanction. Sanción; pena.
Satisfaction of a duty. Cumplimiento de la obligación.
Saving clause. Cláusula de reserva.
Saving to suitors clause. *Véase* saving clause.
Schedule. Inventario (quiebra).
Schedule of property. Lista de bienes.
Scienter. A sabiendas; con conocimeinto.
Scope of employment. Ambito del empleo.
Sea damage. Daño marítimo. Llámase así al daño causado al cargamento por un peligro de mar.
Seal. Sello.
Sealed instruments. Documentos sellados.
Sealed testament. Testamento cerrado.
Seaman. Marinero; miembro de la tripulación de una nave.
Seamen's articles. Contrato de marinero.
Seamen's claim. Demanda de marinero por causa marítima.
Seamen's wage lien. Privilegio sobre la nave de los marineros por jornales devengados.
Searches and seizures. Registros y embargos; registros y aprehensiones.
Search warrant. Orden de registro; autorización de registro; mandamiento de registro.
Seaworthiness. Navegabilidad; buen estado de navegar.
Seaworthy. En buen estado de navegar; navegable.
Seaworthy vessel. Nave en buen estado de navegar.
Secondary boycott. Boicot secundario.
Secondary evidence. Evidencia secundaria.

Secondary obligation. Obligación secundaria.
Secondary party. Parte responsable subsidiariamente.
Secondary sources. Fuentes secundarias.
Secretary of state. Secretario de estado; ministro de relaciones exteriores.
Secured creditor. Acreedor garantizado.
Secured debt. Deuda garantizada; deuda afianzada.
Secured party. *Véase* secured creditor.
Secured transaction. Transacción garantizada; contrato garantizado.
Securities exchange. Bolsa de valores.
Securities regulations. Regulación de valores.
Security. Valor; garantía; resguardo; caución.
Security agreement. Contrato de garantía.
Security devices. Figuras jurídicas de garantía crediticia.
Security for performance. Garantía para asegurar el cumplimiento.
Security, impairment of. *Véase* impairment of security.
Security interest. Derecho de garantía; derecho de rentención.
Security right. *Véase* security interest.
Seisin. Posesión; derecho de posesión.
Seizure. Embargo; aprehensión.
Self defense. Defensa propia; legítima defensa.
Self-executing provision. Norma de efecto inmediato; cláusula de efecto inmediato Dícese de una norma o cláusula constitucional o de una ley orgánica que no necesita legislación adicional para entrar en vigor.
Self incrimination. Autoincriminación.
Seller. Vendedor.
Senate. Senado.
Sentence. Condena.
Separate estate. Bienes parafernales; bienes propios de la esposa; bienes privativos.
Separate maintenance. Alimentos para la esposa después de la separación; bienes privativos.
Separate obligation. Obligación privativa de uno de los cónyugues.
Separate property. *Véase* separate estate.
Separation. Separación.
Separation agreement. Contrato de separación.
Separation from bed and board. Separación de cuerpos; separación legal.
Separation, legal. Separación legal; separación de cuerpos.
Separation of powers. Separación de poderes.
Separation of property, judgment of. *Véase* judgment of separation of property.

Separation of property regime. Régimen de separación de bienes en el matrimonio.
Sequestration. Secuestro.
Sequestration, judicial. *Véase* judicial sequestration.
Sequestration of witnesses. Separación de testigos para que no escuchen las declaraciones de quienes testifican antes de ellos.
Sequestration, writ of. *Véase* writ of sequestration.
Servant. Empleado.
Serve. Emplazar.
Service. *Véase* service of process.
Service by mail. Citación por correo; notificación por correo.
Service by publication. Citación por edicto; notificación por edicto.
Service, long-arm. *Véase* long-arm service.
Service of process. Emplazamiento; citación.
Service, substituted. Véase substituted service.
Servient tenement. Predio sirviente.
Servitude. Servidumbre.
Servitude, affirmative. *Véase* affirmative servitude.
Servitude, apparent. *Véase* apparent servitude.
Servitude, common wall. *Véase* common wall servitude.
Servitude, legal. *Véase* legal servitude.
Servitude, natural. *Véase* natural servitude.
Servitude, negative. *Véase* negative servitude.
Servitude, nonappparent. *Véase* nonapparent servitude.
Servitude of light. Servidumbre de luces.
Servitude of view. Servidumbre de vista.
Servitude, personal. *Véase* personal servitude.
Servitude, predial. *Véase* predial servitude.
Session law. Legislación de una sesión o jornada legislativa.
Set-off. Compensación.
Settle. Arreglar; comprometer; componer.
Settlement. Arreglo; componenda; compromiso; transacción.
Settlement, deed of. Documento (o acto) de arreglo.
Settlor. Fideicomitente; fundador.
Several deaths by the same event. Conmorientes.
Several obligations. Obligación no mancomunada; obligación individual de cada parte.
Severalty. Heredad con un solo propietario.
Severance tax. Impuesto sobre extracción de frutos de la tierra.
Share. Acción (de sociedad anónima); parte.
Shareholder. Accionista.
Share of stock. *Véase* share.
Sheriff. Jefe de policía; alguacil.
Shifting use. Uso o aprovechamiento condicionado.

Shipment. Embarque; envío; despacho; cargamento.
Ship mortgage. Hipoteca naval; hipoteca de nave.
Shipowner. Naviero; fletador; armador.
Shipowners' club. Asociación de navieros.
Shipowner's liability. Responsabilidad del naviero o armador.
Shipper. Expedidor; cargador; embarcador; despachador.
Shipper's export declaration. Declaración de exportación.
Shipper's load and count. Carga de carro no comprobado antes de la firma del conocimiento de embarque.
Shipping and forwarding agent. Agente de embarques.
Ship's papers. Documentos de la nave.
Shipwreck. Naufragio.
Shipyard. Astillero.
Shut-in rentals. Precio pagadero por el arrendador de minas al cerrar un pozo de petróleo o gas para mantener vigente el arrendamiento.
Sight draft. Giro pagadero a la vista; libranza pagadera a la vista.
Signature. Firma.
Silent partner. Socio comanditario; socio que únicamente aporta capital.
Simple trust. Fiedeicomiso simple o libre. Dícese de la cesión de bienes en fideicomiso sin instrucciones sobre su administración.
Simulation. Simulación.
Simulation, absolute. *Véase* absolute simulation.
Simulation, relative. *Véase* relative simulation.
Sine qua non. Acto o causa sin la cual un accidente no hubiere ocurrido.
Slander. Difamación oral; calumnia.
Slave. Esclavo.
Sleeping partner. *Véase* silent partner.
Small claims court. Tribunal de casos de menor cuantía.
Smart money damages. *Véase* punitive damages.
Social Security Act. Ley de seguridad social.
Social security laws. Legislación sobre la seguridad social.
Solicitor general. Procurador general.
Solidary liability. Responsabilidad solidaria.
Solidary obligation. Obligación solidaria.
Solidary obligees. Acreedores solidarios.
Solidary obligors. Deudores solidarios.
Sources of law. Fuentes de derecho.
Sovereign. Soberano.
Soverign immunity. Inmunidad del Estado; inmunidad del soberano.
Sovereignty. Soberanía.

Special agent. Mandatario especial; mandatario con poder limitado.
Special appearance. Comparecencia limitada. Comparecencia del demandado cuando se limita a impugnar la jurisdicción o competencia del tribunal.
Special damages. Daño especial o particularizado. Llámase así al daño que fluye del incumplimiento de un contrato, o de un cuasidelito, pero que no es una consecuencia necesaria del incumplimiento o cuasidelito.
Special endorsee. Endosatario por endoso especial; endosatario por endoso completo.
Special endorsement. Endoso especial; endoso completo.
Special injunction. Prohibición específica. Prohibición de causar daños o desperdicio.
Special mandate. Mandato especial.
Special mortgage. Hipoteca especial.
Special partner. *Véase* limited partner.
Special property. Propiedad provisional. Derecho real provisional que existe para llevar a cabo un propósito determinado.
Special trust. Fideicomiso especial. Llámase así al fideicomiso en que se espicifican actos que el fideicomisario debe realizar.
Specialty. Contrato sellado.
Special verdict. Veredicto detallado.
Specific intent. Intención específica.
Specific legacy. Legado específico.
Specific performance. Cumplimiento específico; cumplimiento en especie.
Spendthrift trust. Fideicomiso en que el beneficiario recibe rentas periodicamente que no pueden dársele anticipadamente.
Spouse. Cónyuge.
Spouse in community. Cónyuge bajo el régimen de propiedad de la sociedad de gananciales.
Springing use. Uso o aprovechamiento futuro.
Standard. Pauta; patrón.
Standard of care. Pauta de cuidado; pauta de prudencia.
Standard of conduct. Pauta de conducta; pauta de prudencia.
Stare decisis. Teoría del caso; teoría del precedente.
State. Estado.
Stated capital. Capital declarado; capital escriturado.
State government. Gobierno estatal.
Stateless. Apátrida.
State of the art defense. Defensa a la responsabilidad civil basada en el estado del arte o conocimiento del problema de que se trata.
Statute. Ley.
Statute law. Legislación; derecho legislado.
Statute of frauds. *Véase* frauds, statute of.

Statute of limitations. Prescripción extintiva de obligaciones.
Statutory. Creado por la ley.
Statutory construction. Interpretación de la ley.
Statutory interpretation. Interpretación de la ley.
Statutory lien. Privilegio o gravamen establecido por la ley.
Statutory policy. Política legislativa; intención del legislador.
Stay laws. Leyes de suspensión o moratoria.
Stay of execution. Suspensión de ejecución.
Stay of proceedings to enforce a judgment. Suspensión del proceso de ejecución de sentencia.
Steal. Hurto; robo.
Stepfather. Padrasto.
Stepmother. Madrasta.
Stipulated damages. Cláusula penal; daño estipulado contractualmente.
Stipulation. Espitulación; admisión.
Stipulation in favor of a third party beneficiary. Estipulación en beneficio de tercero.
Stipulator. Estipulante.
Stock. Inventario (de una empresa); acciones (de una sociedad).
Stock certificate. *Véase* certificate of stock.
Stock, common. Acciones ordinarias (de una corporación).
Stock dividend. Dividendo de una sociedad anónima consistente en acciones de la misma.
Stock exchange. Bolsa de valores.
Stock warrant. Derecho a comprar acciones de una sociedad a un precio determinado.
Stock watering. Dilución del capital societario mediante el aumento de acciones sin aumentar el capital.
Stop order. *Véase* stop payment order.
Stoppage in transitu. Paro de las mercancías en tránsito. Llámase así al paro o embargo de mercancías en curso de ser transportadas.
Stop payment order. Orden de suspensión (de pago); orden de detener el pago.
Straight credit. Carta de crédito que no autoriza la negociación o descuento de giros o letras de cambio a terceros.
Strict constructionist. Intérprete riguroso o estricto.
Strict interpretation. Interpretación en sentido riguroso.
Strict liability. *Véase* liability, strict.
Strictly personal obligation. Obligación personalísima.
Strike. Huelga.
Striking a statement from the record. Borrar una declaración del expediente.
Subcontractor. Subcontratista.

Subject matter jurisdiction. Competencia.
Sub judice. En proceso; ante el juez.
Sublease. Subarriendo; subarrendar.
Sublessee. Subarrendatario.
Sublessor. Subarrendador.
Submission. Acuerdo de someterse a la decisión de un árbitro o un amigable componedor.
Subpoena. Citación a testificar.
Subpoena duces tecum. Citación ordenando que se traigan documentos, libros, u otros artículos.
Subrogation. Subrogación.
Subrogation by operation of law. Subrogación de derecho.
Subrogation, conventional. *Véase* conventional subrogation.
Subscribed capital. Capital suscrito.
Subscription. Subscripción. Promesa de comprar acciones de una corporación o sociedad anónima.
Subsidiary. Subsidiaria; compañía afiliada.
Subsidy. Subsidio; ayuda; subvención.
Sub sigilo. Bajo sello; sellado.
Sub silentio. Bajo silencio; en silencio.
Substantial justice. Justicia; equidad.
Substantive law. Derecho substantivo.
Substituted performance. Prestación substituta; cumplimiento en substitución.
Substituted service. Citación por correo; notificación por correo.
Substitution of parties. *Véase* parties, substitution of.
Subtenant. Subarrendatario.
Succession. Sucesión
Succession, acceptance of. *Véase* acceptance of the succession.
Succession administrator. Administrador judicial de sucesión.
Succession duty. Impuesto sobre la herencia.
Succession, intestate. *Véase* intestate succession.
Succession, opening of. *Véase* opening of the succession.
Succession, renunciation of the. *Véase* renunciation of the succession.
Succession, testate. *Véase* testate succession.
Successive performances (contract calling for). (Contrato de) tracto sucesivo.
Successor. Sucesor; causahabiente.
Successor in interest. Sucesor en el derecho (o interés); causahabiente en el derecho (o interés).
Sue. Demandar.
Sue and labor clause. Cláusula de pleito y trabajo.

Suffer. Permitir.
Sufficient cause. Causa suficiente; causa suficiente para justificar cierta acción (esp. del tribunal).
Suffrage. Sufragio.
Sui juris. Bajo su propia autoridad.
Suit. Juicio; proceso; demanda; litigio.
Suitor. Una de las partes de un pleito.
Sum certain. Suma cierta.
Summary judgment. Sentencia sin juicio oral; sentencia sumaria.
Summary proceedings. Juicio sumario; procedimiento sumario.
Summation. Resumen; resumen del proceso ante el jurado.
Summons. Citación.
Supercargo. Sobrecargo.
Superior force. Fuerza mayor.
Supersedeas. Orden que suspende la ejecución de una sentencia, proceso, o mandamiento.
Supervening cause. Factor interviniente que sobrepasa a otro agente como la causa eficiente del daño.
Supervening frustration. Frustación contractual sobreviniente; imprevisión sobreviniente.
Supplemental pleading. Alegato suplementario.
Supplementary proceedings. Proceso adicional; proceso para interrogar al deudor condenado.
Suppletive law. Derecho supletorio.
Supply contract. Contrato de abastecimiento; contrato de aprovisionamiento.
Support. Manutención; alimentos.
Supremacy clause. Cláusula de supremacía (de la constitución de los E E.U U.).
Supreme Court. Corte Suprema; tribunal supremo.
Supreme law of the land. Ley suprema de la nación.
Surety. Garante; fiador.
Suretyship. Fianza; afianzamiento.
Suretyship, commercial. *Véase* commercial suretyship.
Suretyship, legal. *Véase* legal suretyship.
Suretyship, ordinary. *Véase* ordinary suretyship.
Surname. Apellido.
Surrebutal. Prueba para refutar la prueba de refutación.
Surrogate. Juez de testamentaría.
Surrogate motherhood. Maternidad sustituta o vicaria.
Surrogate motherhood contract. Contrato de maternidad sustituta o vicaria. Contrato por el cuál una mujer se compromete a ser embarazada artificialmente y a entregar al niño después del parto.
Surrogate parenthood. Paternidad sustituta o vicaria.

Surrogate's court. Tribunal de testamentaría; tribunal de sucesiones.
Survival action. Acción sobreviviente. Llámase así a la acción del damnificado que fallece a consecuencia de las lesiones sufridas.
Surviving spouse. Cónyuge supérstite.
Suspends payments. Suspende pagos.
Suspension of payment. Suspensión de pagos.
Suspension of prescription. Suspensión de la prescripción.
Suspensive appeal. Apelación suspensiva; apelación que suspende la ejecución de la sentencia; apelación con efecto suspensivo.
Suspensive condition. Condición suspensiva.
Swear. Jurar.
Synallagmatic contract. Contrato sinalagmático.
Syndicate. Consorcio; sindicato.

T

Tableau of distribution. Lista de distribución; lista de acreedores.
Tacit mortgage. Hipoteca legal.
Tacit reconduction of lease. Tácita reconducción del arrendamiento.
Tacking of possession. Adición del período de posesión de un poseedor a la de su sucesor.
Tail. Limitación de herencia a los herederos en línea recta.
Tangible property. Bienes tangibles.
Tariff. Arancel aduanal; tarifa; arancel.
Tax. Impuesto; tributación.
Taxation. Tributación; imposición de impuestos.
Taxation of costs. Condena al pago de las costas.
Tax avoidance. Evasión de impuestos por medios legítimos.
Tax court. Tribunal fiscal; tribunal de impuestos.
Tax deed. Título sobre propiedad embargada por no pagar impuestos.
Tax evasion. Evasión de impuestos; evasión fraudulenta de impuestos por parte del contribuyente.
Tax law. Derecho fiscal; derecho tributario.
Tax lien. Derecho de rentención por impuestos adeudados.

Tax sale. Venta de bienes embargados por falta de pago del impuesto sobre la propiedad.
Tax title. Título que se le otorga al comprador de bienes embargados por falta de pago del impuesto sobre la propiedad.
Temporary injunction. Prohibición temporal; mandamiento temporal.
Temporary restraining order. Mandamiento provisional de prohibición.
Tenancy. Tenencia.
Tenancy at sufferance. Relación jurídica arrendaticia que surge cuando el arrendatario permanece en posesión del inmueble arrendado después de terminarse el contrato.
Tenancy at will. Arrendamiento terminable por la voluntad de cualquiera de las partes.
Tenancy by the entirety. Condominio o copropiedad conyugal.
Tenancy for years. Arrendamiento de inmuebles por un término de años.
Tenancy from month to month. Arrendamiento de inmuebles por el mes.
Tenancy from year to year. Arrendamiento de inmuebles por uno o varios años.
Tenancy in common. Condominio; copropiedad.
Tenant. Arrendatario.
Tenant at sufferance. Arrendatario que permanece en posesión después de terminado el contrato.
Tenant for life. Usufructuario cuyo término es por su propia vida o la vida de otra persona.
Tender. Oferta de cumplimiento de una obligación.
Tender of delivery. Oferta formal de tradición o entrega.
Tender payment. Oferta de pago.
Tenor. Tenor.
Tenure. Posesión; tenencia.
Term. Plazo; cláusula; término.
Termination. Terminación (p.e.j., de un contrato).
Territorial application. Aplicación territorial (de la ley).
Territorial scope. Ambito territorial de la ley.
Territorial sea. Mar territorial.
Territorial waters. Aguas territoriales; mar territorial.
Territory. Territorio.
Testacy. Testado.
Testament. Testamento.
Testamentary. Testamentario.
Testamentary capacity. Capacidad para testar.
Testamentary guardian. Tutor testamentario.
Testament, mystic. *Véase* mystic testament.
Testament, nuncupative. *Véase* nuncupative testament.
Testament, olographic. *Véase* olographic testament.

Testament, open. *Véase* open testament.
Testament, sealed. *Véase* sealed testament.
Testaments made at sea. Testamento marítimo.
Testaments of military personnel. Testamento militar.
Testate. Testado.
Testate succession. Sucesión testamentaria.
Testate successor. Legatario.
Testator. Testador.
Testatrix. Testadora.
Testimony. Testimonio; declaración.
Theft. Hurto; robo.
Things. Bienes; cosas.
Third party. Tercero.
Third party acting in good faith. Terecero de buena fe.
Third party answer. Contestación del tercero demandado. (*Véase* third party defendant).
Third party beneficiary. Tercero beneficiario; beneficiario de estipulación a favor de tercero.
Third party complaint. *Véase* impleader.
Third party defendant. Tercero demandado. Llámase así al tercero demandado por el demandado en la acción principal. *Véase* implead; third party plaintiff.
Third party demand. *Véase* impleader.
Third party plaintiff. Tercero demandante. Demandado en la acción principal que a su vez actúa como demandante contra un tercero responsable, el tercero demandado. *Véase* implead; third party defendant.
Third party practice. *Véase* impleader.
Third person. Tercero.
Third possessor. Tercer poseedor.
Through bill of lading. Conocimiento de embarque hasta el destino.
Time charter. Fletamento por tiempo.
Title. Título; propiedad.
Title abstract. *Véase* abstract of title.
Title, chain of. Cadena del título. Llámase así a las enajenaciones y otros documentos de traspaso de dominio sobre una heredad.
Title deed. Documento de título. Llámase así al documento necesario para probar el dominio sobre una heredad.
Title, mumiment of. *Véase* muniment of title.
Title, paramount. *Véase* paramount.
Title search. Estudio de título.
Title theory. Teoría del título.
Tort. Agravio; cuasidelito.
Tortfeasor. Persona que comete un cuasidelito o un delito que produce efectos civiles.

Tortious. Conducta que implica la comisión de un cuasidelito.
Torts. Cuasidelitos; Derecho de la responsabilidad civil cuasidelictual.
Total breach. Incumplimiento total.
Total loss. Pérdida total.
Towage. Remolque.
Towage fees. Derechos de remolque.
Trademark. Marcas de fábrica; marca registrada.
Trade name. Nombre comercial; razón social.
Trade regulation. Reglamentación del comercio.
Trade union. Sindicato de trabajadores.
Tradition. Tradición; entrega.
Traffic court. Tribunal de tránsito.
Transaction. Transacción; arreglo; compromiso.
Transactional immunity. Inmunidad total contra el procesamiento penal.
Transcript of record. Compilación del expediente del proceso; compilación de la documentación del juicio.
Transfer. Transferir; traspasar; ceder; transferencia; traspaso; cesión.
Transfer of obligations. Traspaso de obligaciones.
Transfer of possession. Transferecia de la posesión.
Transferred intent. Intención transferida; premeditación transferida.
Transitory action. Acción que puede ejercitarse en cualquier lugar, siempre que exista jurisdicción y competencia en el tribunal.
Traverse. Refutar.
Treason. Traición.
Treasury. Erario; fisco.
Treaty. Tratado; convención.
Treble damages. Tres veces el daño probado.
Trespass. Violación; transgresión.
Trespasser. Violador; transgresor.
Trial. Juicio; proceso; audiencia; vista.
Trial attorney. Abogado de parte en un juicio; *véase* trial lawyer.
Trial by jury. Juicio ante jurado.
Trial lawyer. Abogado litigante; abogado que se dedica a llevar pleitos ante los tribunales.
Trial on the merits. Vista principal; vista decisiva.
Tribunal. Tribunal.
True bill. Acusación del gran jurado.
True copy. Copia fiel.
Trust. Fideicomiso.
Trust company. Compañía fiduciaria; banco fiduciario.
Trust, constructive. *Véase* constructive trust.
Trust deed. Hipoteca; escritura fiduciaria.
Trustee. Fiduciario.
Trust receipt. Recibo fiduciario. Llámase así al contrato mediante el cual el fiduciario

recibe documentos o bienes de un tercero que conserva un derecho de retención sobre los objetos entregados al fiduciario.

Trust, simple. *Véase* simple trust.

Trust, spendthrift. *Véase* spendthrift trust.

Turn state's evidence. Declarar en un juicio penal en contra del acusado.

Turpis causa. Causa vil; causa inmoral.

Turpitude, moral. Acto contra la moral y las buenas costumbres.

Tutelage. Tutela.

Tutor. Tutor.

Tutor of the person. Tutor de la persona.

Tutor of the property. Tutor de los bienes.

Tutorship. Tutela.

Tutorship by effect of the law. Tutela legal; tutela por ministerio de la ley.

Tutorship by nature. Tutela natural.

Tutorship by the appointment of the judge. Tutela por nombramiento judicial.

Tutorship by will. Tutela testamentaria.

Tutorship, dative. *Véase* dative tutorship.

Twilight zone. Zona crepuscular (Der. marítimo).

U

Uberrima fides. El mayor grado de buena fe.

Ultimate facts. Hechos en disputa.

Ultrahazardous activity. Actividad extremadamente peligrosa.

Ultra vires. Acto no autorizado; acto no autorizado por la carta constitutiva de una corporación.

Umpire. Arbitro; árbitro nombrado para logar una decisión mayoritaria cuando las árbitros nombrados por las partes están en desacuerdo.

Unconditional. Incondicional.

Unconditional promise to pay. Promesa incondicional de pago.

Unconscionability. Desproporción en las obligaciones dimanantes de un contrato que impide su cumplimiento.

Unconscionable. Desproporcionado; desmedido. *Véase* unconscionability.

Unconstitutional. Inconstitucional; anticonstitucional.

Unconstitutionality. Inconstitucionalidad.

Underlease. Subarriendo.

Undertenant. Subarrendatario.

Undertutor. Protutor.

Undisclosed principal. Mandante no revelado.

Undivided. Pro indiviso; término genérico aplicado al estado de copropiedad.

Undue influence. Influencia indebida; coacción.

Unearned income. Entradas no ganadas; entradas producto de una inversión capitalista, de una donación, o de figuras jurídicas similares.

Unenforceable contract. Contrato que no puede hacerse cumplir.

Unenforceable promise. Promesa que no puede hacerse cumplir.

Unfair. Injusto.

Unfair competition. Competencia desleal.

Unfairness. Injusticia.

Uniform Commercial Code (U.C.C.). Código de Comercio Uniforme.

Uniform law. Ley uniforme.

Uniform operation of laws. Aplicación uniforme de las leyes.

Uniform Sales Act. Ley Uniforme de Compraventa.

Unilateral agreement. Acuerdo unilateral.

Unilateral contract. Contrato unilateral.

Unincorporated association. Asociación, o sociedad, no incorporada; sociedad que no es corporación.

Uninsured motorists policy. Póliza de protección contra conductores de vehículos no asegurados.

Union. Sindicato; unión.

Unit, compulsory. *Véase* compulsory unit.

Unit, conventional. *Véase* conventional unit.

United Nations. Naciones Unidas.

United States Code. Código de los E E.U U.; compilación de leyes del congreso de los E E.U U.

United States Courts. Tribunales federales de los Estados Unidos.

Unitization. Unificación de varios predios en una unidad minera con el propósito de maximizar el aprovechamiento de un yacimiento de hidrocarburos.

Unitize. *Véase* unitization.

Unit operation. Operaciones de extracción desde una unidad unificada para mayor aprovechamiento del yacimiento. *Véase* unitization.

Unity of interest. Unidad de derechos.

Unity of possession. Unidad de posesión. Dícese de la situación que ocurre cuando el mismo individuo adquiere el dominio y una servidumbre sobre una heredad; derecho de los comuneros a poseer y usar el predio en su totalidad.

Universal agent. Apoderado con poder general.

Universal donee. Donatario a título universal.

Universal legacy. Legado universal; legado a título universal.

Universal legatee. Legatario a título universal.

Universal partnership. Sociedad universal.
Unjust enrichment. Enriquecimiento sin causa; enriquecimiento injusto.
Unlawful. Ilegal; ilícito.
Unlawful arrest. Arresto ilegal.
Unlawful cause. Causa ilícita.
Unperfected security interest. Derecho garantizado sin perfeccionar.
Unreasonable searches and seizures. Registros y embargos irrazonables.
Unrecorded. No registrado.
Unrecorded lease. Arrendamiento no registrado.
Unrecorded mortgage. Hipoteca no registrada.
Unrecorded sale. Compraventa no registrada.
Unseaworthy. En mal estado de navegación; innavegable; en malas condiciones de marinaje
Unseaworthy vessel. Nave en mal estado en navegación; nave innavegable; nave en malas condiciones de marinaje.
Unsecured creditor. Acreedor sin garantía o quirografario.
Unworthiness to succeed. Indignidad para suceder.
Unwritten law. Derecho no escrito; derecho consuetudinario.
Usages. Usos.
Usages of the trade. Usos del comercio; usos del giro.
Use. Uso; fideicomiso.
Useful expenses. Gastos útiles.
Useful improvements. Mejoras útiles.
Use immunity. Inmunidad parcial contra el procesamiento penal; inmunidad de uso.
User. Uso; gozo.
Usufruct. Usufructo.
Usurious. Usurario.
Usury. Usura.

V

Vacant possession. Derecho inmobiliario abandonado
Vacant succession. Sucesión sin reclamantes o herederos conocidos.
Vacate. Desocupar; cancelar; anular.
Vacating a judgment. Anulación de sentencia; invalidación de sentencia.
Valid. Válido; efecto legal.
Validating act. Ley o acto que convalida actos anteriores.
Validity. Validez.
Valuable consideration. Causa; consideración; causa onerosa.
Value. Valor; cuantía.
Valued policy. Póliza valorada; póliza valuada; póliza de valor declarado; póliza tasada.
Value received. Contraprestación recibida; valor recibido.
Variance. Diferencia sustancial; permiso o dispensa a una

finca urbana que la exime de cumplir con los requisitos de un plan urbanístico .
Vendee. Comprador.
Vendor. Vendedor.
Vendor's lien. Privilegio del vendedor; derecho de retención del vendedor.
Venireman. Persona llamada a formar parte del grupo de donde se selecciona el jurado.
Venture, joint. Sociedad para un fin específico.
Venue. Competencia territorial de un tribunal.
Verbal. Verbal; oral.
Verdict. Veredicto; sentencia del jurado.
Verification. Verificación; constatación.
Verify. Verificar; constatar.
Vessel. Barco, nave, navío.
Vested. Adquirido.
Vested remainder. Derecho adquirido al remanente (de un derecho real temporal).
Vested right. Derecho adquirido.
Vesting order. Orden de adquisición.
Veto. Veto.
Vicarious liability. Responsabilidad por los actos de otro, generalmente subordinado al responsable; responsabilidad vicaria.
Vice. Vicio.
Vicecounsul. Vicecónsul.
Vices of consent. Vicios del consentimiento.
Vicinage. Vecindario de donde debe ser seleccionado el jurado.
Violate the law. Violar la ley; desobedecer la ley.
Violation. Violación; quebrantamiento.
Violent possession. Posesión violenta; posesión ejercitada por métodos violentos.
Visa. Visa.
Visitation rights. Derecho del padre o la madre sin patria potestad, o de los abuelos, en su caso, a visitar a los hijos menores de edad después del divorcio o separación; derecho de visita.
Void. Nulo; inválido.
Voidable. Anulable; cancelable.
Voidable contract. Contrato anulable.
Voidable promise. Promesa anulable; obligación anulable.
Voidable title. Título anulable.
Void title. Título nulo.
Voire dire. Interrogación de las personas llamadas a formar parte del jurado.
Voluntary. Voluntario; intencional.
Voluntary bankruptcy. Quiebra voluntaria; bancarrota voluntaria.
Voluntary conveyance. Cesión de bienes sin causa onerosa.
Voluntary dismissal. Anulación de la instancia a petición del demandante; sobreseimiento voluntario.
Voluntary partition. Partición voluntaria o convencional.

Voluntary payment. Pago efectuado voluntariamente.
Voluntary respite. Espera voluntaria (o convencional).
Voluntary, waste. *Véase* waste, voluntary.
Volunteer. Voluntario; gestor oficioso; gestor de negocios ajenos; adquirente de bienes a título gratuito.
Voting stock. Acciones con derecho al voto.
Voting trust. Fideicomiso de votar.
Vouch. Certificar; comprobar.
Vouchee. Persona que ha garantizado el título.
Vouch to warranty. Llamar a defender el título.
Voyage charter. Fletamento por viaje.

W

Wager. Apuesta.
Wages. Jornal; salario; compensación.
Waiver of claim. Renuncia de pretensión.
Waiver of liability. Renuncia de responsabilidad.
Waiver of rights. Renuncia de derechos.
Waiver of warranty. Renuncia a la garantía.
Wanton. Imprudencia enorme; imprudencia dolosa.
Ward. Pupilo; tutelado.
Warden. Administrador de una prisión.
Warehouseman. Almacenista; almacenero.
Warehouse receipt. Recibo de almacén; boleto de almacén; resguardo de almacén.
Warrant. Garantizar; otorgar; exigir; justificar; garantía; libramiento; autorización; comprobante.
Warrantee. Garantizado; afianzado.
Warrant of arrest. Orden de detención.
Warrantor. Garante; fiador; persona que garantiza.
Warrant title. Sanear.
Warranty. Garantía.
Warranty against eviction. Garantía contra la evicción.
Warranty against hidden defects. Garantía contra vicios ocultos (o redhibitorios).

Warranty against redhibitory vices. Garantía contra vicios redhibitorios.

Warranty, breach of. Incumplimiento de la garantía.

Warranty deed. Escritura de garantía; escritura de traslación de dominio mediante la cuál el vendedor garantiza al comprador contra la evicción.

Warranty, express. *Véase* express warranty.

Warranty, implied. *Véase* implied warranty.

Warranty of fitness. Garantía de idoneidad; garantía de aptitud.

Warranty of goods. Garantía de calidad de bienes muebles.

Warranty of habitability. Garantía de habitabilidad; garantía del arrendador de vivienda que la vivienda arrendada está en condiciones habitables.

Warranty of land. Garantía de bondad del título de una heredad.

Warranty of merchantability. *Véase* merchantability.

Warranty of seaworthiness. Garantía de navegabilidad; garantía de que la nave está en buen estado de navegar.

Warranty of title. Garantía de título; garantía de validez del título.

Warranty of workmanlike performance. Garantía de cumplimiento eficiente.

Waste. Devastación; desperdiciar sin derecho una heredad.

Waste, permissive. Daño sufrido por una heredad debido a la imprudencia del poseedor o arrendatario.

Waste, voluntary. Acto intencional del poseedor o arrendatario de una heredad que causa daño a esta última.

Watered stock. Acciones de valor diluído por faltarle respaldo de capital.

Way bill. Documento de vía. Llámase así al documento que identifica la carga transportada en ferrocarril.

Way, right of. Servidumbre de paso; derecho de paso.

Weight of the evidence. Peso de la prueba; valor de la prueba en su totalidad.

Wharfage. Muellaje; atraque; derechos de muellaje.

Whiteacre. Nombre ficticio usado para distinguir una heredad de otra; a la otra heredad se le llama usualmente "blackacre".

Wife. Esposa.

Will. Testamento; voluntad.

Willful. Intencional.

Withdraw. Retirar; retirarse.

Without prejudice. Sin afectar; salvedad que indica que el acto no afecta otros acuerdos o que no implica una renuncia.

Without recourse. Sin recurso.

Without reserve. Sin reserva.

Witness. Testigo.

Words of limitation. Palabras de límites. Dícese de las palabras en una escritura que definen el derecho cedido.
Words of purchase. Palabras de compra. Llámase así a las palabras en una escritura que identifican al adquirente del derecho cedido.
Worker. Obrero; trabajador.
Workers' compensation. Compensación laboral.
Workers' compensation act. Legislación laboral por accidentes de trabajo.
Working capital. Capital de trabajo; capital de explotación.
Work risk policy. Póliza de riesgos de guerra; póliza de contingencia de guerra.
Writ. Auto; mandamiento; orden judicial.
Writ of attachment. Orden de embargo; auto de embargo.
Writ of certiorari. Recurso discrecional de revisión.
Writ of detinue. Auto contra el detentador.
Writ of distraint. Auto de secuestro.
Writ of entry. Acción posesoria.
Writ of error. Recurso de casación; apelación; apelación de derecho.
Writ of execution. Orden de ejecución de sentencia; auto de ejecución.
Writ of fieri facias. Auto de ejecución.
Writ of habeas corpus. Auto de hábeas corpus.
Writ of mandamus. Mandamiento.
Writ of prohibition. Inhibitoria.
Writ of replevin. Auto de desembargo.
Writ of sequestration. Orden de secuestro judicial.
Written interrogatories. Interrogatorios por escrito.
Wrong. Cuasidelito; daño; agravio.
Wrongful. Ilícito.
Wrongful act. Acto ilícito; acto doloso; acto realizado de mala fe.
Wrongful birth. Acción contra al médico por nacimiento indeseado.
Wrongful death. Muerte culposa o dolosa.
Wrongful death action. Reclamación por muerte culposa o dolosa.
Wrongful dishonor. Deshonor injustificado; negación de pago sin justificación.
Wrongful rejection of goods. Rechazo injustificado de mercancías.

Z

Zealous witness. Testigo partidista.

Zoning. Urbanismo.

Zoning regulation. Reglamento urbanístico.